Woody Allen on Walt "Clyde" Frazier:

"Now, a favorite crackpot notion of mine is the following: The Knicks never regained their past championship form because they sinned by trading Walt Frazier to Cleveland. I can't prove this, but those who have read *The Rime of the Ancient Mariner* know what the shooting of that bird did. Not that Frazier was an Albatross. Quite the contrary. He was, in my opinion, the greatest of all Knickerbocker players, and he was for a time not only the soul of their team but one of the spirits of this city.

"I recall him after a routine night of superb basketball, tooling around in his chauffeured Rolls, dressed, to put it mildly, like an extrovert and lighting up the various night spots of Manhattan like he had just lit up the Garden. Clyde came up with the Knicks and was a major (I think the major) cog in the peerless machine that took two championships. It should have entitled him to tenure in New York forever. Dealing him to the Cavaliers upset some balance in the cosmic order, and the fruit of this curse could be felt from the days of Spencer Haywood, through Bob McAdoo, Micheal Ray Richardson, Lonnie Shelton, the Bulls, the Rockets, Rick Pitino, Hubie Brown, Mike Fratello, last year's brawl in Miami, many heartbreaking late baskets by Reggie, by Michael, even by Sam Cassell."

Reprinted from the New York Observer, May 25, 1998

©1998, Woody Allen

Woody Allen on Walt "Clyde" Frazier

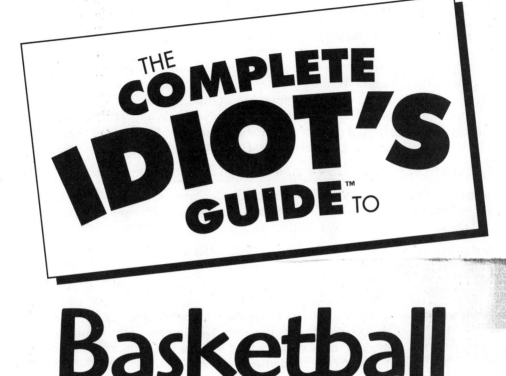

THE COMPLETE IDIOT'S GUIDE TO

Basketball

by Walt "Clyde" Frazier
and Alex Sachare

alpha
books

A Division of Macmillan General Reference
A Simon & Schuster Macmillan Company
1633 Broadway, New York, NY 10019-6785

THE COMPLETE IDIOT'S GUIDE TO and design are trademarks of Prentice-Hall, Inc.

Macmillan Publishing books may be purchased for business or sales promotional use. For information please write: Special Markets Department, Macmillan Publishing USA, 1633 Broadway, New York, NY 10019.

International Standard Book Number: 0-02862679-6
Library of Congress Catalog Card Number: 98-87302

00 99 98   8 7 6 5 4 3 2 1

Interpretation of the printing code: The rightmost number of the first series of numbers is the year of the book's printing; the rightmost number of the second series of numbers is the number of the book's printing. For example, a printing code of 98-1 shows that the first printing occurred in 1998.

Printed in the United States of America

Alpha Development Team

Publisher
Kathy Nebenhaus

Editorial Director
Gary M. Krebs

Managing Editor
Bob Shuman

Marketing Brand Manager
Felice Primeau

Senior Editor
Nancy Mikhail

Development Editors
Phil Kitchel
Jennifer Perillo
Amy Zavatto

Editorial Assistant
Maureen Horn

Alpha Production Team

Development Editor
Lisa A. Bucki

Production Editor
Stephanie Mohler

Copy Editors
Geneil Breeze
Krista Hansing
Howard Jones

Cover Designer
Mike Freeland

Photo Editor
Richard Fox

Color Illustrator
Michael W. Skrepnick

Cartoonist
Jody P. Schaeffer

Designer
Glenn Larsen

Indexer
(to come)

Layout/Proofreading
Angela Calvert
Michelle Lee
Megan Wade

Contents at a Glance

Contents

Foreword

So who needs another guide to basketball?

You do. I do. We all do. And this is the one we've been waiting for.

Basketball is in the midst of an incredible global growth in popularity among people of all ages—men and women, boys and girls. With the technological changes the world is going through, we're changing our playing and viewing habits from slower-paced games like baseball and football to the game of the future—basketball. Basketball embodies everything our culture now craves: excitement, speed, dynamic personalities, up-close relationships with the stars, the exciting physical nature of the contest, and of course, the incredible suspense that is possible with each game. That is why this book is so important.

Basketball for me has always been a celebration of all the elements in life: the joy of teamwork, the pride of skill development, the enthusiasm of the crowd, the running and jumping and cheering and yelling at the refs. All the things that you dream about as a young person are right out there in front of you in basketball. And like everything else, the better you understand the game, the better you're going to be as a ballplayer, and the more you're going to enjoy it as a fan.

What makes this book so special is the fact that Walt "Clyde" Frazier has written it. To me, he embodies everything that is right in the world, and not just the world of sports. He's a man who carries himself with class, dignity, style, intelligence, character, and grace—all the things you want your kids to have.

When I was growing up, I had the dual pleasure of watching and learning from Walt Frazier. Then, because the beginning of my career in the NBA and the end of his overlapped, I had the privilege and honor of playing against him. Finally, due to our continued involvement in the sport and business of basketball, I've gotten to know Clyde as a person—and you could not ask for a better man. What makes the game of basketball so very special is that the people who dominate it, as great as they are as players, are always better people. I'm talking about players like Bill Russell, Wilt Chamberlain, Kareem Abdul-Jabbar, Michael Jordan, Magic Johnson, Larry Bird, Jerry West, Oscar Robertson—and Clyde Frazier belongs, unequivocally, in that group.

As a young man, I was blown away by the skill level and control of the game that Walt Frazier exercised over the NBA—effortlessly gliding over the court, always making the right play at the right time and the biggest play at the most critical moment. The games when the Knicks battled against the Celtics, the Bullets, the Bucks, and the Lakers were when Walt Frazier *had to be at his best*—and was *always at his best*. Those games made me appreciate basketball even more. Like so many others, I was dazzled by Walt's brilliance.

Walt Frazier and his New York Knicks teams in the late 1960s and early 70s scaled heights that had never been attained in the history of basketball. The style with which Clyde led those Knicks teams and the way they conducted themselves, both on and off the court, brought a whole new generation of fans to love the game that has been Clyde's life. We all owe Clyde Frazier a huge debt of gratitude for his contributions—which are ongoing and continue to improve, educate, and draw ever-increasing numbers of fans to the game. Clyde has never really stopped. He just changed his uniform.

This book will take you through Clyde's magical vision of the game that has meant everything to him. The greatest skill that the world's best players possess is the ability to make others better at what they do. This book will make your love, enjoyment, and participation in the world of basketball that much more special.

—Bill Walton, NBC Sports commentator and member, Naismith Memorial Basketball Hall of Fame

Bill Walton, like Walt Frazier, was named by the NBA as "one of the 50 greatest players in NBA history." Regarded by many as the best college player of all time, Walton was Sporting News Player of the Year three straight years and MVP of the 1972 and 1973 NCAA tournaments. Many of his college scoring records stand to this day. As a pro in the NBA, his passing, shooting, jumping, and running skills led the Portland Trail Blazers to the 1977 championship. The following year, he was named league MVP. From 1979–85 he was a member of the San Diego/Los Angeles Clippers, and in 1986 he helped lead the Boston Celtics to the NBA championship. In 1991, he was recipient of the prestigious NBA Players Association Oscar Robertson Leadership Award. Today, Walton can be seen and heard as a basketball television analyst on NBC.

Introduction

May 8, 1970, is a night I'll never forget. Even if I could, the people of New York won't let me.

I still hear it from fans on the street: "Clyde, I'll never forget Game 7 against the Lakers. Great game, man." And you know what? More than 25 years later, it's still the greatest feeling in the world.

NBA champions. No New York Knicks team had ever done that, and with our center, Willis Reed, hobbled by a leg injury, it looked like we'd have our hands full against the Los Angeles Lakers. While the rest of us were out on the court warming up before the game, Willis was back in the locker room getting an injection in his thigh. People still think we planned his last-second entrance onto the court to be dramatic, but the real reason he was late was that it took the doctor so much time to find the right spot for that huge needle.

But there he was, hobbling through the tunnel and onto the court just before tipoff. All the Lakers were stealing glances at Willis, and I remember thinking, "Hm, maybe we've got them." When he hit our first two baskets of the game, that feeling only got stronger. And so did my game—I played what I think was the best game of basketball I've ever played, considering the circumstances: I scored 36 points, handed out 19 assists, and made five or six steals. And when it was over, the scoreboard read Knicks 113, Lakers 99—and we were the champions.

I didn't understand at first what it meant to be world champs and how it would affect my life. But it has, and still does—it has impacted everything that has happened to me since. That Knicks team struck a chord with a lot of people. I think it was a combination of the way we played and the way we conducted ourselves. People respected us, both on and off the court.

I still wear my championship ring on occasion. It makes me feel proud. It reminds me that I did something so many only dream about. For that one shining moment, we were the best. As you can tell by now, I love the game of basketball. I hope this book helps you get to know the game better so that you will come to love it, too.

How to Use This Book

This book is divided into six parts that are intended to build upon one another so that the fan who is new to the game can start with the basics and then make steady progress from there. If you're already a fan who's familiar with the game, however, you can easily pick up anywhere and read whatever strikes your fancy. Either way, I'm confident this book will add to your appreciation for the game.

In Part 1, "What's All the Hoopla About?" I'll explain why basketball is the fastest-growing sport in the world in terms of both popularity and participation. It's a great game to play and a great game to watch, whether in person or on television.

In Part 2, "The Players," I'll give you an idea what each of the players on the court is trying to accomplish, and what skills and savvy he needs to get the job done. I also emphasize here that, especially in the NBA, the players are the show—not the coaches, not the referees, nobody but the players.

In Part 3, "Beyond the Players," I'll introduce you to all those other people who are a part of bringing you the game; they may not be as important as the players, but there wouldn't be an NBA without them. I'm talking about coaches and referees who run things on the court, statisticians who record what happens, media members who report on the game, and front office executives who put the whole show together.

In Part 4, "Basketball Strategy," I'll try to explain what makes a winning team, without getting too technical. I'll go into some basic plays and the thinking behind the offense, as well as some of the tactics used on defense to thwart those tactics. The idea is to give you an understanding of what players and teams are trying to accomplish out on the court. I'll close with a time-out in which I'll answer some of the questions I hear most frequently from fans.

In Part 5, "From the Playgrounds to the Pros," I'll discuss the various settings in which basketball is played, from the NBA and other pro leagues here and abroad, through the college and high school games, to pickup basketball in playgrounds and schoolyards. All have their own lore, their own culture that makes each unique. I'll also look at women's basketball, which is booming both in the United States and abroad.

Finally, in Part 6, "A Fan for Life," I'll give you some tips that should help you become just that, if you aren't already. I'll show you how to get the most out of going to the arena or following your favorite team from the comfort of your den, but I'll also urge you to get out and play, because basketball is a game for all ages.

Acknowledgments

I'd like to thank my parents for their patience and wisdom, my uncle Eddie for providing the impetus, and my former coaches, teammates, and opponents for supplying the tenacity, teamwork, and sagacity that catapulted me to the pinnacle of the NBA.

—Walt "Clyde" Frazier

I am indebted to Randy Voorhees and John Monteleone of Mountain Lion Books and Gary Krebs of Alpha Books for leading this project, Mark Gola of Mountain Lion for his work on the photos, and Lisa Bucki, Stephanie Mohler, Geneil Breeze, Howard Jones, and Krista Hansing for their valuable and precise editing. Special thanks to Bill Walton for contributing the Foreword and to George Kalinsky for his special photography of Clyde. A heartfelt, personal note of thanks to my wife Lori and daughter Debbie for their kindness, patience, and love, which mean everything. Finally, to Clyde, it's been a pleasure working with a Hall of Famer on and off the court.

—Alex Sachare

If You Need An Assist...

In addition to the main text, you'll see many boxes and icons sprinkled throughout. These boxes give you extra information:

Clyde's Rules

Some cautions and warnings to keep in mind, as well as things to avoid.

Clyde's Record Book

Interesting facts and anecdotes to complement the text. Use them to dazzle your friends!

Quote...Unquote

Noteworthy quotes I've picked up along the way that hopefully illustrate a point I'm trying to make.

Clyde's Tip

Tips to understanding a point easily.

Clyde's Chalk Talk

Definitions of common and not-so-common basketball terms.

Part 1
What's All the Hoopla About?

Is there a more exciting play in all of sports than Michael Jordan or Grant Hill or another NBA star faking past his man, huffing and stuffing, shaking and baking, driving to the basket, gliding through the air, then finishing with a slam-dunk?

It's no surprise that basketball, especially NBA basketball, is growing by leaps and bounds…or perhaps I should say rebounds!

It's a sport of non-stop action and perpetual motion, where quickness, agility, and skill are more important than brute force. It's like ballet in its grace of movement and the sheer artistry of its athletes. Invented barely over a century ago, it is the second most popular sport in the world, rapidly closing in on soccer for the number one spot.

NBA stars are tremendously popular with sports fans of all ages—and non-fans, too. Jordan is the best-known and most popular athlete in the world, a man whose popularity transcends sports. How else do you explain the tremendous success of his cologne? Think about that for a moment: a fragrance bearing the name of a man who sweats for a living becomes a best-seller within a year of its introduction, thanks to the popularity of its namesake.

In this part of The Complete Idiot's Guide to Basketball, *I'll explain some of the reasons for basketball's remarkable growth in popularity. I'll also discuss how the game and its rules have evolved, so you'll have the background you need to develop a better understanding and appreciation for this extraordinary game.*

Chapter 1

It's Everybody's Game!

In This Chapter

➤ Everybody's into basketball these days

➤ Any number can play, just about anywhere

➤ Basketball comes across great on TV

➤ It's not just America's game anymore

NBA players are household names, in households around the world as well as in the United States.

Like movie legends or rock stars, only one name or nickname is enough for NBA greats present and past to be recognized: Michael or Shaq, The Mailman or The Dream, Kareem or Magic, Penny or Grant, Wilt or Dr. J, Scottie or Sir Charles. If you don't know who they are, ask any kid or teenager and chances are they'll tell you more than you wanted to know.

Michael Jordan isn't just a basketball player, he's a multi-national corporate figure. He is an icon, perhaps the only living person who could possibly hold his own while starring in a movie opposite that cartoon legend, Bugs Bunny.

How popular is basketball?

NBA videos dominated *Billboard's* 1997 year-end list of Top Recreational Sports Videos, as they have for more than a decade. Nine of the top 20 titles on the chart were NBA videos, including 5 of the top 10, with the No. 1 spot belonging to *Michael Jordan: Above & Beyond.*

A crowd of 37,283 reached into the upper level of the mammoth Pontiac Silverdome for this game in 1979, evidence of basketball's popularity.
Associated Press

Here's another example: Fifth grade students at a school in New Jersey recently were asked if they could name 10 major league baseball players. None could do so. But when asked who could name 10 NBA players, 17 of 18 students raised their hands, and a total of 35 names were listed.

Need I say more?

Hoops, There It Is!

Wherever you look today, you see evidence of basketball. It has become part of the fabric of American life, transcending the world of sports.

If you go to the movies, you'll see people playing basketball. Before, if the movie included any sort of sports play in the background, it was always baseball or football. Now you see basketball instead.

The same goes for television. Paul Reiser of *Mad About You* sits on his sofa and tosses a basketball in the air as he waits for Helen Hunt to come home. When the doctors on *E.R.* seek a way to work off the energy and emotion of a day in the emergency room, they take to a court near their Chicago hospital for some one-on-one.

And how many times have you stood in your office or your room and done your best Kareem Abdul-Jabbar *sky-hook* imitation as you tossed a wadded up piece of paper at a waste basket across the way, letting out a "Yes! And it counts!" when it went in?

Basketball influences the music we listen to. MTV features players from the National Basketball Association, the men's pro league in the United States that was founded in 1946, on its shows, rapping and tapping with the hosts and introducing videos. Kids see NBA guys as cool, because of the movies, the rap music, and the clothes the players wear. That's one of the problems with baseball—the kids do not view their players or the sport as cool, so baseball is losing a whole generation.

Basketball terms have infiltrated our language, too, just as words from baseball and football entered our lexicon in years gone by. Ask a question today that has an obvious answer, and you might well be told, "That's a *slam-dunk*."

Basketball leaves its impression on our lifestyle, our clothes, and our fashions—and not just for young people. The whole country goes casual now. Wherever you go, you see people wearing sneakers as opposed to shoes, warm-up suits in lieu of business attire. It's not like the '70s and '80s when people "dressed." Everybody's very casual now, and basketball jerseys, shooting shirts, and warm-up clothes are ubiquitous.

Basketball embodies the music, the creativity, the action that people crave today. Back in the old days, life moved at a leisurely pace. That's why baseball was the premier sport, the national pastime. People had all day to go out and sit in the

Clyde's Chalk Talk

A *hook shot* is a shot in which a player, standing with his back to the basket, extends his arm high over his head in a sweeping motion as he turns toward the basket in order to shoot the ball over a defender. The term *sky-hook* was coined by Milwaukee Bucks broadcaster Eddie Doucette to describe 7-foot-2 Kareem Abdul-Jabbar's hook shot, which seemed to come out of the sky.

Clyde's Record Book

Michael Jordan of the Chicago Bulls and Shaquille O'Neal of the Los Angeles Lakers are two of basketball's best-known stars, and they've made a dazzling impression with kids off the court as well. Jordan starred in the popular movie *Space Jam*, along with a host of animated characters, including Bugs Bunny. O'Neal has recorded several albums of rap music, including the million-selling *Shaq Diesel*, hosted the award-winning *Nickelodeon Sports Theatre* on cable TV, and starred or been featured in four major movies.

Clyde's Chalk Talk

Don't worry if you can't tell the difference between a *dunk*, a *slam*, a *slam-dunk*, or a *jam*. They all refer to a basket scored by throwing the ball down through the hoop. Once considered bad form because slamming the ball down like that showed up the opponent, the dunk is now seen as a form of self-expression. Players try to out-do one another by devising fancy new ways to approach the basket, improvising and mesmerizing with their dunks.

Clyde's Tip

Parents like basketball because it's convenient, but also because its relatively safe, like soccer is compared to football. While there's some physical contact in basketball, the game is based on movement and calls for a wide variety of skills. It also promotes the values of teamwork and cooperation while enhancing individual creativity.

park. People don't want that now. They want action. They want perpetual entertainment and basketball provides it.

Then you have the celebrities at the games, Jack Nicholson in Los Angeles, Spike Lee in New York, and so on. Having all those movie stars and supermodels sitting in the front row adds to the appeal, illuminating and embellishing the pageantry of the NBA today. It becomes a happening.

That's what basketball is now, a happening.

A Game of Few Limitations

One of the best things about basketball is its accessibility. You don't need 22 people and tons of protective gear to play, as with football; or 18 players and a large park, as with baseball; or expensive equipment and 7,000 yards of sculpted grassland, as with golf; or ice skates, pads, helmets, sticks, and a rink to skate in, as with hockey.

Groups of any number can play basketball. There are no limitations in age, size, or gender. And you can play just about anywhere, indoors or out, wherever there's enough room to hang up a basket. Many a youngster has tacked a cardboard rim over the door to his bedroom and used a balled up pair of socks to work on his shooting prowess.

All You Need Is a Basket and a Ball

Actually, you don't even need a basket. You can always improvise. Ever since my playing days, I've had a second home in St. Croix in the U.S. Virgin Islands, where I've seen baskets made out of milk cartons, garbage cans, or any other good-sized thing that resembles a hoop. Folks in St. Croix lack the sophisticated equipment we take for granted here in the States, but they continue to persevere. Drive down any street and you'll find a makeshift basket tacked up on a 4x4 post. So I guess all you really need is a ball.

Today, in the United States, it seems like every house has a hoop. Take a ride in suburbia or rural America and count the number of hoops you see in the driveways or the backyards. The high numbers are relatively new; it certainly wasn't that way when I was growing up in the '60s.

Who needs a basketball pole? After attaching the basket to a tree, 14-year-old Jason Kelton of Greenfield, Mass., got a running start and climbed its trunk in order to dunk. Associated Press

Parents have discovered basketball is an entertaining way to keep kids at home while letting them get exercise. Parents put up a basket in the driveway so their kids can go outside and shoot whenever they want. The kids don't have to go anywhere. They don't need other kids or planned activities. They can go out there and play by themselves anytime. It's so convenient.

Clyde's Record Book

Until 1969, women's basketball rules called for six players on a team, with three confined to the offensive half of the court and three to the defensive half. That's because when Clara Baer, a teacher at Newcomb College in New Orleans, asked Naismith for a copy of his rules, he also sent her a court diagram showing where players normally were stationed, using six examples. She took this to mean that the players were restricted to those areas of the court, with six players per team.

Clyde's Chalk Talk

Dribbling, or bouncing the ball while you walk or run, is one of the fundamental skills in basketball. Players are taught to practice dribbling until it becomes automatic, so they don't have to look at the ball and can focus their attention on teammates and opposing players. Watch a deft dribbler control the ball—it looks as if it's attached to his hand with a string, like a yo-yo.

Any Number Can Play

While basketball is generally played with five players on a team, there's nothing sacred about that number. The first game of basketball had nine players on each team because there were 18 students in Dr. James Naismith's gymnastics class when he invented the game in Springfield, Massachusetts, in 1891. Shortly thereafter, more than 100 players mobbed the court during a game played at Cornell University in Ithaca, New York. Talk about overcrowding and chaos!

In 1897, rulesmakers decided that five was the optimum number of players for a basketball team, providing enough options for team play and interaction without cluttering up the court with too many bodies, thus restricting the speed and creativity that's so much a part of the game's essence.

But if you don't have 10 players, improvise. Playing three against three (called *three-on-three*) is ideal for half-court play, where the game is confined to one half of a regulation court, thus cutting down on the overall running as well as the area needed for play. With three players, you still have enough for the passing, the ball movement and the basic plays that are the essence of the game. It also works if you play *two-on-two* (two players per team), and if you just want to work on your own individual skills you can play *one-on-one*.

You can even play by yourself. Just take a ball out to the driveway, the backyard, the school gym, or the playground and work on your game. You don't need an opponent to practice your shot, your *dribble*, or your moves. All you need is a vivid imagination as you practice your jumper, your handle, your creativity. You're one-on-one with Michael, the Dream or Shaq, three seconds on the clock, you're shaking and baking as you penetrate the paint for the winning shot—it's good! Pros all have spent countless hours dribbling, faking, and shooting against imaginary opponents just like that.

Be creative in finding ways to work on your game. Magic Johnson tells how his mom used to send him out for groceries, so he combined those errands with *dribbling* practice. As he was walking to the store he would dribble a basketball with one hand, and as he walked back he dribbled with the other.

A Game for All Ages

Watch a toddler dribble a ball with flat palm, then giggle in joy as it bounces back up. Watch him (or her) take a Nerf ball and stuff it through a plastic goal, then clap hands in glee and exchange a high five with a beaming parent. You're (almost) never too young for the joys of basketball.

Or too old. Sure it helps to be young and in peak physical condition, but men in their 40s, 50s, and 60s play religiously every weekend. There are countless frustrated athletes who still hoop it up because they love the game, the physical activity, and the camaraderie. They're addicted. For a long time I thought basketball addiction was just a New York City phenomenon—possibly existing in a few other cities—but now weekend basketball warriors can be found all over the country.

A Game for Women, Too

Women began playing basketball just four months after the game was invented. Basketball creator Dr. James Naismith went on to marry a participant in that first women's game in March, 1892. One year later the first women's intercollegiate game was played at nearby Smith College in Massachusetts, but in deference to prevailing codes of modesty and propriety of those times, men were not permitted in the gymnasium to watch.

Women today hoop it up just like men. There are two women's professional leagues vying for attention in the United States, and women's pro circuits are thriving in countries throughout Europe, Asia, and Latin America. The women's college game has hit the big time, with its Final Four an annual sellout that's nationally televised. Every high school has a girls team, and from the time they enter kindergarten, active participation in sports like basketball is a viable option for girls as well as boys.

Clyde's Tip

Women's basketball has come a long way from the days when no male spectators were allowed in the gym. The United States team that won the gold medal at the 1996 Summer Olympics drew over 30,000 people to each of its games at the Georgia Dome in Atlanta, and more than 5.2 million people watched women's college basketball games in 1995–96 (not counting games that were played as doubleheaders with men's games), the most recent year for which figures are available.

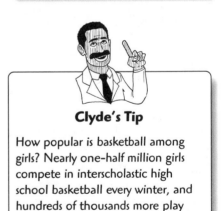

Clyde's Tip

How popular is basketball among girls? Nearly one-half million girls compete in interscholastic high school basketball every winter, and hundreds of thousands more play intramural hoops or compete in gym classes.

Women can take it to the hoop, too, as Georgia's Saudia Roundtree shows in this game against Tennessee in the 1995 NCAA Championships. Associated Press

Girls who participate in a sport like basketball today are no longer singled out as tomboys. I grew up in the South in the '50s and '60s, and a girl was considered a tomboy if she played sports then. Girls weren't supposed to sweat and be physical—it wasn't chic. No girls were pumping iron or going to the gym to work out.

Today there's no stigma attached to girls who want to play sports. Both girls and young women have more and more role models whom they can emulate. Basketball, with its combination of individual skills and teamwork plus its emphasis on movement and creativity (as opposed to power), is very appealing to this new generation of female athletes.

Courts of the Game

From the hardtop playgrounds of Harlem to the dirt driveways of Indiana to the sandy shores of the California coast, the steady thump, thump, thump of a dribbling basketball provides a rhythmic backdrop to the ebbs and flows of American life.

You can play basketball anywhere. Indoors, in shiny air-conditioned arenas or aging school gyms. Outdoors, on floodlit playgrounds or in alleys between houses. Anywhere.

As long as the floor or ground is hard enough for the ball to bounce back up when you dribble and there's a place high enough to tack up a basket, you're in business.

From Hardtop to Hardwood

The surface you play on changes the nature of the game and the equipment you use.

The leather game balls used in the NBA perform well on the hardwood floors in arenas around the league, but would quickly wear out if used on the cement or asphalt that paves our cities' outdoor courts. For those blacktop playgrounds, as well as the courts of clay, gravel, and dirt you'll find in suburbia and rural America, a rubber basketball works best.

A nice, smooth surface is ideal for playing basketball. On a proper surface you get accurate, true bounces, so you don't have to look at the ball when you dribble and can concentrate on things like beating your defender or finding an open teammate. It also helps to be able to run upcourt without worrying about tripping over cracks in the concrete or losing your balance on loose floorboards.

You also want a smooth, even *backboard,* one without dents or pockmarks that can change the angle of a shot that you bank toward the basket. That's why plexiglass has replaced wood or metal as the material of choice for backboards at virtually all levels of competition. And of course, the rims should be smooth and round as well.

Clyde's Record Book

When James Naismith invented basketball in 1891 he used a soccer ball, because it gave a true bounce and because its size demanded finesse in shooting—a player couldn't just throw the ball at a target. An official NBA game ball is made of leather, measures 9 inches in diameter and 30 inches in circumference, and must be inflated to between $7\frac{1}{2}$ and $8\frac{1}{2}$ pounds of air pressure.

Clyde's Chalk Talk

The *backboard* is the surface to which the basket is attached. An NBA backboard is a flat, transparent rectangle measuring 6 feet by $3\frac{1}{2}$ feet, with a smaller white rectangle painted directly behind the basket ring to help shooters aim the ball.

Clyde's Record Book

The backboard has evolved over the years. Dr. Naismith's original baskets were nailed to an overhead running track that encircled the gym in which the first game was played. For several years baskets were attached to or hung atop freestanding poles, until players realized that a backboard would help them sight the target and make it easier for them to shoot.

Quote...Unquote

"When I was playing in the Catholic League, I was Catholic. When I was playing in the Jewish League, I was Jewish. All the while I was really Protestant. I loved basketball so much, I played at whatever opportunity I had."—*Bennie Borgmann, one of the outstanding players of the 1920s.*

Then there's the practice of diving for loose balls, an inevitable part of the game that moms frown upon but coaches love. Dive onto the highly varnished wood floor of a modern gym, and you might emerge unscathed, or with minor floorburns. Dive onto the cracked concrete of an inner city playground or the prickly gravel of a country lane, and you risk bloody cuts, scrapes, and worse.

From Dance Halls to Sports Palaces

In its infancy, professional basketball was a sideshow. Teams and leagues came and went, and so the best players of the early 1900s played for three and four teams at the same time, often using assumed names to conceal their identity.

The top professional teams of the early part of the twentieth century, like the Original Celtics or the Rens, survived not by competing in leagues but by *barnstorming*—packing themselves and their gear onto a bus and traveling from town to town, taking on all comers, stopping anywhere a local team would take them on, and splitting the gate receipts. After the game they'd climb back on the bus, often still in uniform, and head off to another town for another night's competition.

Sometimes a basketball game wouldn't draw enough of a crowd, so it would be combined with other events. One popular combination in many towns and cities during the 1920s and 1930s, perhaps because both activities were well suited for wood floors, was to pair a basketball game with a dance on a Saturday night. Men and women would dance for awhile, then watch from the sidelines as basketball players took the floor and competed in a game. When it was over, the dancing would resume and continue on into the wee hours of the morning. Hey, that sounds like fun!

In the barnstorming era, teams would play wherever they could—in local high schools and colleges, in recreation centers and church basements, in armories and, yes, dance halls. As long as a couple of baskets could be hung 10 feet (more or less) above the floor, you had an arena.

What a dramatic metamorphosis from today's ultramodern sports arenas, which combine multimedia centers, shopping malls, dining establishments, and entertainment centers all in one. Even the venerable multi-purpose arenas that were so much a part of a city's lifeblood through most of the twentieth century have given way to modern replacements.

Boston Garden is no more; the Celtics now play in the splendid FleetCenter, although at least they took the parquet floor and banners with them. Chicago Stadium, the "Madhouse on Madison" that hosted everything from indoor football to the stormy 1968 Democratic National Convention to the acrobatics of Air Jordan, fell to the wrecking ball; the Bulls now play in the gargantuan United Center across the street, an arena which Jordan himself once said had "all the atmosphere of a shopping mall."

There's no denying that many of the new arenas are magnificent. The MCI Center in Washington, America West Arena in Phoenix, the Palace of Auburn Hills outside Detroit, and the Rose Garden in Portland are among the elite. But after awhile they tend to blend into one another, since they lack the quirks and nuances that gave the older arenas such character. The new arenas are dazzling but I miss the hallowed halls of Boston Garden and the cacophony of Chicago Stadium.

A Game That's Made for Television

Basketball and television go together. Maybe not like bees and honey, but just as sweet.

Basketball seems like it was made for television, though the sport was invented long before the tube. The ball is big and easy to see. The game is played in a camera-friendly, confined space—and it's played indoors. You can see the players up close and personal, as they say on TV. You see their bodies, no pads. You see their faces, no caps or helmets. Only tall guys in short pants and tank tops, their emotions from ecstasy to anguish etched on their faces.

Quote...Unquote

"In Philadelphia we played at the Broadwood Hotel. We had a nice place, and we'd draw between 2,000 and 2,500. They charged about $1 for a ticket, which included the game and the dance afterwards. I bet about 50 people met and got married there."—*Moe Goldman, who played professionally in the 1930s.*

Clyde's Tip

Boston Garden was renowned for the dead spots in its parquet floor. I remember dribbling the ball and wondering why the Celtics guards would try to force me to one spot on the floor. Once I got there I knew—the ball hit a dead spot and didn't bounce back up, and before I knew it the Celtics had a steal and a fast break going. That floor made every trip to Boston Garden an excruciating adventure.

That's why whenever they take those polls of the most popular players in sports or the most recognized names, it always seems like seven out of 10 are from the NBA. TV has been the catalyst for propelling basketball players into the most recognized team sports figures in the world.

Nearly every one of the 1,189 games in an NBA season is televised either nationally or locally, over-the-air or via cable. Every single playoff game is nationally televised live over the air or on cable, with each game of the NBA Finals and most of the Conference Finals aired in prime time on NBC. But this is a recent phenomenon—as recently as 1981, the NBA Finals between Boston and Houston were shown nationally only on a taped delay basis, airing after the late-night news because CBS felt they wouldn't get high enough ratings to justify bumping its prime time programming.

Watching basketball on TV is exhilarating. It feels just like being at the game. The camera shows you nearly everything you want to see, often closer than if you were sitting in the arena. It will mesmerize you with the agility, mobility, and hostility of the players. In baseball the camera shows you the pitcher and the catcher, and you lose everything else. You can't feel the ambiance of the field, and you lose touch with the pageantry of the game. The same applies to football, where the camera only can show you a small part of what's going on.

In basketball, when the players go back and forth, you're right there. The cameras capture everything and zoom in for close-ups so you're right in the middle of the hoopla in the paint and you see all the antics and shenanigans that take place, especially if Rodman or Sir Charles is in the house.

One of the best reasons for watching basketball on TV is the replays. With the fast and furious action in basketball, you often need replays to truly appreciate what you have just seen. That's why you see those huge video screens in every NBA arena these days; the fans in attendance can see the same replays on those video screens that you see at home.

Nobody understands the value of television to a sport better than David Stern, the NBA's shrewd and clairvoyant commissioner. He views NBC and the Turner networks as key business partners who are helping to spread the gospel. And when the NBA launched its big international push, it began by making sure its games could be seen in as many countries as possible.

The NBA scrutinizes its television coverage, paying close attention to everything from announcers to camera angles to halftime features, recognizing that for every fan who attends a game live, hundreds more will watch it on TV and form their impression of the league from what they see and hear.

Then there's the ESPN factor. They disdain the mundane. Basketball's dunks, shot-blocks, and no-look passes are perfect for the highlight clips that are so important to ESPN's *SportsCenter* and the other sports news shows that are proliferating today, shows that survive and thrive on the bizarre, the absurd, the most provocative plays of the day.

Clyde's Rules

A strong word of caution for young players: Don't get carried away by what you see on the highlight clips on TV. The flashy dunks and fancy passes fascinate, but remember, those are the pros or the top college players you're watching. Flash and dash is cool, but if you want to be a player, make sure you know the basics. Fundamental skills are what coaches look for at every level, and showing you've got the basics down cold is the best way for you to make the team. Players need more ESP and less ESPN.

In my day, a guy would make a great play and he'd be lucky if there was a picture of it in the newspaper. Now when a guy is ahead of the field for a dunk, you can almost see him thinking about how Chris Berman will describe his huffing and stuffing as he decides what kind of slam he's going to take.

The World Gets a Basketball Jones

Back in the 1980s, when Ted Turner's Atlanta-based TBS started broadcasting NBA games on cable, somebody came up with the phrase "America's Game" as a theme for its coverage. It was a takeoff on football's Dallas Cowboys, who liked to bill themselves as "America's Team."

Ironically, Dr. James Naismith was born, raised and educated in Canada. And while the sport certainly is most popular in the United States, it has long had its avid followers and participants in countries around the world. Students of Naismith at the YMCA Training School in Springfield, Massachusetts, spread word of his game far and wide, so that in a few short years basketball was being played in Europe and Japan as well as throughout the United States and Canada.

Basketball's Canadian roots run deep:

> ➤ The first college team to play basketball against an outside opponent was the University of Toronto, which beat the Toronto YMCA 2-1 in a game played in January, 1893.

Clyde's Chalk Talk

The phrase "Basketball Jones" means an obsession with the game of basketball and stems from 1960s counter-culture, where a "jones" was an addiction of one sort or another. *Basketball Jones* was the title of an album recorded by comedians Cheech and Chong in which the hero, Tyrone Shoelaces, was so into hoops that he related everything in life to basketball.

➤ The first NBA game was played in Toronto, with the New York Knicks beating the Toronto Huskies 68-66 on Nov. 1, 1946. The NBA was known as the BAA (Basketball Association of America) in those days.

So while it might be catchy or patriotic to call basketball America's Game, it's not entirely accurate.

Clyde's Record Book

The United States men have dominated Olympic basketball competition, winning 11 gold medals, 1 silver, and 1 bronze. The United States has played 103 games over the years and lost just 2—to the former Soviet Union for the gold medal in 1972, a game mired in controversy because its ending was twice replayed, and again to the Soviet Union in 1988, when the United States took home the bronze medal.

Quote...Unquote

"I love this game!"—*Gheorge Muresan, a 7'7" center from Romania, speaking one of the few English phrases he knew upon being drafted by the Washington Bullets in 1993.*

Basketball was introduced to the Olympics as a demonstration sport in St. Louis in 1904, but the first medal competition took place in Berlin in 1936. The games were played outdoors in a tennis stadium, and the United States won the first gold medal by beating Canada 19-8 as a thunderstorm turned the clay court to a quagmire.

The fact that more countries entered teams for the basketball competition than any other event in those Olympics shows the scope of the sport's popularity. As *The New York Times* reported, "It is now clear that basketball no longer is merely an American game, but a genuine world game."

Under the guidance of the International Basketball Federation, basketball has enjoyed a steady growth at the grass roots level around the world. This growth mushroomed in the past decade, once restrictions against NBA players competing in international events like the Olympics were lifted and the league began taking an active part in the sport's global growth.

A watershed event in basketball's global growth was the 1992 Summer Olympics in Barcelona, which included the first United States team to feature NBA stars following a rules change in 1989 that opened the door for their participation. That squad, known as the Dream Team, was a global sensation. It didn't matter that the team overwhelmed the competition, winning its games by an average of nearly 44 points. What mattered was that it gave the world a chance to see basketball at its best, as played by living legends such as Michael Jordan, Magic Johnson, and Larry Bird.

Nearly three dozen foreign-born players competed for NBA teams in the 1997–98 season, while hundreds of Americans played professionally in leagues in Europe, Asia, South America, and Australia, leagues that have been operating for 30 years or more.

It is estimated by the International Basketball Federation that around the world, more than 300 million people of all ages, girls as well as boys, are now playing basketball regularly, and this number is growing daily.

Michael Jordan drives to the basket against Angola in the 1992 Olympics. The Dream Team's play in Barcelona gained millions of new fans for the sport of basketball around the world. Associated Press

The Least You Need to Know

➤ Basketball is rapidly becoming a part of day-to-day life in America and around the world.

➤ To today's kids, basketball is in and NBA players are cool.

➤ One of the best things about basketball is its accessibility: Any number, of any age, can play some form of the game virtually anywhere.

➤ Basketball comes across on TV better than just about any other sport because of the size of the players and the ball, the confined nature of the court, the relative simplicity of the game, and the ongoing action.

➤ Basketball is very popular with women, who are more into exercise and physical activity now that ever before.

➤ With an estimated 300 million people regularly playing basketball, it is rapidly gaining on soccer for the distinction of being the world's most popular sport.

Chapter 2

The Object of the Game Is Simple

In This Chapter

➤ How a team racks up points

➤ Everybody has his place on the court

➤ Talk the talk: learning basketball lingo

Basketball can be as simple or as complicated as you want. That's one of the beauties of the sport—you can enjoy it on myriad levels.

One of the keys behind basketball's tremendous growth in popularity in recent years is that it's a fundamentally simple game that anyone can grasp and enjoy the first time they see it. Yet it's a game that has subtleties and complexities that can fascinate a fan for life.

Sometimes, when I'm broadcasting a Knicks game, I look around Madison Square Garden during a timeout and am dumbfounded by the diversity in the crowd. I'll see some guys I recognize from my playing days, season ticket-holders for three decades or more; they're still bantering with the referees during timeouts and trying to distract visiting players when they take the ball out (to restart play after a foul or a timeout, for example). Then I'll see young kids who might be at a game for the first time, staring wide-eyed at the size of the players and talking animatedly to one another about the things they've just seen. Opposite ends of the fan spectrum, yet basketball has more than enough to send both groups home enthralled and enchanted.

Clyde's Chalk Talk

Remember that *basket* and *hoop* both have two meanings. They are used to describe the object at which players aim, consisting of a metal *rim* with a *net* hanging from it. But when a shot goes in, it's often described as a *basket* or a *hoop*, as well. Further complicating the issue, the game itself is often called hoops or even baskets, as in "Let's go shoot some *baskets*" or "Let's see if there are any *hoops* on TV."

Clyde's Chalk Talk

Guard is another of those terms that has two meanings. Used as a verb, as in "try to *guard* your man," it means attempting to prevent an offensive player from scoring, or at least making it as difficult as possible. But it can also be used as a noun (I was a *guard* for the New York Knicks) to describe one of the three basic positions in the sport, as I'll explain shortly.

Whoever Scores More Points Wins

There, is that simple enough?

Five words summarize the game's objective and tell you all you need to know to enjoy basketball at its most fundamental level:

Whoever scores more points wins.

Points, as anyone watching a game quickly sees, are scored by throwing (or *shooting*, if you want to start learning the lingo) that large round ball through the *basket*, which consists of a metal ring (make that *rim*) from which hangs the string (or *net*). *Hoop* is an often-used slang term for basket. Whichever team has the ball tries to score. The second team tries to prevent the first team from scoring until it gains possession of the ball, and the roles of offense and defense are reversed as the second team tries to score by shooting at the basket at the other end of the floor (or *court*).

That's it. You now know enough to survive your first trip to a basketball game without embarrassment, or to watch a game on television without wondering what all those tall guys (or gals) in shorts pants are doing.

Of course, that's only the tip of the iceberg. How a team goes about trying to score, how the opposing team tries to stop it, and what rules the players must obey are what give the game its rich texture, and we'll go into all that later on. For now, let's focus on the basics you need to get started.

Offense: One Point, Two Points, Three Points

Basketball scoring is basically simple, too—not quite as simple as baseball, but not as complex as football.

When a team has possession of the ball, it can score points and is said to be on *offense*. The other team, which is on *defense*, tries to keep the offense from scoring and get the ball so it can be on offense and try to score itself. Defensive players *guard* offensive players to try to keep them from scoring. Teams alternate between offense and defense depending on which team has possession of the ball.

A team that's on offense is credited with either one point, two points, or three points each time it scores, that is, each time the ball goes through the basket. How many points it gets depends on where the ball was shot from (and some other circumstances), which is what some of the markings on the court are for.

Quote...Unquote

"The object of the game is to put the ball into your opponent's goal."—*Dr. James Naismith, the inventor of basketball, in 1891.*

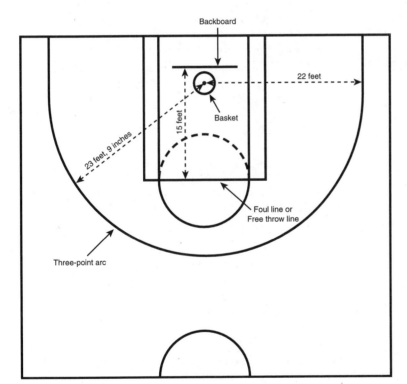

This simplified basketball court diagram shows only the lines that pertain to shooting.

Clyde's Chalk Talk

Fouls come in all flavors, from vanilla to rocky road. The basic "vanilla" foul is when an offensive or defensive player makes contact with an opponent, either with his hand or body. At the "rocky road" end of the spectrum are the *technical foul*, assessed by a referee for conduct detrimental to the game, including verbal abuse; and the *flagrant foul*, assessed for excessive and unnecessary physical contact.

Clyde's Chalk Talk

You might hear the free throw line referred to as the *charity stripe*. That's because coaches feel that letting an opponent shoot too many free throws is like giving them charity. It affords them too many easy opportunities to score without having to earn points against defenders.

One Point at a Time: Free Throws

The offense scores one point for a *free throw*, a shot taken from the *free throw line* (or *foul line*) after a *foul* has been committed. The free throw line is 15 feet from the *backboard* from which the basket is hung. The clock that times the game (called the *game clock*) is stopped while a free throw is attempted, and the player shoots unopposed, without being guarded by a defender—hence the *free* in *free throw*. I'll cover the topic of fouls in more detail in Chapter 11.

The best free throw shooters in the NBA make 85 to 90 percent of their attempts or more, although other players struggle. Wilt Chamberlain, one of the most prolific scoring machines in basketball history and a player who once scored 100 points in a single NBA game, was notoriously inept from the foul line. No matter what shooting technique he used or how much he supposedly practiced, he could never get the hang of it and wound up making barely over half his free throws during his career, retiring with a mediocre percentage of .511 from the line.

Your Basic Field Goal: Two Points

In most cases the offense receives two points for a *field goal*—a shot that's made during the course of play. *Field goals* are also known as *baskets*, just like the targets at which the ball is aimed.

Really adroit shooters make 50 percent or more of their field goal attempts. Obviously the caliber of the defense plays a part in this percentage—if a player is constantly guarded closely by a talented defender, or if the defensive team chooses to *double-team* him (guard him with two defenders), it's that much more difficult to score and the shooter's percentage inevitably goes down. At least, it goes down over the long run—for short periods, when a shooter is hot (or when he's "feeling it" or "in the zone," to use two phrases popular among players), he may continue to make his shots regardless of the defense.

Cha-ching! Three-Pointers

Most field goals are worth two points, although shots that are taken and made from beyond a designated arc painted on the court are worth three points. These are called *three-point shots* or *three-pointers*, also known as home-run balls, bombs, or trifectas.

Three-point shots can enable a team to make up a deficit in a hurry, which is one reason why the rule was adopted. Another was to force defenders to move away from the basket and guard larger areas of the court, preventing them from *"clogging the lane"* or gathering in and around the painted area beneath the foul line directly in front of the basket (the *lane*).

Why is that bad? Because if too many defenders hang around in the lane, offensive players don't have enough space to *drive to the basket*, and those spectacular swoops to the hoop are among the most graceful and exciting plays in the game.

Think of it this way: You know that logo of Michael Jordan sailing through the air, arms and legs outstretched, as he takes the ball to the basket? Well, if the rules permitted teams to line up a picket fence of defenders right in front of the basket, "Air Jordan" might never have gotten clearance for takeoff, there'd be no swooosh symbols, and we'd all be the poorer for it.

The three-point shot has proven popular with fans and is used in all levels of the game of basketball, although the distance of the arc varies. The NBA even changed its distance for several seasons, going to a 22-foot arc all around, before extending it back to 23 feet, 9 inches (keeping it at 22 feet along the sidelines) in 1997. In college ball, the arc is set at 19 feet, 9 inches, while in international ball the distance is 20 feet, 7 inches. Women use a 19 foot, 9 inch arc in both college and professional ball.

The idea of awarding more points for shots made from a greater distance is not a novel concept. The American Basketball League (ABL), which had a brief run in 1961–62, awarded three points for shots made from beyond 25 feet. And the American Basketball Association (ABA), which lasted nine seasons from 1967–68 through 1975–76, had the

Clyde's Chalk Talk

A *field goal* in football is when the ball is kicked through the goal posts above the crossbar. A *field goal* in basketball is when the ball is shot through the basket during the course of play. Would it count as a *field goal* if the ball was kicked through the basket? Only if it happened accidentally, because kicking the ball deliberately is a violation (see Chapter 11).

Clyde's Chalk Talk

You don't need a license to *drive to the basket*, which means taking the ball and dribbling it around or through the defense for a close-in shot at the basket. What you need are quickness, agility, strength, and savvy, with the latter being most important. If you can fake your defender off balance or make him look or step in the wrong direction, your task becomes infinitely easier.

Clyde's Record Book

The first three-point field goal in NBA history was made by Chris Ford, then playing for the Boston Celtics and now the coach of the Milwaukee Bucks, on October 12, 1979. While there were nine games played on the opening night of the 1979–80 season, Ford's three-pointer late in the opening quarter against the Houston Rockets was first and earned him a place in league annals.

Clyde's Tip

If 50 percent is a good barometer for measuring field goal shooting, what's a good number for three-pointers? Try 33 percent, and here's why: Because the long-distance shot is worth an extra point, a player making one-third of his three-point attempts will roughly match the total number of points scored by a player making half his two-point tries. Do the math for yourself and you'll see it works.

same three-point arc the NBA uses today—ranging from 22 feet from the basket along the sidelines to 23 feet, 9 inches along the arc. It took the NBA three years after the demise of the ABA to adopt the three-point rule, but it finally did so beginning with the 1979–80 season.

Dee-fense! Dee-fense!

That invigorating cry, reverberating down from the rafters at Madison Square Garden, was music to my ears as a player with the New York Knicks in the late 1960s and early 1970s. The fans would chant it early and often and it would galvanize us and keep us focused on what was a key element of our success—our ability to play tenacious defense and shut down the opposition.

You could see the frustration building in the other players' eyes when we would deny them, play after play, thwarting everything they tried to do, hounding and pounding them into submission. It would get to a point where an offensive player would be tentative and apprehensive, reluctant to try a shot or make a pass or drive to the basket, and then we knew we had him! The game was ours.

Most fans have to learn how to appreciate defense—the skills and hard work it takes to keep the other team from scoring. In some places, like New York, there's a tradition for supporting the defense. The chant of "Dee-fense!" will rise spontaneously from the Knicks crowd. But fans elsewhere are more offense-oriented and view defense as lackluster action. You have to be indoctrinated into the nuances of defense to appreciate it.

Defense is subtle. Fans pick up the newspaper or watch the highlights and see offense—most sports stories and video clips focus on scoring. These days people want to hear about tangible statistics, and there aren't many of those for defense. Defense is about the intangibles—hustle, tenacity, playing with abandon. You don't need anything extra as far as skills go—oh, it helps to be quick, it helps to be tall or strong maybe. But really all a player needs for defense is the desire to play it. You have to be hell-bent and relentless. You have to really want to play defense.

Defense Wins Championships

There's a saying in golf: You drive for show but putt for dough. Well, in basketball, scoring a lot of points gets you headlines, but defense provides the foundation upon which teams build championships.

The epitome, of course, was the indomitable Bill Russell, the defensive genius who anchored the Boston Celtics juggernaut that won an astounding 11 championships in his 13 seasons. Russell was brilliant at blocking shots, to the point where opponents eschewed driving the lane against him for fear of having their shots swatted back in their faces.

The Los Angeles Lakers of the 1980s, a team that won five NBA titles, also illustrated the impact of awesome defensive play. They were known for their flash and flair, their "Showtime" running game, and Magic Johnson's no-look passes, but they were the most fundamentally sound defensive team in the league, stifling their opponents with regularity.

Individual defense is valuable, but team defense—when five players think and act as one and are committed to giving the effort needed to stop another team—is invaluable.

I was known for my velcro defense with the New York Knicks, but our whole team was a formidable defensive team. We had Willis Reed at *center* to police the paint and make up for any mistakes and Dave DeBusschere at *forward*, another great defensive player. The *guards* I played with, Dick Barnett and Earl Monroe, allowed me the freedom to roam the court like a free safety, using my quickness and anticipation to play the passing lanes and go for steals and deflections and generally create havoc. (You'll learn what centers, forwards, and guards do shortly, in the section titled, "Positions Have Names [and Numbers, Too]".) Our coach, the astute Red Holzman, was a fundamentalist from the old school. He believed in defense and never let us forget about it.

Quote...Unquote

"A guy comes in and you block his shot, and you go down and get an easy layup. You might look at him and smile and say, `Yes, we did that to you.' These things make statements."—*Bill Russell, Hall of Fame center for the Boston Celtics (1957–69), who loved to deliver a message when he blocked a shot.*

Clyde's Record Book

At his peak, Michael Jordan wasn't only the greatest offensive player in the NBA, he was the best defensive player as well. In 1988, he won Most Valuable Player (MVP) honors, led the league in scoring and *steals* (taking the ball away from an offensive player), and was the NBA Defensive Player of the Year. When he hunkers down in his defensive stance, eyes focused on his opponent, beware of Air!

Bill Russell (6), who turned defense into an art form, leaps to block a shot by Tommy Hawkins of the Los Angeles Lakers in the 1968 NBA Finals. Associated Press

Defense 101

There are two basic types of defense in basketball: man-to-man, where each defensive player is responsible for guarding a specific offensive man, and zone, where each defensive player is assigned to an area of the court and guards any opponent who comes into that area. There is also an assortment of trapping and pressing defenses that are variations designed to have two men guard the player with the ball and harass him into losing it, but we'll get into those later in the book.

For now, you need only know that the NBA only allows man-to-man defense. The defensive team can't play zones, because the NBA wants to promote movement and action on the court and doesn't want defensive players standing around close to the basket, taking away those daring drives we talked about earlier. Which would you rather see: Grant Hill of the Detroit Pistons shooting 20-foot jumpers or Grant Hill making dynamic and dazzling swoops to the hoop?

When it all comes together, tenacious defense can be as exciting, exquisite, and entertaining as great offense. Just ask those fans at the world's most famous arena.

Positions Have Names (and Numbers, Too)

There are three basic positions in basketball: *center*, *forward*, and *guard*. Though an NBA team may have as many as 12 players on its active roster, each team can only have five players on the court at any given time—usually one center, two forwards, and two guards. The center is generally the tallest player on the team and plays closest to the basket, while the guards are the shortest and play farthest away. The forwards fall somewhere in between, both in height and where they play.

But if you think you're getting away that easily, forget it! Although Part 2 will deal with each position in detail, the rest of this section covers a few more basics you should know.

The center's job is to score points (generally, although not always, from close to the basket), set picks so other shooters can get free from their defenders, *rebound* the ball, and block shots that are attempted by the opposing team.

Forwards primarily are expected to score and also help the center with rebounding. Guards have the job of orchestrating their team's offense as well as trying to score on their own. Guards and forwards are smaller and quicker than centers and generally have greater shooting range; in addition to shooting from a distance, they also will penetrate to the hoop.

Defensively, a player at any of the three positions is expected to stop the man he's covering from scoring, or at least make it difficult for him to do so. Each position also has additional roles within a team defensive concept. A center generally stays near the basket and tries to block the shot attempt of any opponent who drives toward the hoop. Guards and forwards often move away from the men they're guarding and double-team an opponent who has the ball, trying to force a *turnover* or make a *steal*.

Clyde's Chalk Talk

A *pick* (or *screen*) is when an offensive player positions himself between a teammate and the man trying to guard him, using his body as a barrier in order to allow his teammate to shoot. *Rebound* is another word that serves as a noun or a verb. "To *rebound* the ball" is to gather a missed shot; the missed shot itself also is called a *rebound*. An *offensive rebound* is when you get your own team's missed shot, a *defensive rebound* is when you get the other team's miss.

In recent years, forwards have been separated into two distinct categories: *small forwards* and *power forwards*. While power forwards generally are indeed strong and powerful, small forwards may be anything but small, standing as tall as 6'9", 6'10", or more in some cases. Power forwards tend to combine the size and strength of centers with the traditional skills of forwards, while small forwards often are able to handle the ball and/or shoot from long range as well as any guards.

Meanwhile, guards have been split into *point guards* and *shooting guards*. The point guard is the team's primary ball handler. His job is to bring the ball up the floor toward the basket at which his team is shooting (after the opposing team scores, misses a shot, or commits a turnover) and start the plays, acting as the team's quarterback if you will. The shooting guard's main responsibility is (surprise!) to shoot. Shooting guards are also called *off guards* because they play "off the ball," meaning they don't normally bring it upcourt but rather try to find open space for their shots before catching a pass from a teammate.

Each position is identified by a number, for the convenience of players and coaches when plays are diagrammed (and also, I think, because it sounds cool). These numbers, it should be noted, have nothing whatsoever to do with the uniform numbers players wear, which are strictly of their own choosing. The position numbers are:

> 1—point guard
>
> 2—shooting guard
>
> 3—small forward
>
> 4—power forward
>
> 5—center

Learn those numbers. Use them wisely in conversation. Turning to your companion at a game and saying about a guard who would rather shoot than pass, "He's more of a 2 than a 1," is sure to impress—if used correctly. The following figure illustrates, generally, where the players do their thing.

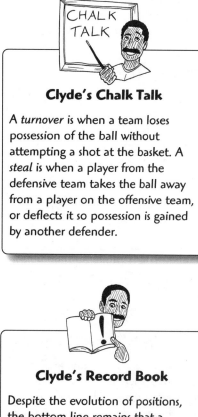

Clyde's Chalk Talk

A *turnover* is when a team loses possession of the ball without attempting a shot at the basket. A *steal* is when a player from the defensive team takes the ball away from a player on the offensive team, or deflects it so possession is gained by another defender.

Clyde's Record Book

Despite the evolution of positions, the bottom line remains that a player is a player. Here's what I mean: Los Angeles Lakers point guard Magic Johnson filled in at center for an injured Kareem Abdul-Jabbar in Game 6 of the 1980 NBA Finals. At various times during the game he played all five positions as the Lakers beat the Philadelphia 76ers 123-107 to wrap up their first of five NBA Championships in the 1980s.

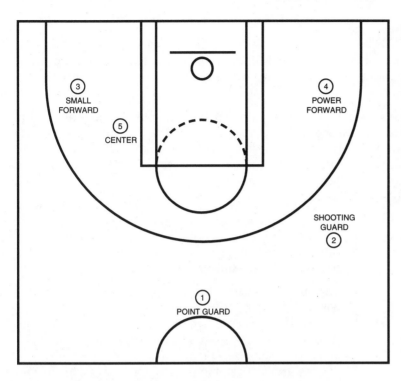

Although anyone can roam anywhere on the court, players playing the different positions generally set up and begin plays in specific areas: 1-point guard, 2-shooting guard, 3-small forward, 4-power forward, 5-center.

You'll also hear talk of "the sixth man," although only five players can be on the court at any time. A team's best reserve player, usually the first substitute to come into the game, is known as the team's sixth man. Good sixth men are very valuable because they can energize a team, offensively or defensively, at a time when the *starters* (the team members who are playing at the beginning of the game) are showing fatigue. The Boston Celtics had a string of great sixth men, including Frank Ramsay and John Havlicek, during their dynasty of the 1960s.

Now that you understand positions, don't get too hung up on them. Asked whether he considered himself a point guard or a shooting guard, Hall of Famer Jerry West quickly replied: "I was a guard. Period."

Clyde's Tip

Not every team follows the accepted mold of having five distinct positions. Some succeed by breaking that mold, if their players are talented enough. The Chicago Bulls, the dominant team in the 1990s, never had a true point guard to serve as a primary ball handler and run their offense. With the multiplicity of skills belonging to Michael Jordan and Scottie Pippen no true point guard was needed.

29

Learning the Lingo

You already know some basic basketball terminology: basket and backboard, rim and net, shots and fouls, and the positions. Now I'll give you a few more key words and phrases to help you follow the action.

The game begins with a *tipoff,* or an opening tip, tap, or jump. One of the three-person refereeing crew (women joined the NBA's refereeing staff in 1997–98 for the first time) will toss the ball up in the center court circle, and one player from each team will jump and try to tip (or tap) it to a teammate, thus giving his team possession to start play.

A player may advance the ball by passing it to a teammate or by *dribbling* (bouncing) it as he runs or walks upcourt. A player may not take two steps without dribbling the ball. To do so is a *violation* known as *traveling,* which results in loss of ball possession.

The object of a pass is to advance the ball to a teammate who may be in better position to get off a shot than you are. A pass may be thrown with one hand or two, on the fly or on a bounce, from over the head, the chest, or just about anyplace else. Often a passer won't even look directly at his target, but make a point of looking in a different direction in order to confuse the defenders— hence the term *"no-look pass."* Sometimes you'll see a player throw the ball one-handed the length of the court to a teammate for an open shot—this is often called a baseball pass because he threw the ball as if it were a baseball.

When a player gets the ball close enough to the basket he may attempt to score by taking a shot at the basket. The type of shot is often dictated by where he is on the court and how closely he's being guarded, but is also affected by personal ability, style, and preference.

A player who's unguarded may dribble all the way to the basket and shoot the most basic shot in the game—the *layup,* where he lays the ball softly onto the backboard and caroms it into the basket. He may also try to flip the ball directly over the rim and into the basket, but this leaves more room for error than laying it off the backboard.

If a player can jump well enough, he may try to *dunk* the ball, or shoot it downward through the basket. Obviously this requires the ability to leap high enough

Quote...Unquote

"It doesn't matter how simple or fancy a pass is. The only good pass is one that is caught by its target."— *Red Auerbach, former coach, general manager, and president of the Boston Celtics.*

Clyde's Tip

It often seems that referees ignore traveling violations, and sometimes that makes sense. If a player is already past his defender and needs two steps before leaping for a rim-rattling slam-dunk, why call a violation and take that exciting play away from the fans? It's when a player is being tightly guarded and he takes an extra step in order to get away from his man that traveling must be called—and too often isn't.

to be able to hold the ball over the rim with either one or two hands and then throw it down, something most people can't do. A dunk is also known as a *slam*, a *jam*, or a *slam-dunk*.

There is no more electrifying play in sports than a Michael Jordan slam-dunk.
Associated Press

The basic shot in basketball today is the *jump shot*, or *jumper*. A player leaps into the air and releases this shot from above his head, thus making it difficult for a defender to block. Until the 1950s players used set shots, one or two-handed shots that generally were released from chest level while both feet were set on the floor. But these became increasingly easy to block as players learned to use their jumping ability, and now the set shot is virtually extinct.

Larry Bird (33) of the Boston Celtics keeps his eyes on the target as he shoots this short jumper against the Sacramento Kings.
Associated Press

There are many types of shots, taken with one hand or two. You'll see shots attempted from all positions and angles, while players are standing still, on the run, or even falling to the floor. You can't take your eyes off the court for a second. Just when you think a player's shot doesn't have a prayer of going in, swish! His prayer is answered.

A shot that goes in is counted as a field goal, or basket. A shot that's missed results in a *rebound* as the ball caroms off the rim or backboard and is grabbed by either a team-mate (an offensive rebound) or an opponent (a defensive rebound). If a shot attempt is knocked away by an opponent, it's called a *blocked shot,* or a rejection. Too many of those and a shooter will find himself pulled out of the game and on the bench very quickly.

If a shooter is hit by a defender while attempting a shot, a *foul* is whistled by the referee and the shooter is awarded two free throws, worth one point each (or three free throws if the attempt was from behind the three-point arc). He thus has a chance to earn, from the foul line, as many points as his shot would have been worth had it gone in. And if his shot goes in while he's being fouled, the basket is counted and he is awarded one free throw on top of it.

After a made basket or free throw, a player from the opposing team passes the ball inbounds to a teammate to resume play. The same goes following a turnover—when a player from one team loses the ball out of bounds, a player from the opposing team tosses it inbounds to a teammate so play can resume.

That's enough for now. When we discuss basketball positions and strategy we'll describe many of the plays teams use to try to score, and you'll get to know terms like *give-and-go* or *pick-and-roll*. And we'll explain how *cherry-picking* can be fruitful, even though it has nothing to do with fruit.

Clyde's Record Book

Joe Fulks, who played for the Philadelphia Warriors in the 1940s and was the NBA's first scoring champion, is considered the first player to effectively utilize the jumper. But while today's jump-shooters are taught to face the basket squarely before going up for a shot, Fulks would spin in either direction before firing or shoot while on the run, often switching the ball from one hand to another while in mid-air.

The Least You Need to Know

➤ The beauty of basketball is that it may be enjoyed on many levels.

➤ Scoring is simple: one point for a free throw, two or three for a field goal, depending on distance.

➤ There are only three basic positions: center, forward, and guard. Centers score, rebound, and block shots; forwards are primarily scorers; and guards set up a team's offense in addition to trying to score on their own.

➤ A player's size and skills determine the position he plays, with the bigger, stronger players playing closer to the basket where their size and strength can be used to the best advantage.

➤ Great defense can turn fans on as much as great offense—just listen to the cheers the next time a team is swarming and smothering its opponent.

Playing by the Rules

> **In This Chapter**
>
> ➤ The birth of basketball
>
> ➤ Understanding the rules
>
> ➤ Why the court looks the way it does
>
> ➤ Rules changes that worked—and one that didn't
>
> ➤ Referees maintain law and order

Unlike other sports, whose roots may be shrouded in myth, basketball's beginnings are well-documented. The game was invented in December 1891 by Dr. James Naismith, who was looking for an activity that would keep an unruly class of physical education students active and involved through the cold, snowy New England winter.

Basketball wasn't always the exciting, high-scoring game we know today. Albeit Naismith intended it to be a non-contact sport and designed the rules that way, early games often turned into rough-and-tumble affairs, especially when a local team would take on a traveling troupe on a barnstorming tour.

Several rules changes served to open up the game and speed up play, including the elimination of the center jump after every basket and the introduction of the shot clock, as well as penalties for excessive fouling. Over the years, basketball has steadily evolved into the fast-paced game we all enjoy today, as you'll learn in this chapter.

The Father of Basketball

James Naismith was a young, Canadian-born instructor at the YMCA Training School (now Springfield College) in Springfield, Massachusetts in 1891 when the head of the physical education department, Dr. Luther Gulick, came to him with a problem. The cold, snowy New England winter was approaching, and the school needed a new game that would hold active students' interest while giving them a chance to work off excess energy and get valuable exercise.

Naismith first considered taking popular outdoor games like soccer and lacrosse and simply moving them indoors, but decided they were too rough and tumble for the confines of a gymnasium. So he set about inventing a new game.

Dr. James Naismith is known as the father of basketball, having invented the sport in 1891. Associated Press

He recalled a game from his childhood called Duck On A Rock, where players tossed small stones at a target that sat atop a large boulder. He also thought of an activity he had devised while a student at McGill University in Montreal, where he helped rugby players stay in shape by having them flip a ball into a box on the gymnasium floor.

Naismith based his game on five principles, as he later explained in his book, *Basketball, Its Origin and Development:*

1. There must be a ball; it should be large, light and handled with the hands.
2. There shall be no running with the ball.
3. No man on either team shall be restricted from getting the ball at any time that it is in play.
4. Both teams are to occupy the same area, yet there is to be no personal contact.
5. The goal shall be horizontal and elevated.

His reasoning was simple. Ball games were popular, but games with a small ball needed gloves or a bat, intermediate equipment that made the games harder to learn. A larger ball was preferable. Next, if players couldn't run with the ball, they would have to develop some other skill to advance it toward its target, which was to be horizontal and elevated to promote skill and finesse over strength and force. No running or contact would eliminate the tackling that made outdoor sports so rough, and having both teams on the court at the same time and permitting any player to touch the ball would keep everybody involved in the game.

Finding a ball was easy. There were plenty of soccer balls left over from the fall season. For targets, Naismith asked school custodian Pop Stebbins to nail a couple of boxes at opposite ends of a wooden running track that encircled the gym, 10 feet above the floor. Stebbins couldn't find any boxes but asked if a pair of round peach baskets would do. Naismith said okay, which is why we play basketball and not boxball today.

One of the students in Naismith's class, Frank Mahan, wanted to name the new game after its inventor and call it Naismith ball, but the shy educator would have none of it. "I laughed and told him that I thought that name would kill any game," said Naismith. "Frank then said, 'Why not call it basket ball?' 'We have a basket and a ball, and it seems to me that would be a good name for it,' I replied. It was in this way that basket ball (later shortened to basketball) was named."

There were 18 students in Naismith's gymnastics class, so there were 18 players in the first basketball game ever played, on December 21, 1891. Naismith wrote up 13 rules for his new game, which was played in a gym that measured 50 feet by 35 feet (for comparison, today's NBA court is more than twice as large, measuring 94 feet by 50 feet).

The first basket in history, and the only one in that initial game, was scored by William R. Chase. It was a 25-foot shot from midcourt and made the final score of that first game 1-0.

Word of Naismith's game spread quickly, because his students went home during the Christmas holiday break and introduced it to friends in gyms and youth centers in their hometowns. Within a year it was being played throughout the United States—and since five of his students were from Canada and one was from Japan, it spread to those countries, too.

This game of basketball took place in 1892. Note that the players hadn't yet figured out that they could speed up the game if they cut a hole in the basket so the ball could fall through, instead of using a ladder to retrieve it after every successful basket.
Basketball Hall of Fame

Dr. Naismith's Original 13 Rules

Dr. Naismith devised 13 rules for his new game and posted them on a bulletin board, so his students could study them before they played. In January, 1892 they were published in the YMCA Training School's newspaper, *The Triangle,* under the heading, A New Game.

They are worth reviewing because they provide insight into Naismith's thinking as he invented basketball—what he was trying to achieve and what he was trying to avoid. The rules have been modified over the years, but the basic principles remain to this day.

Here are those original 13 rules, which Naismith introduced with one sentence about the goal of the game:

Objective: The object of the game is to put the ball into your opponent's goal.

The Rules:

1. The ball may be thrown in any direction with one or both hands.

2. The ball may be batted in any direction with one or both hands (never with a fist).

3. A player cannot run with the ball. The player must throw it from the spot on which he catches it, allowance to be made for a man who catches the ball when running if he tries to stop.

4. The ball must be held by the hands. The arms or body must not be used for holding it.

5. No shouldering, holding, pushing, tripping or striking in any way the person of an opponent shall be allowed; the first infringement of this rule by any player shall count as a foul, the second shall disqualify him until the next goal is made, or if there was evident intent to injure the person, for the whole of the game, no substitute allowed.

6. A foul is striking at the ball with the fist, violation of Rules 3, 4 and such as described in Rule 5.

7. If either side makes three consecutive fouls it shall count as a goal for the opponents (consecutive means without the opponents in the meantime making a foul).

8. A goal shall be made when the ball is thrown or batted from the grounds into the basket and stays there, providing those defending the goal do not touch or disturb the goal. If the ball rests on the edges, and the opponent moves the basket, it shall count as a goal.

9. When the ball goes out of bounds, it shall be thrown into the field of play by the person first touching it. He has a right to hold it unmolested for five seconds. In case of a dispute, the umpire shall throw it straight into the field. The thrower-in is allowed five seconds; if he holds it longer it shall go to the opponent. If any side persists in delaying the game the umpire shall call a foul on the side.

10. The umpire shall be the judge of the men and shall note the fouls and notify the referee when three consecutive fouls have been made. He shall have the power to disqualify men according to Rule 5.

11. The referee shall be judge of the ball and shall decide when the ball is in play, in bounds, to which side it belongs and shall keep the account of the goals, with any other duties that are usually performed by a referee.

12. The time shall be two 15-minute halves, with five minutes' rest between.

13. The side making the most goals in that time shall be declared the winner. In the case of a draw, the game may, by agreement of the captains, be continued until another goal is made.

In reading these original rules, it's clear that Naismith was a law-and-order guy who wanted a non-violent game. His first seven rules discuss what's allowed and what's not allowed; he doesn't get to how a goal is scored until Rule 8!

How the Rules Have Changed

Much has changed in 100+ years with regard to the rules of basketball, yet much remains the same. This says a lot about Naismith's perceptiveness in creating a game that would fill an immediate need but stand the test of time.

Quote...Unquote

"It will be surprising to many to know how little the game has really changed throughout the years. People often believe that much of basketball is comparatively new, whereas in reality, the things that have been considered of recent development were embodied in the game almost from its conception."
—Dr. James Naismith, in 1941.

Clyde's Chalk Talk

Double-dribble is dribbling the ball at the same time with both hands. *Discontinuation*, or a discontinued dribble, is when a player dribbles the ball, stops and holds it, then starts to dribble it again. Both are violations and result in loss of ball possession.

It remains a non-violent game, if not exactly a non-contact game. Over the years, a certain amount of contact became an accepted part of basketball, although how much has varied. The free throw quickly was introduced as a penalty for fouling, and the technical foul for verbal abuse or other misconduct.

It's ironic that Naismith's original Rule No. 5, written over a century ago, covers the same ground as the flagrant foul rule in the NBA today—what to do about excessive use of force in committing a foul.

The biggest change in basketball, according to Naismith himself, who helped mold the game's rules for over 40 years, was the development of the dribble. Because players could bat the ball but not run with it, they soon realized they could stay within the rules by bouncing the ball, moving a step or two and then catching it, or bouncing it again. This quickly became a popular offensive tactic, and it's a good thing. Without the dribble, we wouldn't have the fast-break style of basketball we have today.

In 1898, a rule was introduced barring a player from touching the ball with both hands more than once—what is today called the *double-dribble*. A player was allowed, however, to bounce it with one hand as many times as he wanted. A year later this was clarified to indicate that a dribbler could alternate hands while bouncing the ball, just not dribble it with both hands.

Another key evolutionary development was the introduction of the *pivot*. Naismith's rules state that a player cannot run with the ball, and must pass or shoot from the spot where he catches it. This quickly was seen as too restrictive, and by 1893 a rule was introduced permitting a player to turn around on the spot where he catches the ball. Thus a player could use his body to block off a defender, catch the ball with his back to the basket, turn to face the target, then shoot.

Pivoting rapidly caught on and became a fundamental part of every big man's repertoire. Players like Dutch Dehnert and Joe Lapchick used it to help make the Original Celtics the barnstorming sensation of the 1920s.

The pivot is the foundation of today's game, used by all players, not just centers. A player takes the ball and, with his pivot foot planted, steps in one direction or another with his other foot while going through a series of head and ball fakes. All of this is designed to throw the defender off balance, creating enough space so the pivoter can take his shot or drive to the basket.

Clyde's Chalk Talk

The *pivot* is when a player keeps one foot still, but turns in one direction or another with his other foot. A player who turns toward the basket is said to "pivot to the hoop." The move is used so often by centers that the words became interchangeable. A player who plays center is also said to play the pivot.

George Mikan, who starred at DePaul, for the short-lived Chicago Gears, and then for the Minneapolis Lakers in the '40s and early '50s, was famous for wheeling toward the basket, elbows flailing, and laying the ball in the basket. Because of Mikan the foul lane was widened from 6 to 12 feet in 1952; along came Wilt Chamberlain and the NBA widened its lane again in 1964, this time to the present 16 feet.

Clyde's Rules

Some of today's centers stretch the envelope when it comes to traveling. The NBA rule book says you're allowed to take one step and then go up for the shot, or catch the ball while on the move and come to a jump stop with both feet. Anything more is supposed to be a violation. Next time you're at a game, watch the centers' feet when they get the ball and see if they stay within the rules.

The height of the basket remains 10 feet above the floor, just as it was when Naismith had the first peach baskets nailed to the overhead running track in Springfield. And while players are taller and stronger, there's no great movement to raise the height of the basket. Back in the 1950s, the NBA played one experimental game with the baskets at 12 feet, but the players hated it and it was never repeated.

Former Boston Celtics coach Red Auerbach points out that if shooting percentages went down as a result of the higher basket, as would seem likely it would create more rebounds—most of which would go to the taller players, which would make the big man more important than ever. Besides, does anyone really want to take the dunk out of basketball? Seeing 5'7" Spud Webb soar to the hoop and win the NBA's slam-dunk contest in 1986 was a moment few who were there in Dallas will ever forget.

Quote...Unquote

"Each game has its own evolution, that is somewhat independent of the rules, for we always find, even in the most strictly enforced athletic games, that the actual playing rules do not and cannot conform exactly to the printed rules."—*Dr. Luther Gulick.*

Basketball's rulesmakers have proven receptive to change. Shot clocks, which require a team with the ball to attempt a shot within a specified time limit or else lose possession, were introduced to speed up the tempo of the game, first in the NBA and later at the college level. The three-point field goal was created to encourage outside shooting and open up the court. The NBA has steadfastly prohibited zone defenses, again for the purpose of opening up the floor and promoting player movement, although it seems to be constantly tinkering with what constitutes a legal or illegal defense.

But it's amazing how many things haven't changed. You still can't run with the ball and "holding, pushing, tripping or striking in any way the person of an opponent" remains a foul, just as Naismith wrote back in 1891.

Court Is in Session

The basketball court has undergone a steady evolution, as have the game's rules.

The first game was played on a gymnasium floor that measured just 35 feet by 50 feet, leaving little room to maneuver. Today's pro and college games are played on courts that measure 50 feet by 94 feet, giving players more than twice as much room in which to do their thing. If today's courts were the original size, I might still be playing.

Clyde's Rules

While NBA and NCAA (National Collegiate Athletic Association, the largest governing body in college athletics) courts are 94 feet long, high school games may be played on courts that are 10 feet shorter. Some school buildings, especially older ones, have these smaller courts because space was at a premium when they were built. Most high school games today, however, are played on 94-foot courts.

SPALDING'S BASKET BALL SHOES

Made of selected leather, rubber sole. The suction caused by the peculiar construction of the sole enables the player to obtain a good purchase on the floor, a feature that has made this shoe very popular.

No. **BB.** Pair, **$4.00**

High Cut, best grade Canvas Shoe, rubber sole.
No. **1H.** Pair, **$1.50**

High Cut, Canvas Shoe, with rubber sole.
No. **M.** Pair, **$1.00**

A. G. SPALDING & BROS.

New York	Chicago	Philadelphia	San Francisco
St. Louis	Boston	Buffalo	Baltimore
Denver	Minneapolis	Kansas City	Montreal, Can.

London, England

Some things have changed. Note the price range in this early advertisement for basketball shoes: from $1 all the way up to $4! Today's shoes are a bit more pricey.
Basketball Hall of Fame

Over the years, the look of the court has changed as new rules were introduced. It's gone from a simple wood floor with no markings to one that looks like a road map, with all sorts of solid and dotted lines.

Here are two early examples. In 1894, the free throw line was introduced and was placed 15 feet from the basket; there was no provision in Naismith's original rules for free throws. And in 1932, to prevent stalling, the court was divided in half with a midcourt line that teams were required to move the ball past within 10 seconds or else lose possession.

The dimensions of the free throw lane have changed over the years—various circles have been painted on the court, three-point lines have been introduced, and assorted other markings have been added to the floor.

Knowing what all (or at least most of) these markings mean will go a long way toward helping you understand what's going on.

What Are All Those Lines About?

The official NBA court, as we said, is a rectangle measuring 50 feet wide and 94 feet long. But it wasn't always this way.

In the old days, when the NBA was new, its courts were placed in existing buildings and had to be fitted to whatever space was there, so the dimensions sometimes varied a bit. Today's arenas are built with the playing court as their focus, so there's no problem keeping every court the same.

One thing you'll notice right away is that the baskets and backboards hang over the court. Each backboard is 4 feet from the *baseline,* or end line, allowing room for players to run from one side of the court to the other behind the basket.

The rectangle at each end of the court, with a circle atop it facing the basket, is called the *foul lane, free throw lane,* or *key*, and is always painted a different color from the rest of the floor. This is why, if you really want to impress the person you're watching a game with, you'll refer to this rectangle as the *paint*.

Why is it painted a different color? To make the referees' jobs easier. Offensive players aren't permitted to stand inside the lane for longer than three seconds. This is called a *three-second violation,* and was first introduced in 1935 as a way of keeping players from parking directly in front of the basket in the best shooting position.

The free throw line is 15 feet from the basket. There is also a free throw circle with a 6 foot radius, shown by a solid arc above the line and a broken arc below it. No player may enter this area while a shooter is on the line attempting his free throws.

You'll also see two circles at the center of the midcourt line. The smaller one is called the center circle, and that is where the *jump ball* that opens a game is held. The larger one is called the restraining circle; no players other than the two who are participating in the jump ball may stand within this circle until the ball is tipped.

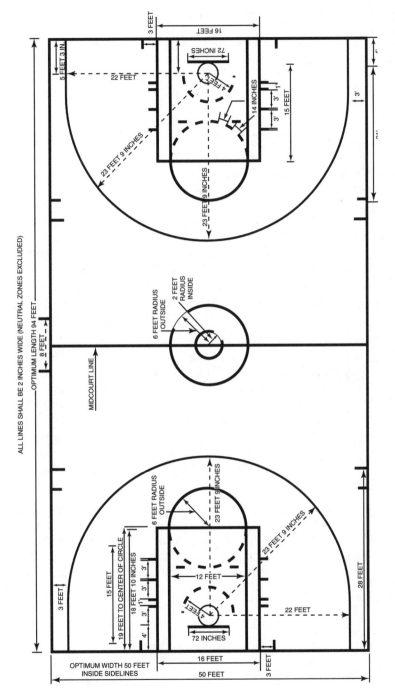

Recognizing the markings on an official NBA court will help you understand how the game is played.

45

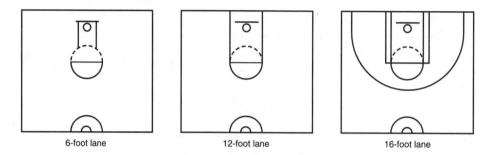

| 6-foot lane | 12-foot lane | 16-foot lane |

The foul lane has gone from (left to right) the original keyhole to the current 12-foot college width to the 16-foot NBA width.

The large arc at each end of the court is the three-point line. A player must have both feet behind that line when he releases the ball in order for his shot to be worth three points. The NBA arc starts at 22 feet along the sidelines and goes out to 23 feet, 9 inches straight away from the basket. In recent years the league tried an arc that was 22 feet all around but this shot was deemed too easy for the pros, so it was extended back to its original distance.

A new addition to the NBA floor markings for the 1997–98 season were the 4-foot dotted semicircles under each basket. This is the so-called "no-charging" area: If a defender is standing inside this area and a player runs into him as he attempts a shot, no charging foul is called. (A charging foul would be called against the offensive player if they collided outside the area.) The purpose of the rule is to encourage players to drive to the basket, one of the most exciting plays in the game.

You'll also see hashmarks along the foul line, which indicate where players may stand while a free throw is being attempted, and along the sidelines, which indicate the areas within which coaches must stay during the game, and where substitutes must stay before entering a game.

Clyde's Chalk Talk

A *jump ball* is when the referee tosses the ball up and one player from each team tries to tap it to a teammate. A jump ball determines ball possession at the start of a game—and determines who gets possession when two players grab hold of the ball simultaneously. In the early years a jump ball also was used after each made basket, but this was eliminated by 1937 in order to provide for more continuous play.

Clyde's Rules

Chances are you will see every coach go outside the designated coach's area in front of the team bench at some time or another, whether to call out a play, give instructions to a player, or offer constructive criticism (ahem!) to a referee. A referee may call a technical foul on the coach for doing so but generally uses his discretion about it, depending on how often a coach strays from the box, how noisy he is about it, and just how constructive his criticism is.

Differences Between NBA and College Courts

Colleges use a court that's the same size as the official NBA court, but you'll immediately notice two important differences in the markings.

The first is in the size of the foul lane. The official NCAA court has a foul lane that's 12 feet wide, 4 feet less than the NBA lane. That permits college players to set up a little closer to the basket without incurring three-second violations.

The second is in the distance of the three-point line from the basket. On the NCAA court, the three-point line is 19 feet, 9 inches from the center of the basket all around. That makes it 4 feet shorter than the NBA distance at the top of the key and 2 feet, 3 inches shorter along the sidelines.

The idea was to bring the shot within the range of more college players, but I think the shorter arc makes it a little too easy. That's why you see so many three-pointers taken in college games—everybody thinks he can make a 20-foot jumper. These guys shoot it all the time. Everything is either a three-pointer or a dunk.

The three-point shot has been a blessing and a curse. It's a blessing in that it gives teams a chance to catch up quickly, which keeps the outcome of games in doubt longer. But it's been a curse in that it has taken the mid-range jumper out of the game.

The worst shot in college basketball is the 18-foot jumper, or the 21-footer in the NBA. Think about it: Why would you want to take a shot from that distance that's worth two points, when you can take one step back and try just about the same shot for three points?

Not only has the three-pointer taken away the mid-range jumper, it's also affected the running game. When you come down on a three-on-two fast break and a guy stops behind the line ready to launch up a three rather than go to the basket, that's bad. Fans want to see guys dashing and slashing, not standing out behind the arc. I know I do.

Note that on the official NCAA court, the three-point arc is closer to the basket than in the NBA and the foul lane is narrower.

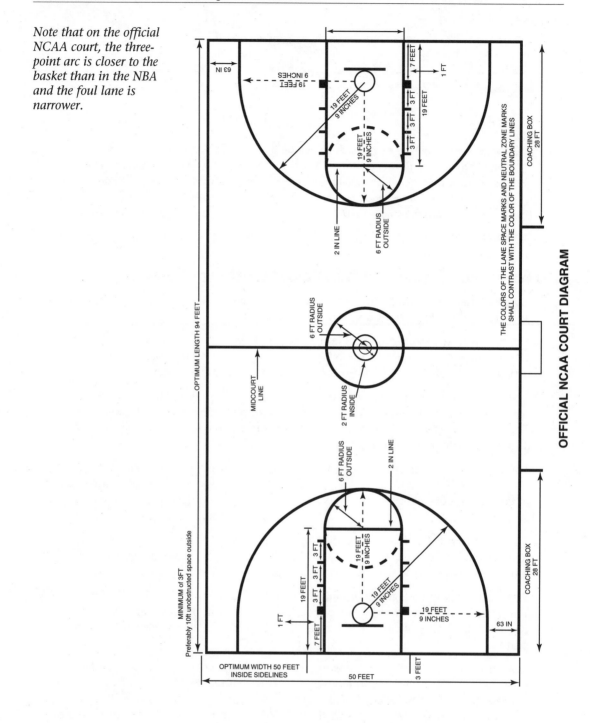

OFFICIAL NCAA COURT DIAGRAM

Why They're Known as Cagers

Just as the court markings have changed over the years, so have the courts themselves.

In the barnstorming era, teams would play just about anywhere they could clear some space on a hard floor and hang up a couple of baskets. As we noted, dance halls were a popular venue. So were high school gyms, armories, rec centers, and auditoriums.

You might hear basketball players referred to as "cagers" or see that term in print, particularly in older books or accounts of early games. It's not because the net on a basket resembles a small cloth cage.

Believe it or not, up until the 1920s many games were played on courts that were enclosed with chain link fences or mesh netting made of wire or cloth. These kept the ball (and players) from bouncing off the court and into the spectators, and also protected visiting players from unruly spectators—not a minor concern in those days.

The rigid cages took their toll on the players, who regularly suffered cuts, scrapes, and bruises when they were slammed into the metal by an opponent, or ran into it on their own. The wire mesh netting was somewhat more forgiving and the cloth was better still, and clever players used the flexible netting to help change directions or build momentum the way circus performers do.

Quote...Unquote

"In the cage, it was common practice if the man with the ball was near the net, you would grab the net on both sides of him and press him into the net so he couldn't pass the ball and they'd have a jump ball."—*Flip Dowling, who played professionally for Cohoes in the New York State League in 1919, describing how defensive players could use the netting to their advantage.*

A Matter of Time

Go to an NBA arena and you'll see three clocks. One gives you the time of day, which is handy if you have to catch a bus or train after the game. Another (the game clock) tells you how much time remains in the game, half, or quarter; its importance is obvious. The third clock times how many seconds the offense has left to attempt a shot; this is the shot clock.

NBA games consist of four 12-minute quarters for a total of 48 minutes of playing time. If teams are tied at the end of the game, they play as many five-minute overtimes as are needed to determine a winner.

Clyde's Record Book

The longest game in NBA history lasted six overtimes, with the Indianapolis Olympians defeating the Rochester Royals 75-73 on Jan. 6, 1951. The Olympians folded two years later, while the Rochester team moved to Cincinnati, then Kansas City, and Sacramento, where it is now known as the Sacramento Kings.

Clyde's Record Book

Stalling in the NBA reached a nadir on November 22, 1950, when the Fort Wayne Pistons beat the Minneapolis Lakers 19–18 in a snoozer. The two teams combined to score only eight baskets in what stands as the lowest scoring game in NBA history.

College and international professional games generally consist of two 20-minutes halves for a total of 40 minutes, although some college conferences have begun experimenting with quarter play. High school games usually consist of four 8-minute quarters for a total of 32 minutes.

The third clock you'll see in the arena is the 24-second shot clock, and it represents the most important rules change in the history of basketball. Without it, the NBA probably wouldn't be around today and I would be working for a living.

Pro ball of the 1940s and early 1950s was marked by rough play, frequent fouling, and stalling tactics. A team would get a lead and then hold onto the ball, forcing its opponent to foul. Then it would foul to get the ball back, and the cycle began anew. Games deteriorated into foulathons with players parading from one foul line to the other—not very exciting, right?

To fix the situation, in the 1954–55 season NBA leaders adopted a 24-second *shot clock* that had been developed by Danny Biasone, owner of the league's Syracuse Nationals franchise. The offense had to attempt a shot within 24 seconds or lose possession of the ball. The league also passed a rule limiting the number of fouls a team could commit in a quarter before penalty free throws were assessed.

The two rules eliminated stalling and cut down on rough play, just what the league's founding fathers wanted. Scores went up by an average of 14 points per team per game in just one year, setting the stage for the fast-paced NBA of today. I'll go into the impact of the shot clock in greater detail in Chapter 19, when I focus on the NBA and its history.

Whoever Said Basketball Is a Non-Contact Sport Never Played the Game

In his original 13 rules, Naismith made it clear he wanted basketball to be a non-contact sport. Nice try.

As a former player, I know differently. And as a broadcaster, I'm reminded every night just how much contact there is in basketball.

Especially in the last five riveting minutes, the pro game involves contact. The whole game is intense and physical. The referees let the players play. You're not going to get the flopping calls that you get earlier in the game. The rebounding is fierce. It becomes more of a half-court game—you have a finite space where all these guys are jockeying and jostling for position, so it becomes more physical.

Next time you're at a game, watch the two centers. See the way they lean on each other as they fight for position on the court. See the pushing and shoving that goes on when a shot goes up and they maneuver for rebounding position. There's contact on every play. They seem to be Kung Fu fighting.

The point Naismith was making in his rules, and that basketball has adhered to over the years, is that contact is neither an object of the game, nor is it fundamental to success. Basketball is a game of speed and quickness, agility and ability, not brute force.

The Day They Outlawed the Dunk

What shot brings fans out of their seats more than any other in basketball? The dunk, right?

So what did the people who run college basketball do in 1967? They outlawed the dunk, taking away the fans' favorite play. Players weren't even allowed to dunk during pre-game warm-ups. Talk about trying to kill the goose that laid the golden egg!

Clyde's Record Book

Be a smart fan, and don't expect a foul to be called every time two players make contact with each other. The NBA's official rules state: "The mere fact that contact occurs does not necessarily constitute a foul." I won't say use the "no blood, no foul" rule, but do what the referees do and try to see whether the contact impeded a player's progress and prevented him from making a play, or whether it was merely incidental to the play.

It was known as the Alcindor rule, after Lew Alcindor, which was Kareem Abdul-Jabbar's original name. The 7'2" center had just finished his sophomore season at UCLA, leading the Bruins to the first of what would turn out to be seven consecutive national championships, and I guess the NCAA thought outlawing the dunk would make him less dominant.

Naturally, it didn't. Alcindor was a great all-around player, as evidenced by the way he perfected his sky-hook, and UCLA went on to win the national title in his remaining two seasons. All banning the dunk did was take one of basketball's most exciting plays away from its players and fans, and inspire Abdul-Jabbar to develop the weapon that would help him become the NBA's all-time leading scorer.

Although nobody liked the rule, it took the NCAA rules-makers nine years before they would admit their mistake and bring the dunk back to the college game for the 1976–77 season.

In the pros, dunking contests have become popular features at All-Star Games and other events, and while the NBA dropped its contest this year, the ABL started one to show that women can dunk, too. You've come a long way, baby! In the 14 years of the NBA slam-dunk contest, players jumped over chairs with relatives sitting in them, dunked blindfolded or with their forearm over the eyes or dunked two balls in one leap. But the most famous slam-dunk contest was the one held by the American Basketball Association in Denver in 1976, its last year of existence (and the last year the collegiate no-dunking rule was in effect). Julius Erving won that one by racing the length of the floor, leaping from just inside the foul line and finishing with a rim-rattling slam. It was one of the Doctor's most spectacular house calls!

Referees Maintain Law and Order

It's a dirty job, and a thankless one, but somebody's got to do it.

Referees (often nicknamed zebras, because on many levels—but not in the NBA—they wear black-and-white striped shirts) are basketball's policemen, maintaining order on the court and ensuring that the sport's laws are enforced. It's not an easy job in a game played by athletes as big, strong, and active as those in the NBA, and where there is contact that could produce a foul call on every play. In fact, it's probably the most difficult job in all of sports.

I'll go into greater detail on the responsibilities of referees and their impact on the game in Chapter 11, but for now it's enough to keep in mind that the hardest thing for a referee is to learn when *not* to blow the whistle. A referee needs good judgment to know what contact to allow and what to penalize.

Quote...Unquote

"The game is the thing. The spotlight should be on the players, not the officials. The players are performers; let them perform as well as they can."—*Chuck Daly, a long-time coach and a member of the Hall of Fame.*

Referees are like kids: They should be seen and not heard. In a well-refereed game, you rarely notice the officials. The game will have a fluidity, a pace. It flows when you don't have too many whistles interrupting play. When you're aware of the zebras, then something's wrong.

I never knew who the referees were when I was playing. I think I knew maybe two or three refs in the entire league. My game wasn't who the ref was, I played the game the way I was supposed to play it. I didn't say, "Oh, Jones is calling the game, I can get away with this or that tonight." That wasn't my game. I still don't know who most of the referees are.

I played 13 seasons in the NBA and I never had a technical foul called on me, not a single one. I grew up under coaches who didn't allow us to talk to the refs, so I never, ever, talked back to them. If a call went against me I just stepped back and played the game that much harder. Being frugal helped, since technical fouls cost you money—I learned to keep my mouth shut and play with more grit than wit. I didn't pay to talk; now I talk for pay.

Which brings me to one of my pet peeves.

Trash Talking: A (Sad) Sign of the Times

I hate trash talking, all that bravado that goes on between players on the court. It's embarrassing. Besides the fact that it's distracting and sets a bad example for kids, who needs it? What purpose does it serve?

When I was a player we never trash talked. That was something you'd get in the Rucker League (in the Harlem section of New York) over the summer, or in the Baker League (in Philadelphia). You didn't trash talk at Madison Square Garden. We viewed this as our profession.

Plus, we let sleeping dogs lie, man. If I'm scoring on you and you're not doing anything about it, why would I want to talk to you and wake you up? It makes no sense. The same thing goes at the other end of the court. Do you really want to get Michael Jordan or somebody like that riled up? If he's not shooting well or playing his best, leave him alone and consider yourself lucky. It's elementary, Watson.

Clyde's Rules

Let sleeping dogs lie. I remember Sam Jones and guys like that were all so political when I played against them. They'd come onto the court and say, 'Hello, Walt, how are you, how's the family?' Then they'd beat you by 50. Nobody wanted to talk you down; they buttered you up and kept you buttered while they beat you.

And the crowd was the same way. They wouldn't tolerate that kind of behavior. It was called hot-dogging. I can remember fans yelling at me in Kansas City, if I passed the ball behind my back, "Hey Frazier, you hot dog, cut that stuff out and play basketball. That's not NBA stuff."

Today there are no parameters to trash talking. Players feel they can say and do whatever they want. And whatever the consequences might be, they'll deal with them at that time. They're out of control. What's a little $500 fine to a guy who's making $2 million a year, or $20 million?

Players today know that silence means anonymity. If you're silent in the NBA, no matter how good you are, nobody's going to know you. You've got to do more than walk the walk, you've also got to talk the talk, like a Charles Barkley or a Dennis Rodman, in order to get the endorsements—the ink, as we used to call it. You've got to be controversial. Otherwise you'll be like David Robinson or Hakeem Olajuwon or the Mailman, Karl Malone, splendid players who don't get the notoriety because they're disciplined—they're from the old school.

I hear the TV guys say it all the time when they're looking for interviews. They say, "We don't want him. He's too boring." They want someone controversial for ratings and appeal. That's what it's all come to.

Who gets the interviews, who gets the endorsements, Rodman or Robinson? It's pretty pathetic, when you think about it.

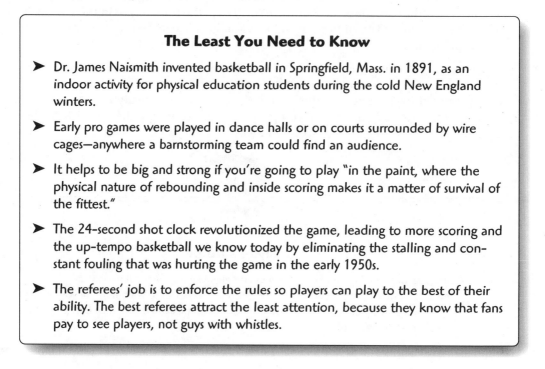

The Least You Need to Know

➤ Dr. James Naismith invented basketball in Springfield, Mass. in 1891, as an indoor activity for physical education students during the cold New England winters.

➤ Early pro games were played in dance halls or on courts surrounded by wire cages—anywhere a barnstorming team could find an audience.

➤ It helps to be big and strong if you're going to play "in the paint, where the physical nature of rebounding and inside scoring makes it a matter of survival of the fittest."

➤ The 24-second shot clock revolutionized the game, leading to more scoring and the up-tempo basketball we know today by eliminating the stalling and constant fouling that was hurting the game in the early 1950s.

➤ The referees' job is to enforce the rules so players can play to the best of their ability. The best referees attract the least attention, because they know that fans pay to see players, not guys with whistles.

Part 2
The Players

Basketball is a player's game, and nowhere more so than in the NBA. In the NBA the players occupy the spotlight, not the coaches or the referees or anyone else. It's the golden rule—he who has the gold rules, and in the NBA the players have the gold. That's different from college ball, where often the coaches are omnipotent because they are the constants in the program while the players change every few years. And because college players aren't quite as skillful as pros, good coaching helps to make up for the flaws of college players. Conversely, NBA players are the greatest athletes in the world. They combine size, speed, strength, and skill in a game designed to highlight their abilities.

The players are the game. They're the reason you turn on your TV set or go out to the arena. And when you think about it, they're the reason you picked up this book—to get a better understanding of what they do, and how and why they do it.

In this part I'll discuss each of the five positions in basketball: point guard, shooting guard, small forward, power forward, and center. I'll also discuss the unique role of the bench player, the reserve who's not in the game at the start but may still play a crucial role in its outcome. In each case I'll go over the player's role and give you some tips on what you can look for to see if he's doing his job well. I'll also tell you my favorites, past and present, at each position.

Chapter 4

Point Guards Are Basketball's Quarterbacks

In This Chapter

➤ A true point guard thinks pass first

➤ You've got to be more than quick

➤ How to run a fast break

➤ What to watch for

➤ My favorite point guards

Point guard might be the most fun position to play in basketball.

You have the ball in your hands on just about every play. You are the orchestrator. You decide the pace of the game, whether to run a fast break or set up the half-court offense. You decide who will get the ball, when, and where. It's a fun position because you're in charge

Many point guards are flamboyant. They play with style, with flair. They're basketball's showmen. They have the mesmerizing quickness fans like. They're creative and dazzling at times—the guys fans really notice the most.

And on the court they look like little guys, at least relatively speaking, so fans can relate to them. Everybody wants to be a point guard. When it comes to shoe endorsements, point guards generally do better than the bigger guys because fans relate to them and want to be like them. The average fan knows he can't dunk or hang in the air, but feels he can handle the ball and run a team. So he pictures himself as the point guard.

Point guards are basketball's quarterbacks, the decision-makers on the court.

Reading that description, I guess it's no surprise that I became a point guard, right?

Clyde's Tip

While the point guards usually are the smallest players on the court, that term is relative. Most NBA point guards are over 6 feet tall and weigh at least 180 pounds. I played at 6'4" and 205, which was pretty big for a point guard back then but only about average today. Magic Johnson took it to another level, playing the position while standing 6'9" He revolutionized the position because of his size!

Clyde's Chalk Talk

The *low post* is the area close to the basket, on either side of the foul lane, where centers often like to position themselves because it's easier to score and rebound from there. Some centers like to set up in the *high post*, along the foul line. This keeps the area near the basket open so other players can run through, take a pass, and shoot from in close.

Dish Before You Swish

A point guard's job is to create situations that lead to a field goal for his team. You have to have a different mentality from most players because you have to think about setting up your teammates before you worry about getting off your own shots. You really have to be unselfish, to think pass first and shot second.

I call it learning to dish before you swish.

The point guard runs the offense. He sets up plays on the court and passes the ball to the teammate who has the best opportunity to score. He must use good judgment in getting the ball to the right player at the right time in a place where he can do something positive with it.

Control and poise are essential in being a point guard because you dictate the tempo of the game. That's why many people feel the point guard position is the most difficult in the game today. If you're erratic and unbridled, your team is going to be likewise. You must minimize the cross-court passes, the foolish plays that are likely to turn the ball over to the other team. You have to be savvy, to know how to use your assets and your team's assets and take advantage of your opponent's weaknesses.

A team generally doesn't look for its point guard to score too often, although there are some exceptions I'll discuss later in this chapter. These I call the *hybrid* guards, who play the point but are really combinations between point guards and shooting guards. Some hybrids have been very successful, such as Nate "Tiny" Archibald, who starred for the Kansas City Kings in the 1970s and won a championship with the Boston Celtics in 1981, and Isiah Thomas, who led the Detroit Pistons to a pair of titles in the 1980s. They were point guards who also scored, but without letting it take away from their essence as set-up men. For the most part, though, a point guard should be more of an assist guy. His job is to use his creativity to help his teammates get open opportunities.

That said, a point guard has to be able to drill the baby jumper, the open shot from 10 to 15 feet. He's got to be efficient with that shot, because he's going to get it a lot in the normal flow of play.

Take Patrick Ewing and Charlie Ward, who play with the New York Knicks. When Ward throws it in to Ewing in the *low post,* invariably his man goes to double-team the big guy. So if Ewing can kick the ball back out to Ward, he'll have a nice open jumper. Ward must be able to can that shot consistently in order to be effective and to stay in the game, because he knows he'll get a certain number of open looks at the basket, especially down the stretch.

"I'm not a point guard who looks for his own shot. I look to create shots for others," said Ward. "But eventually, if you give enough, you also will receive. That's when you must hit your shot."

A point guard has to know who's hot and who's not. If a guy is scoring, the point guard has got to know to keep getting his teammate the ball while he's on a roll. He's got to know who to give the ball to and when to give it to him. You don't give it to a big guy 20 feet from the basket when he's running toward the basket, because you don't want to make him catch a pass, dribble a few times, and then shoot. That's too much to ask of most big guys when they're on the run. You don't want to make them dribble, so you make sure that when he catches the ball he can just dunk it or lay it in.

To me the point guard is also like a catcher in baseball—he knows different "pitchers" and he moves the "outfielders" around. He's orchestrating the whole game. This is what the real, bona fide point guard has to do—be like a coach on the floor.

Quickness Is Nice, but It's Also Over-rated

You must be elusive to be a point guard. Quickness helps, but to be elusive you do not have to be quick. Most kids don't understand that. They think you have to have blazing speed, but what you really need is savvy. Many players are quick, but they go at one speed and so they aren't effective. In order to be elusive you have to have a change of pace.

Clyde's Record Book

Bob Davies, a Hall of Famer who played professionally in the 1940s and 1950s, is considered the father of the behind-the-back dribble, using the maneuver to help him change directions. Davies was one of the first point guards to play with flair and showmanship, with "crowd appeal," as teammate Red Holzman put it.

Clyde's Record Book

One of the greatest point guards of all time was Bob Cousy, who starred for the Boston Celtics in the 1950s and early '60s. Cousy was nicknamed "the Houdini of the Hardwood" because he was truly a magician with the ball. He was dribbling between his legs and throwing no-look passes long before those plays became commonplace.

Quote...Unquote

"As a point guard, being a player-coach came easy to me because I knew who should have the ball, who had a hot hand and who we should go to. So I was successful at it."
—*Lenny Wilkens, a Hall of Fame point guard, has won more games than any other coach in NBA history after beginning his coaching career as a player-coach with Seattle in 1969–70.*

When I played, people sometimes thought I was slow. Then all of a sudden I would put on a burst of speed and go around them. They were baffled because I used different speeds as the key to my elusiveness. A guy who was always going full-speed, helter-skelter, was easy for me to defend because I knew he'd always be going at that one speed.

Dexterity also contributes to elusiveness. A point guard must be able to create opportunities off the dribble, to make a sharp pass while he's dribbling the ball upcourt, often on the run. To elude the defender who's guarding you, you have to go left or right, dribble between your legs, or whatever it takes to give you the space you need to set up the play.

A point guard also has to *have a handle*, and I don't mean a nickname. He must be able to handle the ball, to dribble and pass instinctively and without second thought, as if the ball is an extension of his own arm and hand. He can't look at the ball when he should be looking for an open teammate, or a defender who's out of position.

Clyde's Rules

Don't be fooled by pure speed; look for a player who knows when to turn it on and off, who knows how to change his pace. Also, if you see a point guard looking at the ball while he's dribbling, chances are you won't see him in the NBA for too long.

Staying tuned in to your teammates likewise is important to success as a point guard. A lot of times a guy is trying to get open and when he comes off a screen, the point guard has his head turned the other way and can't see him. What good is that? The point guard has to know what his teammates are trying to do on the court, to anticipate their moves, and to reward them with the ball when they get open. When you have a team that's been together four or five years, the point guard develops a kind of instinct, what I consider ESP. He knows what certain players are going to do in certain situations, and can react in a way that leads to scoring opportunities.

Not having to look at the ball while he dribbles has helped John Stockton of the Utah Jazz become the NBA's all-time leader in assists.
Associated Press

John Stockton of the Utah Jazz is a great example. He seems to know what Karl Malone is going to do before Malone himself! The two have played together for so long, 13 seasons now, that they have developed a bond, a sixth sense. Stockton always seems to know where Malone is on the court and when to get him the ball. It's hard to think of one without the other, and it would be apropos if they retired together and were inducted into the Hall of Fame together.

When I played for the Knicks, I often felt that connection with my teammates. I knew what Bill Bradley would do when he was running his man around a double-screen and when to get him the ball. I knew that Willis Reed liked a bounce pass rather than a chest pass when he was over along the baseline.

And it was reciprocal. They knew when I liked to gamble on defense. They knew that in certain situations, if I got the chance, I'd go for the steal, so they knew when to be ready to back me up.

Coach on the Court?

When I played, and earlier, the point guard was something of a coach on the court. In fact, several point guards also served as player-coaches, including Lenny Wilkens, who went on to become the coach with the most wins in NBA history. The point guard really was seen as an extension of the coach, a guy who would call the plays and keep the team on an even keel while the game was going on.

Clyde's Chalk Talk

Two phrases you'll often hear in describing running an offense are *in transition* and *setting up*. In *transition* refers to when a team is moving from defense to offense and heading toward its goal. Players are on the move and the object is to try to get into good shooting position before the defense has time to react, which can lead to easy baskets. If a team can't beat the defense downcourt and get off a good shot *in transition*, it will *set up* its offense and the point guard will call a play with his teammates moving to predetermined spots on the floor and areas and moving along specified routes. It is often more difficult to score when *setting up* the offense, because the defense has time to *set up*, too.

It's not as common to see a point guard calling plays today. Many college coaches and some NBA coaches call all the plays from the sideline every time the team comes downcourt, so that responsibility has been taken away from the point guard. His job is to adjust, if necessary, and execute.

This can hurt a team at the end of a close game. If a team can't call a timeout, what happens? Invariably guys are looking toward the sideline to find out what to do, instead of acting instinctively and taking advantage of what the defense might be giving them in transition. Often the better, more experienced teams push the ball up the court instead of calling a timeout, because they know they can get a better shot on the fly than if they give the other team a chance to get set.

What a coach tries to do is get a point guard who thinks the same way he does. When I was in high school, my coach would always say, "Now Walt, I would run this play." As I was learning the game, he would drill me to run certain plays that he would call in certain scenarios.

Running a Fast Break

Getting easy shots is essential to winning basketball, and one way to get an easy shot is to beat your opponent downcourt. That's a no-brainer—if you have the ball and you get to the basket before he does, there's no way he can stop you from scoring.

That is the philosophy behind the *fast break* or the running game.

There are two advantages you can gain by running. First, you can achieve a manpower advantage, getting more offensive players in the attacking zone than defenders. Basic math should tell you that two defenders are going to have a hard time trying to guard three offensive players. Second, you increase your chances of getting open shots by running and pushing the ball up the floor toward your goal. By running, an offensive player can get into position to shoot before the other team has time to set up its defense.

Some teams thrive by running; it becomes their basic offensive philosophy. However, even teams that don't usually run but prefer to play a *set-up* or *half-court offense* must run once in awhile to get easy shots. It's too grueling to try to win exclusively the other way.

Many point guards today don't know how to run a fast break properly. Here are two things you can watch for.

Clyde's Chalk Talk

The object of a *fast break* is to move the ball up the floor toward your basket quickly to get an easy shot in transition, either because of a manpower advantage or because the other team hasn't had time to get in position to defend. The opposite of the fast break is the *set-up* or *half-court offense*.

Man the Middle

The player with the ball, generally the point guard, should try to get to the middle of the floor when running the fast break. Being in the middle gives you the option of going straight to the basket or passing to a teammate on either side. The diagram on the next page shows the proper positioning for the offensive players in a quintessential three-on-two fast break.

You can see that if the point guard (1) running the break takes the ball to the middle of the floor, it puts the pressure on the defenders. If they spread out to cover the men (2 and 3) on each side, or *wing* as it is called, the point guard can go to the basket himself; if a defender comes up to guard him, he can dish the ball to the teammate left open on that side.

In a properly executed three-on-two fast break, the point guard (1) keeps the ball in the middle of the court so he has the option to pass to a player on either side (2 or 3) or go straight to the basket himself.

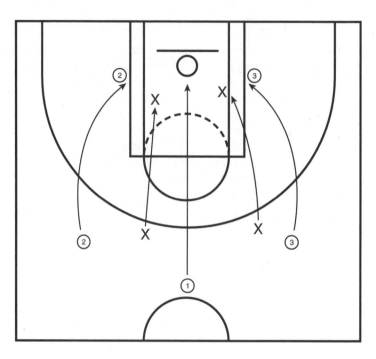

1 – Point Guard
2 – Shooting Guard
3 – Small Forward
4 – Power Forward
5 – Center
X – Defenders

Clyde's Chalk Talk

While the point guard takes the ball down the middle of the floor on a fast break, the players who run down the sides of the court are said to be *filling the lanes*. The sides of the court are also known as the *wings*, as in: Frazier feeds the ball to Monroe on the right wing for the open shot.

Now look at a three-on-two fast break where the point guard brings the ball up the sideline, as shown in the diagram on the next page.

All of a sudden his options are limited. He only has one direction in which to pass the ball. That makes life easy for the defenders, one of whom can guard the man with the ball while the other can guard both of his teammates. The offensive team has lost its advantage because the point guard didn't take the ball to the middle of the floor.

Don't Get Hung Up in the Air

OK, the point guard has taken the ball to the middle of the floor on the fast break. He has a teammate on each wing and there are two defenders back to try to stop them. Now what?

64

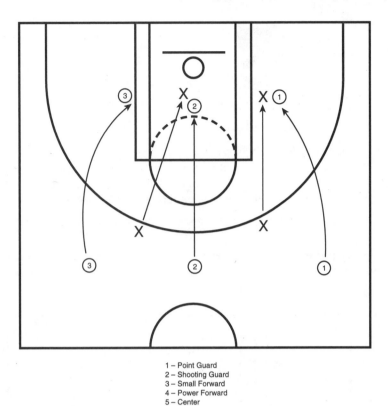

By bringing the ball down one side of the court, the point guard (1) has let the defenders off the hook by surrendering the man-power advantage he should have in a three-on-two fast break.

1 – Point Guard
2 – Shooting Guard
3 – Small Forward
4 – Power Forward
5 – Center
X – Defenders

He should keep the pressure on the defenders for as long as possible by dribbling the ball straight toward the basket. By the time he reaches the foul line, chances are good that at least one of the defenders will have left his man to come over and stop him, so he can flip an easy pass to his open teammate for a layup.

If the defenders haven't committed themselves by the time the point guard reaches the foul line, he should stop right there and avoid the temptation of going all the way to the basket or jumping into the air. At that point, the area under the basket will be too crowded to get an easy shot, with three offensive players and two defenders in a relatively small space. Stopping at the foul line ensures enough space for an open shot, either for the point guard or one of the players on the wing.

But if the point guard is unbridled and makes the cardinal mistake of jumping into the air, he limits his options—he now has to pass or shoot before he lands or else it's a violation and his team loses possession of the ball.

Clyde's Rules

Remember, a player with the ball isn't allowed to jump in the air and come down with it. Once both feet leave the floor, the player has to pass or shoot before either foot touches down, or else it's a violation and the other team gets the ball. A player may, however, pick one foot up and down as often as he wants, as long as the other foot (his pivot foot) remains planted.

If the point guard just stands at the foul line, however, he can get an easy 15-foot jump shot for himself, because the two defenders generally peel back to keep the two men on the wing from getting layups, as the following diagram indicates:

As the defenders keep backing up, the point guard (1) who stops at the foul line is left with an open shot.

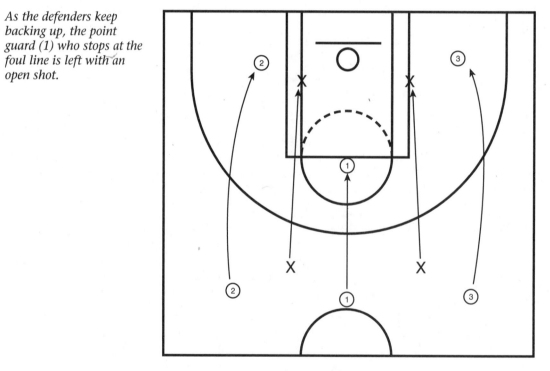

1 – Point Guard
2 – Shooting Guard
3 – Small Forward
4 – Power Forward
5 – Center
X – Defenders

The rule of thumb for defenders is to give up anything but a lay-up (or dunk), which is the easiest shot in the game. But if one of the defenders elects to confront the point guard at the foul line and contest the jumper, that leaves a man on a wing open to take a pass for a layup, as this diagram shows:

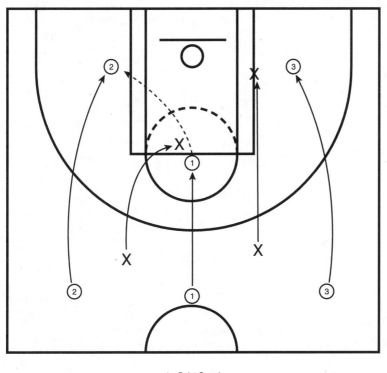

If a defender elects to pick up the point guard (1) at the foul line, that leaves an open teammate (2) on the wing for a lay-up.

1 – Point Guard
2 – Shooting Guard
3 – Small Forward
4 – Power Forward
5 – Center
X – Defenders

This gets back to savvy, poise, and control. A point guard who keeps his cool and stops at the foul line has an easy shot and usually scores. A point guard who's out of control and hell bent on getting to the basket charges frantically into the teeth of the defense and will probably lose the ball. Watch for it.

The Hybrids

Too many of today's point guards don't look to dish before they swish. When they come downcourt they're looking for their own shot as much as to create a shot for their teammates. I call these guards *hybrids*—a cross between a point guard and a shooting guard.

Allen Iverson of the Philadelphia 76ers is a perfect example. He's really a scorer, a two guard or shooting guard, but because he's so quick and handles the ball so well, he plays the point guard position. But he doesn't have a point guard's mentality—he'd rather swish than dish.

Iverson is so talented he'll get his points, but his team suffers when he becomes too offensive minded and would be better off with a pure point guard. Players love to play with a point guard who looks to pass—who wouldn't like a guy who's always thinking about how to get you the ball so you can shoot?

The most discouraging thing for a player, especially a big man, is when you hustle, run the floor hard, and get open—then don't get the ball because your point guard stopped and popped a jumper from 25 feet out. Even if that shot goes in, it can hurt the team in the long run because when a big man sees that happen once too often, he's going to stop hustling and running because he is not being rewarded. Then where are you?

Let me be clear: I have nothing against hybrid guards. As I said earlier, when I was playing with Earl Monroe or Dick Barnett, or when guys like Oscar Robertson of the Cincinnati Royals and Jerry West of the Los Angeles Lakers were playing in the 1960s and 1970s, we considered ourselves guards. Not point guards or shooting guards, just guards. We were versatile and the positions hadn't evolved into today's specialized roles. So in effect we all were hybrids.

Also, there have been great point guards who also were scorers. I've already mentioned Nate Archibald and Isiah Thomas, both of whom were among the NBA's 50 Greatest Players of All Time. They were small, quick guards who knew how to run a team and orchestrate a game but also had the knack for scoring.

The problem comes when the point guard thinks too much about shooting and not enough about setting up his teammates. If you can do both, that's great. If you create your own shots while also keeping your teammates happy by setting them up, you've got the best of both worlds. But that's difficult, and if he has to give up one or the other, a point guard must learn to give up his shot and focus on his teammates. That makes for a happier, more productive team.

Quote...Unquote

"Isiah Thomas was a point guard that could score 20 to 25 points a game and he could control the tempo. Down the stretch he was going to find a way to beat you. I don't care if he made the last-second shot or he set up one of his teammates, he was going to find a way to beat the opposing team."—*Sidney Moncrief of the Milwaukee Bucks, a guard who played against Thomas from 1981 to 1991.*

Watching Point Guards

I scrutinize point guards when I watch a game, partially because I played the position myself. Other players I tend to just watch, but I pay extra close attention to point guards because they have such a compelling presence on the court.

I've already discussed things to look for when a point guard is running a fast break. There are also a few keys to watch for when a point guard is setting up his team's half-court offense.

As I indicated, control and poise are essential for a point guard. He should exude confidence, so it spreads to his teammates. Look for this when you're watching a game from the stands or on TV. Whether he's racing upcourt in a fast break or just walking the ball up the floor, watch the point guard and see how much control he has, over himself, his teammates, and the entire game.

A good point guard must always keep his cool, even when he's double-teamed—as I was here by Brian Winters and Bobby Dandridge of Milwaukee. Associated Press

Does he pass the ball confidently, with command? Does he get into a play quickly, without meandering and wasting time? If a teammate is not where he wants him, does

69

he have the presence to move him around? If a defender guards him tightly or he is double-teamed, does he start to panic or does he calmly figure his way out of the problem?

A point guard's job is to create scoring opportunities, and there are two basic things he can do to maximize his creative opportunities: keep the dribble alive and stay in the middle of the floor. It baffles me how many of today's players are negligent in these regards.

One thing that epitomizes a good point guard is being able to keep your dribble alive. Once a point guard—or any player, for that matter—starts to dribble, he should do so until he makes something positive happen. Once you stop your dribble you can't start it again, so you're basically anchored to that spot on the floor. Your options become limited to shooting or passing, and that invites a defender to come up and guard you closely. It also makes you vulnerable to the double-team.

So in watching point guards, see how well they keep their dribble alive. If a point guard stops dribbling for no apparent reason, he's inviting trouble—and a quick hook from his coach.

Also watch where a point guard goes when he brings the ball up the court. He should always try to keep the ball in the center of the court so he can capitalize on breakdowns in the defense. Too many guys veer over toward the sideline; then if something happens on the other side of the court, it's too late for them to get back to the middle to try to take advantage and create something.

Clyde's Tip

Remember the rule on discontinuation? If a player starts to dribble, stops, and then starts again, it's a violation and his team loses possession of the ball.

My Favorite Point Guards

Gary Payton of the Seattle SuperSonics is one of the quintessential point guards in the league today. He orchestrates on offense and he plays relentlessly on defense. He plays with gusto and with savvy. He's tenacious on the court. He ignites his team. He's the catalyst for so much that happens for Seattle. I'd say he's the consummate point guard.

Another in that category is John Stockton of the Utah Jazz, the NBA's all-time leader in both assists and steals. He's not as fiery or as explosive as Payton; when you think of Stockton you think of poise and control. Nobody runs an offense more efficiently. And despite his angelic choirboy face, he's as tough and audacious as they come with regard to setting screens or running through them.

I'd have to put Tim Hardaway of the Miami Heat and Terrell Brandon of the Milwaukee Bucks up there among the best of today's point guards as well. Damon Stoudamire of the Portland Trail Blazers is a young point guard who creates havoc and I like Stephon Marbury of the Minnesota Timberwolves a lot, too. I like Marbury more than

Allen Iverson because to me he's more of a pure point guard, whereas Iverson really is more of a two guard.

The best point guard ever would have to be Magic Johnson of the Los Angeles Lakers. He revolutionized the position. He was a guy at 6'9" who could do what Oscar Robertson and I did at 6'4", 6'5". His height and his court sense gave him a tremendous advantage and his knack for the dramatic made him indefensible. I don't know if there will ever be another guy as exciting as he was, breaking down the defense, shaking and baking to the basket, electrifying the crowd, and frustrating his opponents. He always tried to make the pass before he looked to score. I believe in Magic!

I'm not putting Oscar in this category even though he had a lot of assists, because I think of him as more of a shooting guard. I don't think he'd be running a team today. He'd be more like Jordan— inside, outside, wherever he wanted to go, doing everything on the court. Same with Jerry West. They'd be looking for their own shot opportunities as much as their teammates. I guess you could call them hybrids, but in the best sense of the term.

Nate Archibald was another hybrid, a point guard who really could score. "Tiny" was remarkable. His feat of leading the league in assists as well as scoring in the same season is truly amazing. Someone will break Wilt Chamberlain's record of scoring 100 points in a game before anybody does what "Tiny" did over a full season.

Isiah Thomas was another point guard like that who could score as well as set up his teammates, a hybrid in a positive sense. He also played with fire and swagger, like Payton does today.

Quote...Unquote

"I don't think there will ever be another 6'9" point guard who smiles while he humiliates you.—*James Worthy of the Los Angeles Lakers, on long-time teammate Magic Johnson.*

Clyde's Record Book

In 1972–73, Nate "Tiny" Archibald, a 6'1", 160-pound quicksilver point guard playing for the Kansas City/ Omaha Kings, averaged 34.0 points and 11.4 assists per game, leading the NBA in both categories. No player has ever matched that feat. Because each assist led to a basket worth two points, Archibald directly played a part in 56.8 points per game (ppg).

Lenny Wilkens, who is now the leading coach in NBA history in terms of victories, epitomized the point guard during his fabulous playing career. He was always slashing into the paint, trying to create opportunities or draw fouls, and was always among the leaders in assists—a real dish before you swish guy. Another guy like that was Maurice Cheeks with the great Philadelphia teams of the early '80s. The same goes for some of the earlier point guards, guys like Bob Cousy, Slater Martin, Dick McGuire, and Bob Davies. They were pure point guards, positive and provocative.

The Least You Need to Know

➤ A point guard must think pass first—dish before you swish—to make the offense run smoothly and keep everybody on the team happy.

➤ Poise and savvy are more important than speed and quickness, because a point guard must make split-second decisions and make the most of opportunities as they arise. He must be unflappable and adaptable.

➤ A good point guard is an extension of the coach and his will, since he's the man who runs the team on the floor.

➤ A point guard should always be under control, whether running the fast break or the set-up offense.

➤ Magic Johnson revolutionized the position of point guard because of his size as well as his skills, while Gary Payton is today's best because he plays great defense as well as superb offense.

Chapter 5

Shooting Guards: Michael Jordan and So Much More

In This Chapter

➤ A shooting guard's job is (what else?) to shoot

➤ You can be a scorer even if you're not a shooter

➤ How this position has changed over the years

➤ Two of the game's most basic plays

➤ What to watch for

➤ My favorite shooting guards

Who wouldn't want to "Be Like Mike," as the saying goes?

You take off from the foul line and soar through the air for a slam-dunk. You drive past your man along the baseline and put in a wraparound layup. You hang in the air for what seems like an eternity till your defender is out of the way, then put in a soft jumper. You beat your man off the dribble and switch hands in midair to elude another defender as your scoop shot finds the net. You force your man to back up with a ball fake and then toss in your sixth three-pointer of an NBA Finals game, then turn to the NBC cameras and shrug.

Millions of youngsters around the world have watched the dazzling exploits of Michael Jordan and pictured themselves in his Nikes, shooting and slamming the lights out and leading their team to yet another championship. Jordan is the preeminent athlete of our generation, the most radiant star in the basketball galaxy, so it's no wonder that shooting guard has become such a glamorous position.

Shooting guards are also known as *two guards* (remember the way positions are numbered?) or *off guards*, because when the play starts they're off (or away from) the ball, which is usually in the point guard's hands. They then catch a pass and take their shot or else create a shot by driving against their defender.

Swish Before You Dish

If you want to play shooting guard, you've got to look to swish before you dish. Shoot first and ask questions later. This is no position for the bashful.

Quote...Unquote

"When you are struggling with your shot, the only way to succeed *is* to keep shooting."—*Kerry Kittles, shooting guard of the New Jersey Nets.*

Clyde's Chalk Talk

By *touch* I mean that softness that allows a shot to be slightly off target but still go in. A shooter with touch will often have his shot hit the rim and bounce in, what we call a shooter's bounce. A shooter without touch has shots that bounce off the rim with a resounding "clang." He's known as a *bricklayer,* and the shots he puts up are called *bricks*—not a hint of softness there.

It's precisely the opposite mentality from that of your backcourt mate, the point guard. His role is to get his teammates involved and keep everyone happy. The shooting guard's role is to score.

Selfishness is a virtue for shooting guards. Confidence—to the point where it borders on cockiness and sometimes crosses that border—is a requirement. You've got to have serious attitude. "You can't guard me, you can't stop me," is the approach shooting guards must bring to the table. That's why players like Reggie Miller of the Indiana Pacers or Steve Smith of the Atlanta Hawks rank up there among the league's premier shooting guards—they have unbridled confidence.

If a shooting guard misses a shot or two, or five or six, he doesn't stop shooting. The only way to get out of a shooting slump is to keep firing away. The difference between the smart shooting guards and the reckless ones is that when they're in a slump, the sagacious ones become a bit more selective about their shots. They'll look to score on a layup or break open for a short jumper, the type of high percentage shot that's likely to go in. And once one goes in, they could erupt.

It's a wonderful role for guys who like to shoot—which covers about 98 percent of the guys who lace up sneakers.

Shooter vs. Scorer

Pure shooters are a pleasure to watch. Their form is mesmerizing. They use their legs for strength, their hands and arms for direction and *touch.*

One of the sweetest sounds in sports is that "swish" that comes when a ball sails cleanly through the net. For years now, TV crews have mounted microphones on the basket supports so they can bring that sound into your living room.

Some shooting guards, however, aren't good shooters. Some may be better described as scorers, guys who manage to get their points even though their shots aren't picture-perfect.

Scorers make their living by taking the ball to the basket. They generally have a quick first step that's enough to get them free from their man. Then they take it strong to the hoop and either score or get fouled. Many scorers feast at the foul line.

Work out the math for yourself. If you drive to the basket and get fouled even just once each quarter, that's eight free throw attempts. Hit six or seven of them, as you should, and you're well on your way to a double-digit scoring game. Add a couple of baskets in each quarter and you've got 22, 23 points—prodigious numbers indeed.

A good scorer also is a good garbage man. By that I mean a guy who picks up loose balls around the basket and puts them in, or scores off offensive rebounds. A good scorer has a nose for the basketball.

How Shooting Guards Have Evolved

Shooting guards today are usually 6'5" to 6'7". Besides being tall, they have to be elusive and prolific in their scoring. Usually they're good rebounders who can go to the offensive *glass* and get some points that way, often scoring off offensive rebounds.

Ideally, two guards will be diversified in their style of play. If all they can do is shoot, they'll be limited in their effectiveness. The best two guards can either play catch-and-shoot, where they catch a pass and immediately take a shot, or else create, where they catch the ball and put a move on their defender in order to get free for their shot.

Jordan is the prototype. Earlier in his career he constantly drove to the basket, using his agility and athleticism. But he knew he could not be one-dimensional or defenders would eventually adjust, so he worked to improve his perimeter shot. Later in his career, when defenders started making it more difficult to drive to the basket, he began swishing from outside.

Clyde's Chalk Talk

Glass is another term for backboard, because today's best backboards are made of clear Plexiglas. A good rebounder is said to be adept at *cleaning the glass.* Earlier backboards were made of wood; for durability, you'll often find metal backboards in playgrounds or school yards.

Having beaten his man, Michael Jordan uses his agility to drive past Miami's Alonzo Mourning to the basket.
Associated Press

A shooting guard has to take what the defense gives him. If they guard him tightly, the shooting guard fakes and goes around them to the basket. If they guard him loosely, a shooting guard makes them pay by canning the open jumper.

Two guards should have some defensive prowess, because the other team's two guard likely will be a good offensive player. That's an area in which some of today's shooting guards are lacking. For all of Jordan's scoring and his spectacular dunks, you tend to overlook what a tremendous defensive player he is. He won the NBA's Defensive Player of the Year award in 1988, when he also won the league scoring title—an unprecedented feat.

Today we're in an age of specialization, but in earlier years you really had to be versatile to play shooting guard. You had to handle the ball as well as be able to shoot, rebound, and defend. And you had to be durable, because the game was more physical then. In our days you could *hand-check* players—put your hand on a player as he was moving so as to impede his progress—and the referees seemed to allow more freedom in setting picks.

We'll go into offensive strategy more deeply later in the book, but for now I'd like to introduce you to two simple, fundamental plays typically involving shooting guards—the pick-and-roll and the give-and-go.

Clyde's Record Book

When I played, Jerry Sloan of Chicago (now the coach of the Utah Jazz) was a defensive stopper at two guard. He and Norm Van Lier, the point guard on those Chicago teams, made for a brutal defensive combination. Nobody liked to play against them because they were talented and physical and intense. They didn't concede you a thing. You always knew you were in for havoc and mayhem when you went up against those two.

Pick-and-Roll

The *pick-and-roll* is one of the oldest plays in basketball, because it only requires two offensive players. Any two players can work this play, but usually it involves a big man, like a center, and a player who can handle the ball well and shoot from outside, like the shooting guard.

The big man establishes his position and sets a pick, usually somewhere in the high post area. The player with the ball drives directly toward the pick until his defender faces a dilemma. If he tries to run behind the player setting the pick and his man, it leaves the player with the ball open long enough to get off his shot, as the following figure illustrates:

If a defender elects to try to run behind a pick, it usually leaves the player with the ball (2) open long enough for him to get off an easy shot.

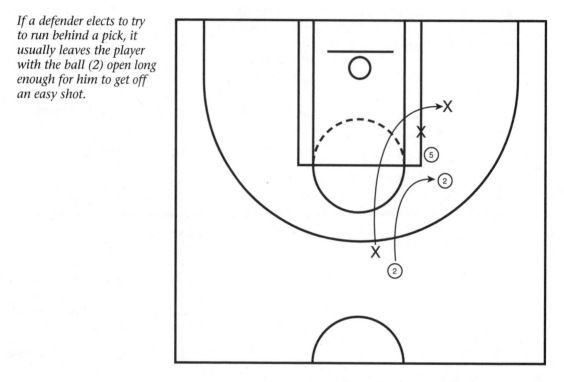

1 – Point Guard
2 – Shooting Guard
3 – Small Forward
4 – Power Forward
5 – Center
X – Defenders

Another way for the defender to play is to try to *go over the pick*, which we also call *fighting through the pick*. Instead of taking the circuitous route behind the player setting the pick, the defender steps up and forces the issue by trying to get in between the man with the ball and the man setting the pick. If he's successful, he keeps the man with the ball from getting open for his shot, as you can see here:

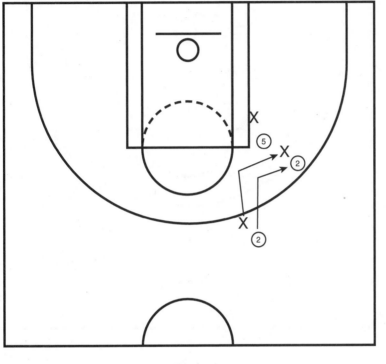

Rather than give up an open shot, the defender squeezes through the pick set by (5) and stays with his man (2).

1 – Point Guard
2 – Shooting Guard
3 – Small Forward
4 – Power Forward
5 – Center
X – Defenders

This only works because the offensive players didn't run the play the way they should. The player with the ball (2) must drive straight toward the player setting the pick (5) and get right up to him, so there's no room for the defender to fight through without causing contact, which is a foul.

Another way to try to defend the pick-and-roll is for the defenders to *switch* and guard each other's man. By stepping out from behind the man setting the pick, the second defender often can prevent the man with the ball from having enough open space to get off his shot. Here's the way that looks:

If the defender steps up from behind the pick, he often can keep the player with the ball (2) from having enough room to shoot.

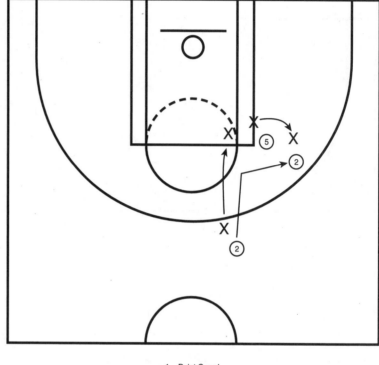

1 – Point Guard
2 – Shooting Guard
3 – Small Forward
4 – Power Forward
5 – Center
X – Defenders

This is where the "roll" part of "pick-and-roll" comes in. If the defenders switch, that generally leaves a smaller defender guarding the man who set the pick (5), and he'll probably be out of position. The player who set the pick should then move, or roll, toward the basket, where he should be able to take a pass from his teammate and get an open layup or dunk. Here's the way it should work:

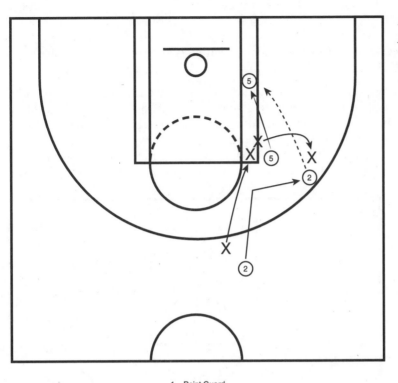

If the defenders switch, the player setting the pick (5) can roll toward the basket and take a pass for a close-in shot.

1 – Point Guard
2 – Shooting Guard
3 – Small Forward
4 – Power Forward
5 – Center
X – Defenders

The pick-and-roll is elegant in its simplicity, which is why it still works after more than 100 years. If executed properly, the offensive players should be able to score one way or another.

Clyde's Rules

While setting a pick, the offensive player must remain stationary. He may not move at all. If he moves his foot a little, or sticks his hip out, or leans into the defender with his elbow or shoulder, it's an offensive foul and his team loses possession of the ball. Watch carefully for this— often players seek to gain an edge with a very slight movement.

Give-and-Go

A variation of the pick-and-roll is the *give-and-go,* which is another of the most basic plays in the game. It also involves just two players and is both elegant and lethal.

This play can work anywhere on the court, but is very effective if you start on one side. The player with the ball, such as the shooting guard, passes it to a teammate who's in a pivot position, with his back to the basket. After he releases the pass he fakes as if he's going to come outside for a jump shot. Once the defender reacts, he immediately changes direction and cuts straight toward the basket, taking a short pass from his teammate for an open layup or dunk. Here's the way it works:

After passing the ball to his teammate (5), the originating player (2) makes a quick fake and then immediately cuts to the basket to take a return pass for an open shot.

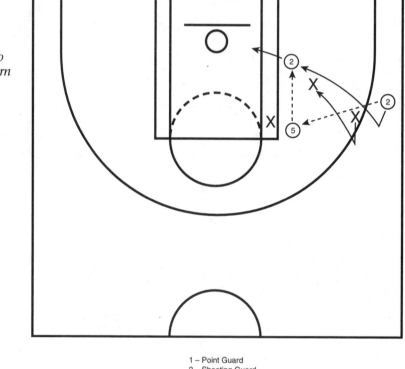

1 – Point Guard
2 – Shooting Guard
3 – Small Forward
4 – Power Forward
5 – Center
X – Defenders

This is a basic misdirection play that works because the offensive player knows where he's going, but the defenders do not. If the defender bites on the fake, there's no way he can react quickly enough to prevent the cutter from getting his easy shot. As long as the ball is handled properly, the play is virtually unstoppable.

Like so many plays in basketball, the give-and-go requires ESP, timing and precise execution. Timing is everything—if the passes are crisp and the player originating the play cuts quickly toward the basket, the defenders inevitably can do little but watch.

Watching Shooting Guards

Obviously, the first thing you look for in evaluating a shooting guard is whether he can shoot. At the NBA level you would think this would be a given, but it's not. Calbert Cheaney of the Washington Wizards is an example of a shooting guard who isn't a potent shooter. But he's a decent scorer and a very good defender who plays well within their team concept, so he has a job.

Shooting range is important for two guards. They should be able to drain jumpers from beyond the three-point arc, from 25 feet or more. If they can do that, they open up the court for their teammates by forcing defenders to come out and guard them far from the basket. That also opens up driving lanes for them to take the ball to the hoop.

Clyde's Tip

Kareem Abdul-Jabbar and Magic Johnson of the Los Angeles Lakers were masters of the give-and-go in the 1980s, while John Stockton and Karl Malone of the Utah Jazz use it effectively today. In both cases the players were teammates for so long that they could anticipate each other's intentions without having to call out a play, making something as simple as th · give-and-go a formidable play to stop.

Next, you should look to see if a player can catch-and-shoot or create his own shot off the dribble, or both. This is critical in determining how effective a shooting guard can be. Just about every team runs a curl play, where the shooting guard runs around a pick set by a bigger player, curls toward the man with the ball, catches a pass and then shoots. A shooting guard must be able to catch-and-shoot to make this play work—if he has to stop and take a dribble to get set up, the defense has time to adjust and will catch up to him. On the other hand, teams often have plays where they let a shooting guard work one-on-one against his defender and create his own shot. A good shooting guard should be able to score both ways.

Some players are superb spot-up shooters, meaning they like to run to a spot on the floor, catch a pass, and shoot right away. The Chicago Bulls had a string of them who played alongside Michael Jordan, including Craig Hodges, John Paxson, and Steve Kerr. Because Jordan inevitably drew a double-team, these guys would just slide to open spots on the floor and wait for the pass to come to them, then drill the open jumper.

You may get open shots because you play alongside Jordan, but you still have to make those shots. Left open, Paxson hit a three-pointer in dramatic fashion to close out the 1993 NBA Finals against Phoenix, while Kerr took a pass from Jordan and nailed a jumper that was the clinching basket in the 1997 NBA Finals against Utah.

Guys like Paxson and Kerr are catch-and-shoot players. The Knicks had a guy like that a few years ago, Trent Tucker. He was a lethal shooter when given room, but he couldn't create a shot for himself. A lot of players are like that and it limits their careers. They can still contribute, but more as specialists and role-players than as all-around front-line players.

The best two guards also can create, like Jordan. Clyde Drexler, who played so well for the Portland Trail Blazers and Houston Rockets before retiring after the 1997–98 season to become the coach at the University of Houston, was another. Reggie Miller is a great shooter who also can create his own shot, especially when he's feeling like he's in that zone.

I like to watch the way the two guard moves to get open to catch a pass and take his shot. This is called "moving without the ball" and I'll discuss it at greater length in the next chapter.

Quote...Unquote

"Am I the greatest? I think I could have played against anybody and played very well against anybody. I think I'm the greatest—look at my record."—*Oscar Robertson.*

Quote...Unquote

"We always went to Jerry West for the last shot because we knew he was going to make it. His nickname was Mr. Clutch and he carried that moniker well because every time we were in that situation, boom, he'd make the shot."—*Lakers teammate Hot Rod Hundley.*

Finally, try to see what kind of defender he is. Does he play his man closely, fight through picks and contest every shot? Or is he content to coast a bit and reluctant to give that extra effort and commitment that defense demands? It's daunting, but the best two guards—like the best players at every position—play both ends of the floor.

My Favorite Shooting Guards

Two of the greatest guards of all time were Oscar Robertson and Jerry West, who were teammates on the great 1960 U.S. Olympic team and played against each other for more than a decade.

They were both all-around guards. They could handle the ball, and Robertson especially had a ton of assists, but if you have to stick them in one category or another I would consider them shooting guards because they were such dangerous scorers.

Robertson was a versatile player who could do everything, as he proved when he averaged a triple-double for a full season. He was big and strong and loved to back you in methodically toward the basket, little by little, before putting up his shot.

West was a bit smaller than Robertson but every bit as prolific a shooter and scorer. He was "Mr. Clutch," the man who always seemed to come through when the game was on the line. We had some memorable confrontations, including the 1972 All-Star Game when he nailed a jumper over me at the buzzer to give the West team the victory.

I got caught flat-footed and had a nice view of this layup by Oscar Robertson, playing for Milwaukee against the Knicks. (Or was it trick camera-work creating an optical illusion?) Associated Press

Earl "the Pearl" Monroe, whom I played with, also ranks up there among the greatest shooting guards of all time. He was a showman, a guy with a million moves who could really create his own shot and loved to play to the crowd. He was the master of the spin move, the shake and bake, who electrified fans with his shenanigans.

Sam Jones was another dominating two guard, a mainstay of those great Boston Celtics teams in the 1960s, and Bill Sharman filled the role there before him. Jones was very steady and tended to get overlooked because he was on such a good team. But he was deadly.

Jerry West was a superb jump shooter, but he could also take it to the hoop, as he does here against the Cincinnati Royals in 1962.
Associated Press

Quote...Unquote

"Sam Jones showed up at the most crucial times to get the good shot. He was a great shooter, a great defensive player and he had great speed. There wasn't anything Sam Jones couldn't do. If he had played with a team other than the Celtics, he'd be held in the same esteem as Jerry West or Oscar Robertson."
—*Celtics teammate John Havlicek.*

Hal Greer, who starred for the Philadelphia 76ers in the 1960s, has to rate up there, a guy with a masterful mid-range jumper. The Iceman, George Gervin, who won four scoring titles with the San Antonio Spurs in the 1970s and 1980s, was another who could really fill it up. Dave Bing of the Detroit Pistons, another great player from the 1970s, has to be included, although he was a point guard as much as a shooting guard—he really ran his teams.

Today, of course, you start with Michael Jordan, the greatest player in the game, a true basketball icon. Guys like Reggie Miller and Clyde "the Glide" Drexler also personify the two guard position, and I enjoy watching their prowess. I'll miss Clyde and I wish him the best in his coaching career.

The Least You Need to Know

➤ A shooting guard comes out of the locker room firing and never lets up—swish before you dish—because he often is his team's primary scoring weapon.

➤ A great shot isn't enough to make a great shooting guard; you also must be able to shake free from one or more defenders and create your shot.

➤ Two of the simplest plays in basketball are the best because they are so hard to defend—the pick-and-roll and the give-and-go.

➤ Michael Jordan, Oscar Robertson, and Jerry West top my list of favorite shooting guards because no single defender could stop them and they seemed immune to pressure.

Chapter 6

Small Forwards: Masters of Offense

In This Chapter

➤ Small forwards must be prolific

➤ They're not necessarily small

➤ Ability + agility = shot opportunities

➤ What to watch for

➤ My favorite small forwards

In the modern era of basketball specialization, we no longer have forwards. We have small forwards and power forwards.

Small forward is a misnomer, for among the players who play the position in today's NBA are 6'9" Shareef Abdur-Rahim of the Vancouver Grizzlies, 6'10" Detlef Schrempf of the Seattle SuperSonics, and 6'11" Kevin Garnett of the Minnesota Timberwolves. One of the definitive small forwards of all time, former Boston Celtic Larry Bird, stands 6'9". These men are hardly small, even by basketball's skewed standards.

Also, small forwards may be every bit as powerful as power forwards. Larry Johnson of the New York Knicks, Charles Barkley of the Houston Rockets, and Anthony Mason of the Charlotte Hornets are all rock-solid physical specimens who ask no quarter and give none, yet all have been starting small forwards during their NBA careers (in addition to also seeing time as power forwards).

But while the physiques and skill sets may vary, there is one common denominator among virtually all the men who play this position in the NBA: They all can score.

They both are primarily scorers. In fact, the positions are pretty much interchangeable so you're not going to see a heck of a difference in their descriptions. Many players play both positions. I can try to use slightly different language, but that's the bottom line. There isn't much new "hard" information to give.

Like the shooting guards I discussed earlier, they are masters of offense.

20 Points a Game

Some of the most talented and exciting players of the modern basketball era have played the small forward position, from Elgin Baylor of the Los Angeles Lakers in the 1960s to Julius Erving of the New York Nets and Philadelphia 76ers in the 1970s and 1980s to Grant Hill of the Detroit Pistons in the 1990s. They all have had one thing in common, and that is the ability to put the ball in the hoop.

Small forwards must be able to score if they're to succeed in today's NBA. Much like shooting guards, they've got to be prolific—in fact, the positions are somewhat interchangeable and many players play both spots. Small forwards must be able to put 20 points on the board every night, so a lot of them don't really assert themselves on the defensive end as much as they should.

Small forwards actually are even more offense-oriented than shooting guards. Which raises a very logical question: Why aren't they simply called shooting forwards? I have no answer. It's certainly a more accurate description of the position.

As I mentioned, the way many teams use small lineups today there's really little difference between the two and the three positions, between shooting guard and small forward. Kendall Gill of the New Jersey Nets, Glen Rice of the Charlotte Hornets, and Rex Chapman of the Phoenix Suns are examples of players who have been starters as shooting guards and small forwards, and there are many more around the NBA. As long as you can score, you have filled the main requirement for playing small forward.

One exception to the notion that leading small forwards aren't necessarily feared on defense was Larry Bird of the Boston Celtics. He wasn't the fastest player, he wasn't much of a jumper, and he wasn't known for his one-on-one defensive prowess, but he was so savvy within the team concept that he was an excellent defensive player. He was perceptive and knew how to anticipate plays, so he came up with creative steals and blocks that way.

Clyde's Record Book

Tom Heinsohn was a high-scoring forward for the Boston Celtics in the late '50s and early '60s who always averaged in double figures. Heinsohn's nickname was "Ack-Ack" after the sound made by a machine-gun, because he never stopped firing away. They say Heinsohn never met a shot he didn't like, or didn't take.

Quote...Unquote

"Larry's mind takes an instant picture of the whole court, and he sees creative possibilities."—*Bill Fitch, Larry Bird's first pro coach with the Boston Celtics.*

Larry Bird was both an offensive master and outstanding team defensive player. Here he passes the ball between two defenders.
Associated Press

One play that illustrates this came during Game 5 of the 1987 Eastern Conference Finals between Bird's Celtics and the Detroit Pistons. Detroit led 107-106 and had the ball out of bounds in Boston's frontcourt with five seconds left. That's when Bird anticipated the direction of Isiah Thomas's inbounds pass, stepped in front of Detroit center Bill Laimbeer and picked it off. Then, in one motion, he turned and whipped the ball to teammate Dennis Johnson, who was cutting down the lane for the game-winning layup.

Bird's savvy, his anticipation, his tenacity, and his clairvoyance are what made that play possible.

Don't Call Me Small!

Kevin Garnett of the Minnesota Timberwolves was a star center in high school—so good, in fact, that he was able to skip college, go directly to the NBA, and after a couple of years sign a multi-year contract for more than $20 million a season. Garnett stands 6'11", yet he's so agile and mobile that he often plays the small forward position in the Wolves' lineup.

It's not that he can't play effectively around the basket. He certainly can, and he has shown it with his shot-blocking and interior moves. It's that he's so talented he's completely comfortable playing small forward, where he becomes an almost impossible matchup. He's too quick and elusive for the big guys and too tall and strong for the smaller guys.

They're not the only towering small forwards. Juwan Howard of Washington, Antonio McDyess of Phoenix, Keith Van Horn of New Jersey, Shareef Abdur-Rahim of Vancouver, and Detlef Schrempf of Seattle are all 6'9" or taller, yet many of them are as efficient, if not more so, as small forwards rather than power forwards.

Clyde's Rules

Nothing against the smaller guy, but the bottom line is if you've got the skills, height never hurts. At the very least, it gives a player the chance to shoot or pass over a defender. If two players of equal ability are trying out for a team, the coach will inevitably pick the taller one.

Standing Tall, Playing Small; Standing Small, Playing Tall

Some players are tall but they play small. By that I mean they don't rebound well, are reluctant to mix it up inside, and prefer to stand on the perimeter and shoot.

Other players stand small but play tall. They're physical and unrelenting on the glass, obliterating bodies in the paint. They may not measure up against a ruler, but they never back down from a challenge.

You can guess which type of player most coaches prefer, although a smart coach will find a way to utilize both.

I mentioned how small forwards, like shooting guards, are expected to score and that the positions are somewhat interchangeable. If there is a real difference, it's that small forwards would get a few more rebounds and be prepared to go under the boards more, while shooting guards must be conscious of getting back on defense and so may tend to stay on the outside more.

When I was playing, there was a 7-footer by the name of Mel Counts who started his career with the Boston Celtics. As tall as he was, he was also very thin and couldn't take the pounding under the boards, especially early in his career. But he was a terrific outside shooter who could stand in the corner and hit the 20-foot jumper all night long. He was tall, but he played small, so Red Auerbach used him as a designated shooter. Counts would come off the bench and shoot over smaller defenders, and if he was hitting, other teams would be forced to adjust their lineups by putting in another big man to guard him. That juggling of personnel often took them out of their rhythm.

Charles Barkley is an audacious example of a player who plays tall. He's listed as 6'6" in sneakers, but measures only about 6'4½" in his bare feet. But he's broad and strong and he relishes physical contact, so he's always taking the ball to the glass or muscling his way in for rebounds. Tenacious and loquacious, he has been a starter at both forward positions during his career, but he's so quick and such a fine scorer and ballhandler that he's especially effective at small forward.

Scorers Who Cannot Be Denied

Small forwards have to be masters of the nuances, understanding and executing on offense. They must know how to get their shots, and they must make them once they get them. As I said with regard to shooting guards, this isn't a position for the meek or the bashful.

Clyde's Record Book

The tallest player in NBA history, 7'7" Manute Bol, loved to stand outside and shoot. And the fans loved to watch the slender giant fire away from long range, even though he enjoyed only spotty success. He attempted 205 three-point shots during his career and made 43 of them, a mediocre .210 accuracy mark.

Clyde's Record Book

Charles Barkley was nicknamed the "Round Mound of Rebound" during his college days at Auburn University, when his weight was said to have ballooned past 300 pounds. When he turned pro he quickly realized he needed to shed some of that poundage if he wanted to have a long and successful career, and to his credit he did just that. In fact, he lost the weight faster than the nickname—some writers were still using it after Barkley, who prefers to go by "Sir Charles," had dropped some 50 pounds.

Al Attles, who coached the Golden State Warriors to the NBA title in 1975, tells a story about his forward, Rick Barry, one of the all-time prolific scorers. It explains what I call the shooter's mentality.

"Rick was 2-for-15 shooting going into the fourth quarter," said Attles. "And I'll be darned if he didn't come out in that fourth quarter and make five straight shots and lead us to victory. That typifies what Rick Barry was all about."

I look at Bernard King, when he played for the New York Knicks in the 1980s, as the quintessential small forward. He was an offensive master, a guy you just could not deny. He was so quick he seemed to mesmerize his defender as he swooped to the hoop.

Quote...Unquote

"Bernard King was like a swooping bird on the fast break. He had that incredible capacity to end the break with a quick dunk, and you would blink because you didn't even see it happen."—*Hubie Brown, former coach of the New York Knicks.*

The 6'7" King was such an incredible offensive player that even after he tore up his knee he was able to come back and play well enough to make the All-Star team. He once spoke eloquently about the feeling he got when he was on top of his game, and I think it's a feeling all of the best offensive players have shared:

"Talk to any guy who's a scorer and he'll tell you there are times when you go into a zone," King said. "When I was averaging 30 points a game, I didn't have to think about anything. Everything is happening on a very instinctual level. On a particular night, no matter what you do, there's a feeling it's going to work. It's an incredible feeling. There's nothing like it."

Small forwards get some of their shots through set plays, where teammates set screens for them so they can get open for their shots. Most of the time when teams run plays, it's for their shooting guards or small forwards, who are usually their most potent scorers. They'll also get some shots in transition, just like shooting guards.

But they also must have the individual ability to create their own shots. A small forward should be able to take the ball and face his man, one-on-one, and be able to get his shot off. Whether he drives all the way to the basket or takes one dribble, stops, and pops a jumper, the important thing is that he's able to create enough open space to get a good shot at the basket.

Bernard King (driving the ball to the basket) was a consummate small forward, an offensive master who would not be denied.
Associated Press

Moving Without the Ball

If you're seated close enough to a team's bench, sooner or later you're bound to hear the coach scream: "Move! Move! Move!"

Basketball is a game of perpetual motion. The most effective teams are the ones whose players are always on the move.

You'll often hear the phrase "moving without the ball," and it's an important one to understand. If a player keeps moving—not just running aimlessly about the court but moving with a purpose in

Clyde's Tip

Stationary targets are easier to hit than moving targets. The same goes for basketball players. Players who stand still are much easier to guard than players who keep moving.

95

mind—chances are that before long he will lose his defender. That's when a good point guard will spot him and dish him the ball for an open shot.

The Boston Celtics epitomized movement, and the continuity it creates to get open shots, during the years they were winning all those championships. They were just perpetual motion. "Hondo" John Havlicek was always moving around, Sam Jones was always moving around, getting open shots.

We had two of the finest at moving without the ball on the Knicks: Cazzie Russell and Bill Bradley.

Quote...Unquote

"He was like the bionic man. People at Harvard were doing studies on his heart rate because he appeared to have this great stamina, because he never stopped running."—*Tom Heinsohn, talking about Boston Celtics teammate John Havlicek.*

Cazzie was the best guy I ever saw at knowing where to go and how to get his shot. Even if you tried to freeze him out, he would somehow end up shooting. You knew when you passed him the ball you weren't going to get it back, because he had the knack for going to the spots that would get him uncontested shots.

Bradley was more like Havlicek because he was always in motion. He was constantly running the baseline, weaving his way inside and outside, moving until he got open. And once he got open he was deadly.

Guys like Bradley and Havlicek were proficient at using picks. On the next page, I've drawn up a frequently used play in which a small forward will start in one corner and run his man through two picks along the baseline to get open for a shot on the opposite side.

Phil Chenier, who played for the Washington Bullets in the '70s, was adept at losing his man in picks. I should know, because often I was that man! He used to run behind picks set by Wes Unseld and Elvin Hayes and come along the baseline for open shots, just as diagrammed, and I'd have a hard time finding him let alone catching up to him.

I think moving without the ball has become something of a lost art. Today, guys tend to go and get the ball and then try to create. We had guys like that, too, but it's more prevalent today because too often the game is characterized by one-on-one play rather than teamwork. Many of today's players are so gifted individually, or think they are, that they would rather create their own shots than run the disciplined patterns you need to get open by moving without the ball. Their motto seems to be: Disdain the mundane!

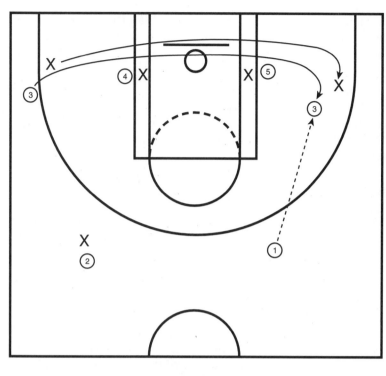

The small forward (3) runs his man through two picks (set by 4 and 5) along the baseline, then curls back to take a pass from the point guard (1) for the shot.

1 – Point Guard
2 – Shooting Guard
3 – Small Forward
4 – Power Forward
5 – Center
X – Defenders

Point Forwards

Because of their versatility, some coaches have their small forwards bring the ball up the court for their teams much of the time. Don Nelson did this with the Milwaukee Bucks when he had a player named Paul Pressey, who handled the ball like a point guard. Since Pressey played the small forward position, Nelson called him a "point forward."

Scottie Pippen played this role for the Chicago Bulls during their championship run. Because Pippen and Michael Jordan were such good ballhandlers, Bulls coach Phil Jackson never used a true point guard. He preferred to get another shooter like B.J. Armstrong, Craig Hodges, John Paxson, Ron Harper, or Steve Kerr into the lineup, and let Pippen bring the ball up and get the Bulls into their offense.

Quote...Unquote

"Scottie Pippen has got to be considered one of the best all-around players in the game. When one phase of his game isn't on key, he's able to contribute in other ways. I think that's the sign of greatness."—*Michael Jordan, on his long-time Chicago Bulls teammate.*

Pippen is an aberration. He isn't just a set-up man, he's Mr. Versatility. He's a much better scorer than Pressey and he's also an outstanding defensive player, a great exception to the rule for small forwards. His defense, and that of Michael Jordan, were keys to the Bulls' success that tended to be overlooked because the two of them were so good offensively.

Grant Hill of the Detroit Pistons is another example of a small forward who's Mr. Versatility. Not only does he rank among the league's leading scorers, he's among the team leaders in rebounding and assists. He brings the ball upcourt most of the time for the Pistons and gets them into their offense.

Watching Small Forwards

Look for players who want the ball, who want to take the big shot when the game is on the line. That's the essence of a scorer, which is what you want your small forward to be.

Remember the story Al Attles told about Rick Barry, how even though he was shooting 2-for-15 he kept on shooting and made five in a row to win the game? That's the mentality and fortitude a small forward should have.

Clyde's Tip

This isn't a position for altruists. Players who want to make it as NBA small forwards must be willing to exhibit fire and desire. They must have aptitude and attitude. You want your small forward to have a bit of an edge to him.

Another thing to watch for is motion. Bill Bradley bewildered opponents by running back and forth along the baseline, from one side of the court to the other. Eventually they got tired of chasing him, which of course was exactly what he wanted. I always knew to look for Bill later in the game, because by then the guy trying to guard him was exhausted.

Finally, look to see what a small forward is doing besides scoring. If you make it a given that a front-line NBA small forward should score 20 points a game, what separates the best from the rest is that they contribute in other areas. Pippen plays tenacious defense and brings the ball up. Barkley is a relentless rebounder, as was Elgin Baylor. Barry was a brilliant passer.

Having that added dimension puts them a cut above the rest, so look for it when you're watching small forwards.

My Favorite Small Forwards

I already mentioned Bernard King, who might not have been the most complete player but who was an unstoppable scorer, which made him a quintessential small forward.

Today, a guy I'd put in that category is Glen Rice. He's a lethal shooter who's going to get 20+ points every night unless he's constantly double-teamed or triple-teamed.

Chris Mullin of the Indiana Pacers, who played so many fine seasons for the Golden State Warriors, is another player like that. He was a deadly shooter, still is. And Charles Barkley, in his prime, was a prolific scorer who was also a productive rebounder.

Scottie Pippen and Grant Hill are both consummate because of their versatility. They handle the ball, they break down defenses, they set up their teammates, and they also score on their own—what more could you ask? And Pippen gives you that added element of being one of the game's greatest defensive stoppers.

Larry Bird was the best of the '80s. He could dish and swish and was an outstanding team defender. He also had an unusual court sense, a mental telepathy that enabled him not only to see a play as it was developing but to anticipate the play that was about to develop and where his teammates would be at that time. And he was as indomitable as anyone who ever played the game, another quality you need to stand out.

Going back a little further, Julius Erving certainly rates among the best of all time. He was a brilliant offensive player, especially in his younger days when he had no peer at taking the ball to the hoop. Later, as his legs began to go and he lost a half-step, he became a strong outside shooter, much the way Michael Jordan has become. He showed his resolve by augmenting his game with the perimeter shot.

Finally, one of the greatest of all time was Elgin Baylor, who played so brilliantly for the Lakers in the 1960s. Baylor was one of those players who took the game off the floor and into the air, who pushed the limits with his creativity and his flair. His stats are spectacular—career averages of 27.4 points and 13.5 rebounds per game. But it was the way he played, combining speed and power, that was even more spectacular.

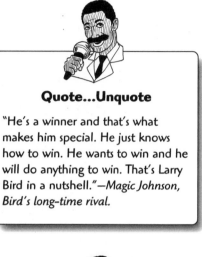

Quote...Unquote

"He's a winner and that's what makes him special. He just knows how to win. He wants to win and he will do anything to win. That's Larry Bird in a nutshell."—*Magic Johnson, Bird's long-time rival.*

Quote...Unquote

"People talk about today's modern players. Elgin Baylor was one of the first modern players. He was one of the first players that had that incredible knack to not only do the right thing but the most spectacular thing."—*Jerry West, long-time Lakers teammate.*

"Dr. J," Julius Erving, shown here stuffing the ball, possessed the most intoxicating moves I've ever seen. He was a master of offense whose game was marked by creativity and flair.
Associated Press

The Least You Need to Know

➤ A small forward must be an offensive machine, capable of scoring 20 points or more every night, since he usually is one of his team's primary scorers.

➤ Two keys to success are moving without the ball and being able to create your own shot. Being able to do those things will give a small forward ample opportunity to score.

➤ All small forwards should be able to score, but the best help their teams win in other ways as well, such as rebounding, handling the ball, or playing defense.

➤ Bernard King epitomized the small forward to me because he was an unstoppable scorer, a true offensive machine.

Chapter 7

Power Forwards: Wimps Need Not Apply

In This Chapter

➤ Let's get physical!

➤ They're the enforcers

➤ The new breed: long and lean

➤ What to watch for

➤ My favorite power forwards

Power forward is a position that has evolved over the years and is still evolving, perhaps more than any other position.

In the early years of the NBA, power forwards were often big and slow. They weren't quite big enough to play center, however, and they were too slow and not prolific enough as scorers to play small forward. But because they usually contributed something to their team's success, they had a place in the lineup.

Most often that something was muscle. Power forwards were the protectors, making sure none of their teammates got pushed around, particularly in the rough-and-tumble early years, when much more physical play was the norm. They called them the goons. These guys would go in the game and rough people up.

Over the years, power forwards became more athletic. Some were scorers, others excelled on defense, but they remained rugged rebounders who relished the banging of bodies under the boards. Today's power forwards are the most athletic of all, often combining the best qualities of centers and forwards.

Nasty, Sassy Dudes

That's the best way I can describe power forwards: nasty, sassy dudes. They ask no quarter and they give none.

These guys are ferocious. They like physical play. If point guards must be able to handle the ball and shooting guards and small forwards have to be able to shoot, power forwards must be physical and indefatigable. Those are the primary requisites for this position.

Take Rick Mahorn. In the early '80s, the late Johnny Most, legendary radio voice of the Boston Celtics, dubbed the Washington Bullets' tandem of center Jeff Ruland and power forward Mahorn "McFilthy and McNasty" because of their rugged play under the boards. Most reprised the nickname several years later, after Mahorn had moved on to the Detroit Pistons and teamed with Bill Laimbeer on the "Bad Boys" who won the 1989 crown. Mahorn is still around because of the intensity and savvy he brings to the game.

Crashing the boards, banging bodies, setting picks—such is the life of a power forward. It's not easy and it's not glamorous. If you like to shoot the ball and crave the spotlight, learn another position. These are the warriors, players who often have all the finesse of a bulldozer.

Power forwards must be rugged rebounders who delight in cleaning the glass. On many NBA teams, the power forward is the leading rebounder, hauling down more boards than even the team's taller center. That's because centers usually are expected to score more and can't always focus on rebounding and the positioning it requires. Also, two teams' centers often cancel each other out, leaving a place for a hungry, hell-bent for leather power forward to swoop in and dominate the boards.

NBA power forwards are expected to score from in close, whether inside the paint or along the baseline. Often their points come on offensive rebounds as they follow up missed shots by teammates. Defensively they are expected to play tough inside and hit the boards. It's great if they can block shots as well, but that's really the center's responsibility. It's more important that power forwards provide a physical presence.

Power forwards are the NBA's blue collar workers. Many of them lack refined scoring skills, meaning they're not great pure shooters or don't have tricky moves to get away from defenders. Frankly, most of them possess a blacksmith's touch when it comes to shooting and have

Clyde's Chalk Talk

You may hear an announcer say a player is collecting *garbage points,* and that player is often a power forward. What he's talking about are points that are up for grabs—loose balls that are bouncing around near a basket. Many of these are offensive rebounds, when a player puts in a teammate's missed shot. These are hustle and muscle plays, and that's what a power forward must have.

just two moves—forwards and backwards. But they can rebound and block shots, because those are effort plays. Power forwards always give 110 percent.

The Prototype

The term "power forward" didn't really enter the hoop lexicon until the late 1970s, when the prototype of the modern power forward, Maurice Lucas, teamed with Bill Walton in Portland.

The muscular, 6'9" Lucas was the consummate power forward. He's the guy who would knock you on your backside and then stand over you, glowering.

Lucas, who once knocked down 7'2" Artis Gilmore, one of the strongest men ever to lace on sneakers, during a fight in an American Basketball Association game, was a physical, no-nonsense player. Lucas's strength was a perfect match for Walton's finesse. Lucas provided the inside scoring and rebounding support Portland needed, and he also gave the team a rough edge. Nobody tried to muscle up on the Blazers when Luke was on the floor.

Yet Lucas had wit with his grit, brains to go with his brawn. He always knew what he was doing. Every bump and grind, every glare and stare, was performed to enhance his persona.

Quote...Unquote

"Maurice Lucas was the heart and soul of that team. He gave us toughness, that never-say-die attitude."—*Herm Gilliam, a teammate of Lucas on the 1977 NBA Champion Portland Trail Blazers.*

Quote...Unquote

"To Luke, basketball was a contact sport—all con and no tact."—*Lionel Hollins, on his Portland Trail Blazers teammate, Maurice Lucas.*

"My image has given me a license to play physical," he said late in his career, which lasted 14 bone-jarring seasons that included stints with the Spirits of St. Louis and Kentucky Colonels of the ABA as well as the New Jersey Nets, New York Knicks, Phoenix Suns, Los Angeles Lakers, Seattle SuperSonics, and Portland Trail Blazers. "I play a physical game, but it's really a mental game. Intimidation. Getting a guy thinking about me, not his game."

Maurice Lucas (20) was the prototype power forward, a nasty, sassy dude who never backed down and was always looking for a body to bang. Associated Press

Power Forwards Complement Their Centers

Centers and power forwards enjoy a unique relationship. Together it's their job to dominate the paint under the basket, whether it be from the standpoint of scoring, rebounding, setting picks, or shot-blocking. It doesn't really matter who does what—so long as between the two of them, the job gets done.

Get a center and a power forward who work well together, like Walton and Lucas, and you have a solid foundation for a championship team. Remember that the closer you get to the basket, generally speaking, the easier it is to score. So if you get a center/power forward combination that can dominate play around the basket both offensively and defensively, you'll have a very happy coach.

Long before the term "power forward" was invented, the players who filled that role enjoyed a symbiotic relationship with their respective centers, feeding off one another's strengths and masking each other's weaknesses.

Go back to the league's first dynasty, the Minneapolis Lakers, who won five titles in six seasons from 1948–49 through 1953–54, and you find a pair of Hall of Famers flourishing side by side in those two positions, George Mikan and Vern Mikkelsen. Mikan was the high-scoring center, the team's superstar, while the 6'7" Mikkelsen ranked among the league's leading rebounders and provided the inside muscle and scoring to support Mikan's brilliance.

Perhaps the best example of such a combination in the NBA during the 1990s was on the New York Knicks, where Patrick Ewing and Charles Oakley teamed up for nearly a decade, until Oakley was traded last summer. Ewing, the 7-foot center, is the high scorer and agile shot-blocker, while Oakley, a 6'9" block of granite, was the tough defender and rugged rebounder whose inside skills gave Ewing the freedom to roam the floor.

In the Patrick Ewing–Charles Oakley tandem, Ewing clearly was the shining star, a future Hall of Famer and an 11-time All-Star. Oakley thrives on intangibles. He's role-playing personified, one who has played his role well enough to earn All-Star recognition and universal respect among his peers.

That relationship isn't unusual. The Los Angeles Lakers won five championships in the 1980s with the brilliant Kareem Abdul-Jabbar at center and the blue-collar worker, Kurt Rambis, at power forward. The 6'8" Rambis was a perfect fit, constantly badgering opponents under the basket, careening for rebounds, and tapping in missed shots. He knew his role and played it well.

One of the Lakers' primary rivals of the early 1980s, the Philadelphia 76ers, had a similar makeup. They had the league's MVP, Moses Malone, at center, and opportunistic Marc Iavaroni at power forward.

Clyde's Tip

Centers and power forwards should bring out the best in each other, like peanut butter and jelly or syrup and pancakes. Their skills should complement one another; if one is primarily a scorer, the other should be primarily a rebounder.

Quote...Unquote

"We had a power forward before we knew what to call him."—*Vern Mikkelsen, who played the position for the Minneapolis Lakers in the late 1940s and early `50s.*

Clyde's Record Book

It's no coincidence that in Patrick Ewing's three seasons in New York prior to Charles Oakley's arrival, the Knicks averaged 28.3 wins; in the next nine seasons (throw out 1997–98, when Ewing was injured for most of the year), they averaged 51.4 wins.

105

A player of limited skills who had been cut in previous tryouts and played in Europe when he couldn't land a job in the NBA, Iavaroni banged the boards and played rugged defense, tiring out opponents and keeping them from getting too physical with some of the team's finesse players.

Clyde's Record Book

On our Knicks teams, Dave DeBusschere complemented center Willis Reed well, even though he wasn't a classic power forward. DeBusschere stood about 6'6" and actually had played guard early in his career, so he wasn't the intimidator Maurice Lucas was. But Reed was so strong and such a dominating presence that we didn't need another intimidator on the floor. DeBusschere was an outstanding defender and a dangerous scorer from inside or out, and he fit into our team's style perfectly.

In the 1970s, the Celtics won a pair of championships with Dave Cowens and Paul Silas as their anchor. Cowens was the dynamic scorer, an under-sized 6'9" center who made up in hustle what he lacked in height, while Silas was the power forward who provided the muscle under the boards. Later that decade, Silas took his strength and savvy to Seattle, where he helped a team built around young center Jack Sikma win a championship in 1979.

The Celtics of an earlier generation, the dynasty that won 11 titles in 13 years from 1957 through 1969, featured one of the game's all-time great centers—Bill Russell, a superb rebounder who revolutionized the concept of team defense. The Celtics had plenty of scorers, too, and a couple of power forwards who played their roles to perfection: "Jungle" Jim Loscutoff and his successor, Tom "Satch" Sanders.

Sanders could nail the clutch jumper, but his biggest contribution was as a defender, both one-on-one and within the Celtics' team concept. His battles with stars of the '60s such as Elgin Baylor were classics.

Loscutoff, meanwhile, brought muscle to the Celtics in the late '50s, a time of wide-open play when bumps and bruises were worn like badges of honor. Jungle Jim loved to push people around.

As Times Changed, So Did Power Forwards

Times have changed since Jungle Jim's day. The position of power forward has evolved, partially because the rules have changed. Referees don't allow as much contact anymore and players have had to adjust.

You can't lean on each other and push and shove like you used to. You can't even put your hand on a player—if a ref thinks it impedes his progress he'll call it hand-checking, which is a foul nowadays.

Instead of just being physical specimens, power forwards now have some agility as well; none more so than Karl Malone of the Utah Jazz.

Karl Malone has raised the standards for power forwards with his prolific scoring.
Associated Press

For more than a decade, Malone has been the game's dominant power forward. He combines a chiseled 6'9", 256-pound physique with quickness and scoring ability. In fact, Malone's really an aberration because he's such an explosive scorer. He's more like a three, where the emphasis is on scoring, yet he's so strong he's an ideal four.

Shawn Kemp, who starred for Seattle and now stars for Cleveland, is another power forward in that mold. He's strong and a nasty, sassy dude, but he's also a real scorer.

Perhaps the most unusual power forward in the NBA is Dennis Rodman, and I don't say that

Clyde's Chalk Talk

Karl Malone got his nickname, "the Mailman," from a sports writer in Louisiana, where he grew up and played college ball at Louisiana Tech. Why "the Mailman"? Because he always delivered.

because of his hair colorings, his tattoos, his unique wardrobe, and his lifestyle. I'm talking about the way he plays the game. He seems to shoot only when forced to, yet he still can be one of the most effective players in the league because he's a relentless rebounder, as his record string of seven consecutive rebounding titles attests. He's one of the few players in the league who truly impacts a game without taking a shot.

Oakley is more of a traditional power forward. The same goes for the Davis boys in Indiana, Dale Davis and Antonio Davis. The youngster who began his career in Sacramento and is now with Portland, Brian Grant, is another in the traditional mold.

The New Breed Is Lean, But Is It Mean?

Those traditional power forward types are becoming rare—these days you have a different kind of player coming into the NBA at that position.

The new breed of power forward is long and lean instead of really muscular. Guys like Chris Webber of Sacramento, Vin Baker of Seattle, Antonio McDyess of Phoenix, and Elden Campbell of the Lakers are examples.

None is really a classic power forward. Each seems to combine a little of what you'd expect to find in a center, a power forward, and a small forward into one versatile package. They're more agile than hostile and better scorers than the typical power forwards, but whether they fill that enforcer role is dubious.

Often you'll find guys who you think would be power forwards playing center because there's such a dearth of quality big men these days.

Clyde's Tip

You've surely heard the saying, "Always keep your eye on the ball." But if you do that as a fan, you're going to miss a lot of what goes on in an NBA game. One of the great things about seeing a game in person is that you can look away from the ball and watch what you want—like the battle between two power forwards for position under the boards.

Alonzo Mourning of Miami would be an ideal power forward because he's strong and mean and loves to get physical, but he plays center even though he's only about 6'9". And Jayson Williams of New Jersey is another guy who's out of position at center; he's more of a power forward who brings aggression and enthusiasm to the game.

Watching Power Forwards

To appreciate power forwards, you have to learn to take your eyes off the ball and watch some of the other action on the court. So when a shot is attempted, don't watch the flight of the ball. Watch the bodies under the basket instead.

Also look under the basket. Watch the way a player like Karl Malone or Charles Oakley tries to jockey and jostle his way into rebounding position. Notice the hostility that goes on, the pushing and shoving that's the accepted norm as players contest in a battle of bodies and wills.

When a point guard calls out a play, find the power forward and see what he's doing. Sometimes, because he may not be much of a scorer, he'll stand away from the ball and wait for the shot to be taken, then race in and crash the boards for a possible rebound. Other times he'll be in the middle of the play, setting a pick so that one of his teammates can flash open for a scoring opportunity.

Look at the intensity the power forward brings to the game. Check out his face. Watch his stride. He should exude strength, forcefulness, confidence. Ask no quarter and give none.

Quote...Unquote

"You know why I like Malone? Because he never stops. He never stops playing, he never stops working. He came at you the first day he was in this league and he's still coming at you. How the hell aren't you going to respect that?" —*Red Auerbach, former coach of the Boston Celtics, on Karl Malone's work ethic.*

My Favorite Power Forwards

You have to start with the prototype, Maurice Lucas. He really defined this position, more than any other player. He would get some points, but he was primarily a rebounder and an intimidating guy.

Late in Game 2 of the 1977 NBA Finals between Portland and Philadelphia, Lucas and Darryl Dawkins got into a fight. Lucas stood up to the bigger Dawkins and chased him all around the court, and that seemed to change the momentum of the series. It ignited a fire under the Blazers and seemed to defuse the Sixers. After losing the first two games, Lucas' Portland team won the next four and the title.

"I thought that changed how we felt about ourselves," Lucas said of the incident. "It changed their game for sure. It let them know that we were going to play them, regardless of who they are and what they've done."

Like I said, a nasty, sassy dude.

Quote...Unquote

"He broke the mold. He incorporated the post game with outside jump shots and just took it to another level. He has taken it about as far as it can go—offensively, defensively, all ways."—*Buck Williams, power forward of the New York Knicks, after Karl Malone was named the NBA's 1996–97 MVP.*

Since 1985, the gold standard for power forwards has been Karl Malone. But he's an aberration because he's such a prolific scorer—31 points per game in one season and over 25 points per game for 11 years in a row.

As a Knicks broadcaster I had the opportunity to watch Charles Oakley night after night, and it's impossible not to appreciate the way he plays the game. He's a real classic power forward who personifies the position and leaves it all on the court every game. I would be remiss if I did not acknowledge his tremendous work ethic and indomitable spirit.

The Least You Need to Know

➤ By his sheer physical presence, a power forward is like a big brother in that he makes sure nobody picks on any of his teammates.

➤ When a power forward and a center work in tandem, it makes a powerful combination because together they can dominate the area close to the basket both offensively and defensively.

➤ Today's power forwards are more active, agile, and athletic than their predecessors, who tended to be slow-footed and not skillful enough to contribute as scorers.

➤ Maurice Lucas established the mold for power forwards with his rugged play, and Karl Malone has broken that mold by adding the dimension of scoring.

Chapter 8

Centers: The Men in the Middle

Basketball is a big man's game. It has been that way ever since Dr. Naismith chose to elevate the target and had those peach baskets nailed from an overhead running track, 10 feet above the floor.

Why does a taller man have an advantage? It's simple. A tall man is closer to the target than a shorter man. His shot has less distance to travel. He starts out closer to the rebound. And because he can reach higher into the air, he has a better chance of blocking a rival's shot attempt.

The biggest man on a basketball team invariably plays center. On offense he sets up close to the basket, where his shot won't have to travel so far, and uses his height advantage to shoot over opponents. A 7-footer who shoots the ball from 25 feet away forfeits his God-given advantage over the 6-footer (from that distance, shooting skill matters more than height). A center may also venture out to the foul line or the corners if he's a good shooter, or if he's being used to set a pick and free up a teammate for a shot. On defense the center hangs around in the painted area in front of the basket as much as possible. That way he's in a good position for potential rebounds and to use his height to block shots and discourage opponents from trying to drive to the basket.

In the early years of pro ball, most centers were only slightly taller than forwards, standing perhaps 6'5" or so. There were some players who were significantly taller, but they generally lacked the quickness to keep pace with smaller opponents. That changed in the 1940s, when 7-foot Bob Kurland and 6'10" George Mikan dominated the college game with a previously unseen combination of size and skill.

Mikan went on to serve as the cornerstone of the NBA's first dynasty, the Minneapolis Lakers, who won five championships in six years, from 1948–49 through 1953–54. Centers served as key figures on two other dynasties, with Bill Russell leading the Boston Celtics to eight titles in a row and 11 in 13 seasons from 1956–57 through 1968–69, and Kareem Abdul-Jabbar helping the Los Angeles Lakers to five championships in the 1980s. And Wilt Chamberlain was a dominant figure on two of the NBA's most winning teams, the 1967 Philadelphia 76ers who went 68-13 and the 1972 Los Angeles Lakers who went 69-13.

As for the NBA's team of the '90s, the Chicago Bulls, it's true they're led by a guard, Michael Jordan. But it's also true they didn't win until they acquired Bill Cartwright, a veteran 7-footer, to play center on their first three championships teams. They stayed on top thanks in part to the acquisition of another big man, 7'2" Luc Longley, to succeed Cartwright in the middle.

In this chapter I'll look at some of the reasons why centers are so important to a basketball team's success.

Clyde's Chalk Talk

The *pivot* is another name for the center position, as in "Patrick Ewing plays the *pivot* for the Knicks." The *pivot move* is also one of the staples in the center's repertoire. He'll catch the ball with his back to the basket and a defender behind him, then spin (or *pivot*) quickly in either direction and drive past the defender to the basket for a shot.

Pivotal in Many Ways

Centers play the pivot, use a pivot move, try not to move their pivot foot, and are pivotal to their teams' success. Let me explain.

The center position is often referred to as the *pivot* because the center generally plays in the middle of the floor, whether on offense or on defense. In some basic plays, such as the give-and-go I described in Chapter 5, the center gets the ball and remains stationary as teammates cut toward the basket or run to designated spots on the floor. He is the hub around whom everything revolves.

If a team's starting and backup centers are playing well, that team is said to be getting "good pivot play" from them.

The *pivot move* is fundamental to every center's game, and in fact every player's game. The center will station himself with his back to the basket, his defender behind him, and catch a pass from a teammate. He will then spin quickly in either direction, or fake one way and spin the other, so he can get past the defender and drive toward the basket.

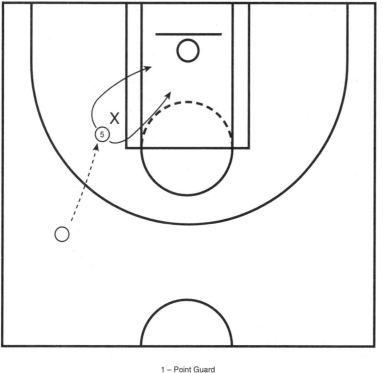

In the pivot move, the center (5) takes an entry pass from a teammate and then spins around his defender toward the basket to get off his shot.

1 – Point Guard
2 – Shooting Guard
3 – Small Forward
4 – Power Forward
5 – Center
X – Defenders

Every player—whether playing in the pros or on the weekend—should learn how to use the pivot move effectively, because there will be times when you are matched up against a shorter opponent and you'll want to back him in close to the basket and use your height advantage to get off a short shot. For a center, the pivot move is vital. That's because the center is usually called upon to set up with his back to the basket, while other players generally play facing the basket. A center must know how to pivot around his opponent to get off his shot.

You'll also hear about something called a player's pivot foot, which is important to understand. The pivot foot can be either the left foot or the right foot, whichever remains anchored to the floor before a player starts to dribble. He can pick up the other foot and put it down as many times as he wants, moving it in as many different directions, as long as the foot that he has established as his pivot foot remains on the ground. Once he picks up that pivot foot, he must shoot, pass, or dribble before it comes down or else it will be considered two steps and thus a traveling violation.

Clyde's Tip

Don't always watch the ball, because there's so much else going on. When the center has the ball with his back to the basket, try to watch his footwork. Notice which foot he establishes as his pivot foot and which way he spins toward the basket. Then check it out next time and see if he does it again. A really effective player will vary his routine so as not to be predictable, making himself tougher to defend.

All players should know how to use their pivot foot effectively, because that can help them fake out their opponents and create space to get off shots. But it's especially important for centers, who so often start off with their backs to the basket and must literally pivot before they can see their target.

By now it should be clear that a center can be crucial to his team's success. As a scorer, a rebounder, an offensive fulcrum, and a defensive stopper, a center can influence the outcome of a game in many ways.

It's no coincidence that great teams often feature great centers. NBA stars like George Mikan, Bill Russell, Wilt Chamberlain, Kareem Abdul-Jabbar, Willis Reed, Wes Unseld, Bill Walton, and Moses Malone all were center-pieces, literally, on some of the league's most winning teams.

Who are today's best centers? Hakeem Olajuwon, David Robinson, Patrick Ewing, Shaquille O'Neal, Alonzo Mourning, and Dikembe Mutombo head the list, and all play for strong, winning teams.

Having a first-rate center is even more important at lower levels of competition. In the college or high school ranks, a good big man virtually guarantees a winning season, which is why talented big men are so heavily recruited. Landing a top center also helps in further recruiting, because other players like to play with a good big man on their side. Coaches know that a good center can mean the difference between a successful program and one that struggles.

Combining strength and agility, Hakeem Olajuwon of the Houston Rockets has been one of the premier centers of the past decade. Associated Press

Dominate the Paint

While the center position has evolved over the years, one thing remains constant: A center must be able to dominate the paint.

Defensively, a center should be an intimidator against penetrators. He is a team's anchor, its last line of defense. He's somewhat like a goalie in hockey or soccer. He's responsible not only for guarding his own man, but for guarding anyone else who ventures into his territory. If an opposing point guard gets away from his man and drives to the basket (called *penetrating the defense*), the center must be able to slide over, clog the middle, deny the opponent's path, and block his shot.

115

Clyde's Record Book

Dikembe Mutombo of the Atlanta Hawks is a great shot-blocker who delights in playing defense. After he blocks an opponent's shot, he'll often end the play by wagging his finger as if to say, "No, no, no, don't try to do that against me."

Clyde's Chalk Talk

There can be *offensive goaltending* as well as *defensive goaltending*. While defensive goaltending involves illegally blocking a shot, offensive goaltending means touching a shot while it is above the rim to help guide it into the basket. This, too, is illegal, at least in the NBA; in events governed by international rules, like the Olympics, players can guide a shot into the basket.

Shot-blocking is a subtle art that is mental as well as physical. A center doesn't waste his energy trying to block every shot, but instead picks his spots and goes for blocks that will have the greatest impact. When a player beats his man and drives down the lane thinking he's going to get an easy dunk, the center should come over and send it back in his face. If the center does that a couple of times, pretty soon the opponent will get discouraged, and he and his teammates will think twice about trying to drive to the basket.

In basketball's early years, players were allowed to block any shot they could reach. But in the early 1940s, 7-foot center Bob Kurland of Oklahoma A&M became so proficient at blocking shots that he forced a rule change. Kurland would stand in front of the basket on defense and swat away just about everything he could reach—and he could reach just about everything. So a rule was passed outlawing *goaltending*, which basically means blocking a shot on its downward path toward the basket. Without that rule, a player could simply stand in front of the hoop, jump, and slap away any shot that came close.

Shot-blocking is legal; *goaltending* is illegal. Technically speaking, goaltending means blocking a shot after it has reached the top of its arc and has begun heading downward toward the basket. Blocking a shot after it hits the backboard or pinning a shot against the backboard also are considered goaltending.

The Utah Jazz used to have a center named Mark Eaton. He could hardly move, barely got off the floor when he jumped and couldn't shoot a lick. But he was the size of the Wasatch Mountains that surround Salt Lake City, standing 7-foot-4 and weighing close to 300 pounds. He could change the course of a game just by standing out on the court. He would lay back in the middle on defense and dare anybody to try to drive to the basket against him. Few were so foolhardy.

One of the best shot-blockers of all time was Bill Russell of the Boston Celtics. At 6'10" he wasn't particularly huge for a center, but he was very quick and had a sense for shot-blocking. And that was his role on the team, since the Celtics had plenty of other scorers. The result was the greatest dynasty in NBA history.

Russell was among the first to focus on not just blocking the shot, but blocking it so that it stays in play and ideally is recovered by a teammate. If you block a shot and it goes out of bounds, the other team retains possession of the ball. If you block a shot and your teammate recovers, you not only deny your opponent a chance at scoring but set up a chance for yourself.

Shot-blocking is only part of what I mean when I say a center must dominate the paint. He also should be a tenacious rebounder, cleaning the glass at both ends of the floor. In the past a center would have to get at least 10 rebounds a game in order for his team to stay competitive and for him to keep his job, and both Russell and Chamberlain averaged over 22 rebounds a game for their careers. You don't see numbers like that today, partially because teams don't take as many shots but also because the rebounding chores often are divided between the center and the power forward.

Clyde's Tip

Watch what happens after a shot is blocked. Does the ball go out of bounds? Is it recovered by a teammate of the shooter, for another attempt at the basket? Or does the defensive team recover and start a play of its own the other way? A great shot-blocker not only denies the shot attempt, but also directs the ball to a teammate.

Depending on the team, a center may also be called upon to score points. Chamberlain averaged over 50 points a game one year, 1961–62, playing on a team that didn't have many other offensive weapons. When Chamberlain went to stronger teams, he found he could help them more by rebounding, blocking shots, and setting up his teammates rather than always looking for his own shot. Russell, by contrast, never scored that much, at least partly because the Celtics always had so many scorers on their teams.

Even if he isn't the focus of his team's offense, a center still should get several points a game just by being in the right place at the right time. He should be adept at battling for loose balls in the paint and turning them into baskets or by scoring off offensive rebounds. And he should be alert to take passes from driving teammates who suddenly are double-teamed, and convert those passes into points.

A center also can set picks, using his big body to brush off a defender and free a teammate for a shot. Wes Unseld and Wayne Embry weren't especially tall, but they were wide as trucks and great at setting picks, which has become something of a lost art. Unseld also was terrific at throwing the outlet pass—grabbing a rebound, whirling, and firing the ball to a teammate near midcourt so that he could get into the offensive zone before the defense had time to get set.

Clyde's Rules

Remember that when a player sets a pick, the rules say he must be stationary or else any contact is called as a foul against him. Many players try to slide their body ever so slightly into an opponent's path when setting a pick, or stick a hip or elbow into his way. If the referee catches him, it will be called as an offensive foul and his team will lose possession of the ball.

Clyde's Tip

A case in point about a center being stagnant came last season when Patrick Ewing of New York broke his wrist. All of a sudden you saw Allan Houston going to the basket more and you saw Larry Johnson prospering in the paint. If Ewing had been there, playing normally, these players wouldn't have gotten those opportunities, because Ewing's stagnant. As great a player as he is, Ewing posts up on one side of the lane and regardless of what happens, he doesn't move to the other side.

Finally, mobility is a key asset for a center, and a center who's stagnant on offense can create problems. Some centers come downcourt, set up on one side, and clog up everything for their teammates. They never move out instinctively to clear up an area for someone else. Unfortunately, some guys are only comfortable on one side of the court. But that's a fault of today's system, which has prevented players from becoming complete players and made specialists out of everybody.

When we played, we'd start a play on one side of the court just to free Willis Reed on the other side. That's how much he moved. The Lakers did it with Abdul-Jabbar all the time. He'd start out on one side, they'd move the ball, he'd move to the other side and boom, he'd have the ball where he wanted it.

Today's players are lazier—they don't move and they don't understand the nuances of the game. They don't know how to get a shot or when to get a shot. That's the type of savvy that the coaches have taken out of the game by calling all the plays, instead of enabling the players to develop their own instincts.

Low Post, High Post

To describe where a center sets up on offense, you'll frequently hear the terms low post and high post. But don't look for any posts out on the court to serve as landmarks.

The post area is just outside the foul lane, on either side of the paint or above the foul line. Remember, an offensive player isn't allowed to stay in the foul lane for more than 2.9 seconds (which is why a lane violation also is called a three-second violation), so in order to set up for any length of time he must do so outside the paint. We say a player is "posting up" when he comes downcourt and sets up on either side of the lane, with his back to the basket. A player who moves into the lane must get the ball and shoot it within three seconds, so that move is often described as "flashing into the paint."

The low post is the area closest to the basket, on either side of the lane, as represented by (A) on the following diagram. The high post is further from the basket, either at the foul line or at the so-called elbows where the foul line intersects the outside border of the free throw lane (B).

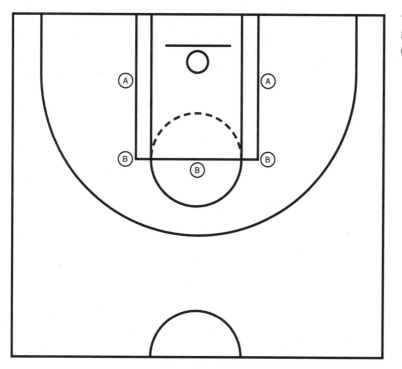

The low post (A) is near the basket, the high post (B) is farther away.

The bigger centers usually set up in the low post, as close to the basket as possible, so their shots don't have to travel far and they can be close to the rim for potential rebounds. In fact, the NBA has twice widened the lane to keep first George Mikan and then Wilt Chamberlain from setting up too close to the basket, where they were virtually unstoppable.

Mikan, playing at a time when the lane was just 6 feet across, would catch the ball in the low post and wheel toward the basket, fending away his defender with his body and free arm and then flipping the ball into the hoop. Chamberlain, playing with a 12-foot lane, developed a pet shot called the finger-roll where he would set up in the low post, back his man toward the basket, lean over his defender, and roll the ball off his fingertips into the basket.

119

Clyde's Chalk Talk

The *hook shot* is taken with a sweeping motion across the body, arm outstretched high above the head, so it is nearly impossible to block. A shooter can take a hook shot from a set position, wheeling toward the basket to put up the shot. In the jump-hook variation, instead of turning and facing the basket to shoot, a player jumps into the air from a set position and flips the ball toward the basket from high above his head. A player also can take a hook shot on the run, dribbling across the court until he feels comfortable enough to shoot. This is referred to as a running hook.

Clyde's Record Book

Bill Russell of the Boston Celtics, known for his rebounding and shot-blocking, was underrated as a passer. With the Celtics' movement, he'd pick out the open man all the time. Willis Reed was the same way on our Knicks teams. He was a good passer who was unselfish, so we all knew that if we kept moving and got open, we'd see the ball and get our shots.

Now the lane is 16 feet wide, and even the biggest centers like Shaquille O'Neal (7'1", 303 pounds) have to take at least one dribble to get from the low-post area to the basket. Which leads me to ask: Whatever happened to the *hook shot*?

The hook shot was the most potent weapon in the game for Kareem Abdul-Jabbar, the leading scorer in NBA history and one of the greatest players of all time. Yet today you don't see anyone in the league using the hook shot regularly except for some players who grew up in Europe like Arvydas Sabonis or Zydrunas Ilgauskas. That's because coaches in places like Europe stress the fundamentals when they teach the game, whereas in the United States players rely more on their athleticism and don't work on fundamentals as much as they should.

Centers who set up in the high post are usually quicker and more agile than low post centers, so they're more comfortable running around farther from the basket. They also are better outside shooters, so that if they are left unguarded they can turn to face the basket and put up a quick jump shot from 15 to 18 feet.

High-post centers also should be good passers, because they're called upon to pass the ball farther than centers who set up in the low post. Actually, passing is something that's important for all centers, but it's a skill that's often overlooked.

Today's teams sometimes get very inactive. A team member passes the ball in to a center like Shaquille O'Neal, and then everybody stands around and watches. Guys don't cut through the lane because they know Shaq isn't a good passer and he's not going to get them the ball, so they stand around outside. With Abdul-Jabbar, as great a scorer as he was, his teammates knew he could drop the ball out to guys like Magic Johnson for easy shots, so they kept moving.

The better passer the center is, the more continuity and movement a team will have in its offense, which obviously helps for balanced scoring and happier players, because they get easy opportunities to score. It creates harmony. It creates hustle in transition, because guys know if they get out and get open, the center will fire an outlet pass and get them the ball.

Bill Walton, when he played for the Portland Trail Blazers in the late 1970s, was the ultimate high post center. The guy was such a phenomenal passer that the Trail Blazers ran a motion offense with everything going through Walton while the other players ran their patterns around him. They had tremendous movement.

Kareem Abdul-Jabbar of the Los Angeles Lakers, the leading scorer in NBA history, releases a sky-hook over the outstretched arms of Boston Celtics center Robert Parish.
Associated Press

Where Have All the Centers Gone?

There's a dearth of talent at the center position today. In the old days just about every team had a real center: Chamberlain, Russell, Reed, Unseld, Embry, Nate Thurmond, Zelmo Beaty. And I almost left out Abdul-Jabbar, the greatest of all time.

Today many guys are compelled to play the position because there's a shortage of true centers. Even some of today's top centers, guys like Alonzo Mourning and Jayson Williams, aren't really centers in the old sense. They're more like power forwards who have to play center because their teams don't have traditional, back-to-the-basket centers like Shaquille O'Neal, Patrick Ewing, Hakeem Olajuwon, or David Robinson.

There are more than three times as many teams in the NBA now, yet the number of true, first-rate centers is about the same as it was 20 or 30 years ago. That's because with the wider exposure of the game through television, kids growing up don't want to be centers. They all want to handle the ball and shoot facing the basket. They don't want to set up down low with their backs to the basket. They all want to be forwards or guards.

That's why you have 6'9" point guards like Magic Johnson, or 6'11" small forwards like Kevin Garnett.

Today you see many teams go with smaller lineups. They'll have three guards on the floor at the same time, or instead of using a center on their front line they'll go with three forwards. Big guys are no longer as prominent as they were in the '60s and '70s because of the types of defenses you can play today. You can take a big man out of the game. You can double- and triple-team him like the Chicago Bulls do to Patrick Ewing late in the game, when they need to make a run. They deny him the ball for five, six minutes at a stretch and take him out of the game and make one of the other Knicks try to beat them from the perimeter.

Quote...Unquote

"There are no great centers anymore. The Kareem-type centers who could do it all are dead and gone."—*Hall of Famer Oscar Robertson, who starred for the Royals in the 1960s and the Bucks in the early '70s.*

Guys who play the two or the three can't be taken out of the game because they're more elusive and they're versatile enough to get to the perimeter and create their own shots. You can't devise a defense that's going to deny a Jordan his shot opportunities for very long, because he's elusive enough to beat the double-team.

As a result, the thinking seems to have changed now. Look at the Bulls with all their championships—they never had a great center on their team, although they did find they needed to have 7-footers. The only great center to win a championship from 1989 through 1997 was Hakeem Olajuwon with the Houston Rockets. But you look at Hakeem and he's not the quintessential low-post center, as effective as he is around the basket. He does it with quickness and agility, not power. He's a guy that's elusive. He has the agility of a small forward—he can shake and bake, he's good in transition. If you deny him inside he can come out on the perimeter and create shots. He's a prototype big guy for today's game, just like David Robinson, who can come out 15 or 18 feet and shoot the jumper. That's the direction centers are going today.

Shaq is more of a throwback to the Chamberlain type of center, a guy who posts up inside and uses power moves. He's deceptively quick and elusive, but basically he's a power center and you can take him out of the game by double- and triple-teaming him. Hakeem has more versatility.

The Ultimate Center Rivalry: Chamberlain vs. Russell

The greatest individual rivalry the NBA has ever seen was that between centers Wilt Chamberlain and Bill Russell.

Chamberlain was the ultimate offensive center, a scoring machine, while Russell revolutionized the pro game as far as defense was concerned.

Chamberlain retired as the game's all-time leading scorer (he now ranks second behind Kareem Abdul-Jabbar), and his 100-point game and average of 50.4 points per game for a season are records that have withstood the test of time. "He was the most unbelievable center to ever play the game in terms of domination and intimidation," said Hall of Famer Jerry West.

Russell, meanwhile, taught us all the importance of team defense as he led the Celtics to 11 championships in his 13 seasons as a player, including two titles as a player-coach. "Bill Russell took defensive basketball and made it an art form," said teammate Tom Heinsohn.

In the 1960s, there were only eight or nine teams in the NBA so these guys played each other 13, 14 times in the regular season alone. Add the pre-season and playoffs and Chamberlain and Russell may have gone against each other 20 times or more in one season. Even when I was playing we'd see them 9 or 10 times a year.

There was a time when it seemed like they were playing each other every Sunday on the national TV Game of the Week. They were the marquee players and the NBA was struggling to attract fans, so naturally they put them on TV as much as possible. And the fact is, that's one rivalry that really embellished the NBA and made many new fans for the league and the sport of basketball.

Quote...Unquote

"During my time, they knew the ball was coming in to me and they would put two and three guys in that position before the ball ever came to me. I would love to play right now. I honestly think if I played right now vs. my time, I'd average 70, 75 points a game."—*Wilt Chamberlain.*

In the NBA's greatest rivalry, Bill Russell (6) of the Boston Celtics leaps to try to block a finger-roll shot by Wilt Chamberlain (13) of the Philadelphia 76ers.
Associated Press

When they played each other, I always wanted Chamberlain to win. I considered him the underdog, even though he was the bigger player, because of all the championships the Celtics were winning. I respected them as a team, but I didn't like them. I felt Chamberlain was unfairly maligned because he didn't win. There was always something they said he should have done that he didn't do. The fact is that most of the time he wasn't on very good teams, and when he was, he won and won big.

The game suffers when you don't have that kind of rivalry. It was something that captured the attention and the imagination of fans everywhere. It also suffers when you don't have a dominant team like the Celtics, or today's Bulls. You need a team like that to create interest in the game, a team fans love to hate like the Cowboys or the Yankees. You've got to have it.

The same thing goes for a dominant player, like Jordan today or Chamberlain back then. Wilt was the NBA's Goliath. People loved to hate him, but they came to see him and they paid their money to do so. They came to boo him at the foul line. As much of a giant as he was, he was vulnerable at the line and fans could get their kicks by saying, "Send him to the line, I can shoot free throws better than Chamberlain." The game needs that. It suffers when you don't have those kinds of personalities.

Quote...Unquote

"The art of defense is really an art based on hard work. Scouting the offense of the other team emotionally, intellectually, and physically. Knowing things about the character or personality of the opposition. But just knowing is not sufficient. The great defensive players have to be great athletes also." —*Bill Russell.*

Watching Centers

Watch for mobility and agility. Centers who are stagnant may compile impressive statistics and succeed in the short term, but their teams tend to suffer over the long haul. Basketball is a team game and a great center, like a great point guard, should bring out the best in his teammates.

After the ball is passed to the center, do his teammates stand around and watch or do they keep moving? There are enough spectators in the building without having more of them on the court.

Notice where the center sets up, and whether he stays there. Is he mobile enough physically, and flexible enough mentally, to move to another spot on the floor if the defense covers his position and takes away his favorite shot?

Beware of centers who are Bermuda Triangles—the ball goes in but never comes out. In today's NBA, defenses almost automatically double-team the center as soon as the ball is thrown into the low post. A smart center quickly passes the ball back out, forcing the defense to disperse, then takes a return pass and makes his move against a single defender instead of trying to beat a double-team all by himself.

As with any other player, watch how the center reacts in transition. Does he get back quickly on defense, to prevent easy scoring opportunities? Does he hustle to try and beat his opponent downcourt on offense so he can set up in his favorite spot?

And if he needs a breather, where does he take it—on offense or defense? Most players tend to relax on defense, but some centers do just the opposite. They catch their breath while their team has the ball, figuring someone else will be glad to take the shot and they can save a trip downcourt by staying back at the defensive end. Bill Russell frequently did this with the Celtics, because they had so many other players on the team who could score.

Offensively, see whether a center likes to play in the low post or high post, and what types of shots he likes to take. Defensively, watch to see how adept he is at leaving his man to confront an opponent who tries to drive the lane. And at both ends of the floor, see how effectively and energetically he goes to the boards.

My Favorite Centers

When someone asks me about my favorite center, I ask back, "What criteria do you use to pick the best?" If you go with winning, Bill Russell had 11 championships, so it's hard to argue with that. If you go with physical dominance, Wilt Chamberlain was in a league of his own.

But for the overall package, I go with Kareem. To me, Kareem Abdul-Jabbar was the greatest of all time.

He won six championships with two different teams. He's the all-time leading scorer in the game. He's among the leaders in rebounds and blocked shots. He was a great team player, and he lasted 20 seasons.

He was a winner. He won everywhere he played—at Power Memorial High School, at UCLA, at Milwaukee, and at Los Angeles. He was unselfish. If he was a selfish player, he would have scored 50,000 points or more. But he would do whatever it takes to win.

If I was forced to pick one player as the greatest center of all time, it would be him. Chamberlain and Russell I'd give a tie for second place because where one had something, the other had something else.

Nate Thurmond, who starred for the Golden State Warriors in the '60s and early '70s, was the most underrated of the great centers. If you ask the players of that time who was their toughest opponent, most would probably say Nate Thurmond. He could guard you, he could block shots, he could pass, plus he averaged 15 points and 15 rebounds a game for his career. He was a very underrated guy.

Wes Unseld of the Bullets in the '70s and Wayne Embry of the Cincinnati Royals in the '60s were the best at setting picks. Moses Malone, who led Houston to the NBA Finals in 1981 and won a championship with Philadelphia two years later, dominated the game for several seasons and may have been the best offensive rebounder I've ever seen. Bob Lanier, who played for the Detroit Pistons in the 1970s and later for the Milwaukee Bucks, and my Knicks teammate Willis Reed were perhaps the best shooters among the great big men—you could put Bob McAdoo, who played for Buffalo and several other teams, in that category, too, but he was more of a forward than a traditional center. Same with Boston's Dave Cowens. And Portland's Bill Walton, when healthy, may have been the best passing center I've ever seen.

The Least You Need to Know

➤ Everybody's always looking for a big man, but they're not easy to find because there just aren't that many skillful 7-footers around.

➤ A center should dominate the paint and be an intimidator against penetrators, using his size to best advantage.

➤ Mobility and passing ability are often overlooked when it comes to rating centers, but not by those in the know because a center who is fluid and can handle the ball keeps an offense from getting stagnant and creates opportunities for his teammates.

➤ The rivalry between Wilt Chamberlain and Bill Russell was special, but to me the greatest center of all time was Kareem Abdul-Jabbar.

Chapter 9

The Bench: They Also Serve Who Sit and Wait

In This Chapter

➤ It's not who starts that's important, but who's on the court at the end when the game is on the line

➤ It takes special skill and attitude to be a good sixth man

➤ There's a thin line between a seat on the end of the bench and a seat in the stands, so every player must know how to contribute

➤ What to watch for

➤ Clyde's top bench players

You must have a strong bench to win in the NBA. Because no player plays a full game, reserves must be able to step in for starters without causing the team to miss a beat. The caliber of play must stay high. And bench players have to be reliable, just like starters—a coach has to know what he'll get when he takes out his regulars and calls on his reserves.

Just because a player begins the game on the bench doesn't necessarily mean he's not good enough to be a starter. Most of the time that's true, but there are some players who simply are better suited to coming off the bench than starting. They can immediately get into the flow of a game, while other players need a few minutes to find their rhythm.

Danny Ainge, who now coaches the Phoenix Suns after a long playing career, came up with the perfect nickname for Vinnie Johnson, a star bench player on the Detroit Pistons' 1989 and 1990 championship teams. Ainge nicknamed Johnson "the Microwave" because he heated up in a hurry—exactly what you want in a bench player.

Johnson wasted no time adjusting to the pace of the game. He came off the bench firing—heck, he left the locker room firing. Shoot first, ask questions later, that was Vinnie's approach. And that made life easy for his coach, Chuck Daly, who would simply leave Johnson in when he was hitting and take him out when he was missing.

In this chapter I'll look at the importance of a strong bench to a team's success, the rich tradition of the sixth man, and what makes a good bench player.

It's Not Who Starts But Who Finishes That Matters

Red Auerbach said that. The former coach and patriarch of the Boston Celtics was among the first to recognize the importance of bench players and give them their due. He pioneered the concept of the sixth man, the reserve who enters a game and not only maintains the level of play of the starters, but often picks it up a notch.

Auerbach's logic was simple. More games are decided in the last five minutes than the first five minutes, so he felt it was more important to have his best players on the court at the end of the game than at the beginning. Of course, many of those players played both at the beginning and end of the game—but not all.

Auerbach reasoned that it would be to his team's advantage to have at least some quality players on the court at all times. So he designated one of his better players as the Celtics' sixth man and kept him on the bench at the start, bringing him in when a starter got tired and needed a breather. That way, Boston had some top players on the floor at all times and there was no noticeable drop in play quality.

Of course, Auerbach had plenty of talent to work with on his Celtics teams. He could afford to keep Hall of Famer John Havlicek as a sixth man for years because he had Sam Jones and Tommy Heinsohn, two more Hall of Famers, starting.

Because of the lack of offensive prowess in today's players, teams really can't afford to keep good men on the bench. Look at Detlef Schrempf. He was a great sixth man, but for some time now he's been a starter because even a strong team like Seattle can't afford to leave him on the bench. Many teams have that same problem—they don't have enough scoring power, so they can't keep a productive player out of the starting lineup.

Clyde's Tip

John Starks is a perfect sixth man, an explosive scorer who comes off the bench shooting and has all the confidence in the world. But for years Pat Riley had to use him as a starter with the Knicks because, other than Patrick Ewing, the team didn't have anybody who could score. Riley couldn't afford to keep Starks on the bench.

Generally, reserves lack certain qualities that enable them to start and play long minutes. Now and then you'll find some who develop into starters, like Kevin McHale or Detlef Schrempf, often because they worked hard to overcome their weaknesses. The games of most reserve players tend to be one-dimensional rather than well-rounded. They may not be strong rebounders or play tough defense. They may not handle the ball well. These weaknesses would be exposed if they were starters and had to play long stretches of the game, but as reserves they can still be effective as long as they can do one thing exceptionally well and usually that one thing is shoot.

What Makes a Good Sixth Man?

Tenacity and audacity, that's what a good sixth man needs to be effective—in addition to some skills, of course.

What makes these guys go is that they have supreme confidence that when they come into the game, they can get some points on the board in a hurry. Whether they make their first couple of shots or not, they're going to keep pumping them up. That's the key to sixth men.

This is called a shooter's mentality. Most players don't have that mentality—if they miss four or five shots, they're not going to keep pumping it back up. Some players stop after one or two misses.

But good sixth men have confidence. They believe that sooner or later they're going to get hot, no matter what they're doing now. No matter how many they're missing, soon the shots are going to start falling.

When you think of sixth men you think of the Celtics. The first guy you think of is Hondo, John Havlicek, even though he wasn't the first sixth man—Frank Ramsey came before him and was the first great Celtics sixth man (actually, Auerbach used others in that role even before Ramsey). But Hondo was a guy who would come into the game running and gunning off the bench and not only keep pace with the starters but pick up the pace. He also was a great defender, unlike so many other sixth men, which is why he became a standout as a starter, too.

Clyde's Tip

If you're a defensive back in the NFL and you get burned, it doesn't matter, you've got to come right back. You get beat long, you've got to forget about it and get right back out there. The same thing applies to sixth men. They may keep missing their shots, but they have to keep shooting. Like gamblers, they think that sooner or later they're going to get hot.

Kevin McHale was another outstanding sixth man for the Celtics, an offensive weapon off the bench. Ricky Pierce, who played for Milwaukee in the 1980s and Seattle in the early '90s, has been an effective sixth man for many years. World B. Free, who averaged over 20 points per game in a 13-year career that saw him play for six teams in the late '70s and '80s, was another, and the Microwave, Vinnie Johnson, used to come in and light it up right away for Detroit's championship teams.

131

John Havlicek (17) of the Boston Celtics, the most famous sixth man in NBA history, drives past fellow Hall of Famer Billy Cunningham of the Philadelphia 76ers. Associated Press

Cazzie Russell played that role for us on the Knicks. He could come in and fill it up, get some points right away. Bill Bradley was better suited to be a starter because he was always in motion. There was continuity to the offense when he was in there because he was always moving, moving, moving. He was perpetual motion, and he also was an excellent passer so the ball was always moving as well. He was a deft shooter if we could get him open behind a screen or two—he couldn't create his shot on his own, so he kept moving until he got an opening. Cazzie was much more of a creator and that's why he made a better sixth man.

Right now, Kobe Bryant of the Lakers is the most prolific sixth man in the league. He's an exciting player with many moves who knows how to get his team going as soon as he steps onto the court. He scores points in a hurry and makes things happen. At 19, his all-around game isn't completely developed, which is why he's more effective as a sixth man than as a starter. But in his case it looks like that's only a matter of time.

Kobe Bryant (8), who went directly from high school to the NBA, was voted a starter in the 1998 NBA All-Star Game at the age of 19, when he was the dynamic sixth man of the Los Angeles Lakers. Associated Press

Clyde's Record Book

Dale Ellis is a shooter with three-point prowess who was a starter for a while but has been an effective sixth man. That role has extended his career, because if there is one thing he can still do, it's shoot the ball, which is what you want from a sixth man. There's a place in the NBA for a guy like that, even though he's one-dimensional. At 6'7" and 215 you'd think he could rebound for you, but he doesn't. Defensively he can be exploited, he has no handle, and he can't really create scoring opportunities—but he can shoot.

Quote...Unquote

"You carry 12, you play 8 or 9, you win with 5."—*An old coaches' saying about the risks of playing your bench.*

Many sixth men are one-dimensional. Dell Curry of the Charlotte Hornets has been a great sixth man for almost his entire career because he's a tremendous shooter. Why wasn't he a starter? He can't really handle the ball well and his overall game is kind of weak, so they prefer having him come off the bench. Look at Trent Tucker, who played for the Knicks in the '80s—he was a lethal shooter, but he just didn't have the handle so he never became a starter.

The Rest of the Bench

Many NBA coaches like to play as few as eight players—five starters plus one reserve each at guard, forward, and center—even though they have 12 players on the roster. For one thing, the deeper down the bench you go, the more significant the drop-off in skills. For another, there are only so many minutes in a game and players need a certain amount of time to get used to the game and perform. It's impossible to spread those minutes among 12 players and still give your stars the minutes they deserve.

Of course, in today's age of specialization, coaches usually have to go 9 or 10 players deep whether they like it or not. Their best reserve guard, for example, might be too slow to play the point, so another reserve is needed there. If the backup forward isn't a strong rebounder, someone else is needed when the power forward has to take a breather. And of course, injuries also come into the equation—a team is bound to lose at least one or two key players for periods of time over the course of a season, creating further opportunities for bench players to show what they can do.

Once you get past your first eight players, it's vital that the remaining reserves understand and accept their roles. That's why they call them role players. It has a lot to do with articulation—a coach has to make sure the player knows exactly what is expected of him, and that he has the right skills for that role.

Take Matt Bullard, who has played for the Houston Rockets (among others). Some games he might not play at all, but once in awhile you'll have an opportunity to really utilize what he brings to the table. In Bullard's case, he's a big guy with three-point range. He can spread a defense and bring an opposing big man away from the basket because of his long-range shooting ability. He can't do much else, but that's not important. His role on the team is clearly defined, he understands it and he accepts it.

Motivation is a key factor with these guys. Many of them have been in the CBA, or in Europe, or out of basketball altogether. They know what that's like and how much better it is in the NBA and they don't want to go back.

Often it's serendipitous—just a matter of luck, of being in the right place at the right time and having a specific talent that a team can utilize. Sometimes a team is looking for an extra ballhandler or another big man or an outside shooter, and if you have that talent you might win the job over a player who's better overall but lacking the specific talent the team is looking for. Your skills have to match the team's needs at that time.

Pete Myers was a perfect example last year. He'd been up and down with a number of teams for a number of years—in fact, he was the player who succeeded Michael Jordan in the Bulls' starting lineup when Jordan went off to play baseball a few years ago. Anyway, he was in the Knicks' training camp last summer and New York made some trades at the start of the year and was short on bodies, so Myers opened the season on their roster. He's a good defensive player, and that was something they figured they could always use. But when Patrick Ewing got hurt the Knicks needed offense, so Myers' defense became expendable and they cut him and signed first Anthony Bowie and then Brooks Thompson, who are better scorers. The philosophy changed, so Myers was out of a job.

Players at the end of the bench—the ninth, tenth, eleventh, and twelfth men—must have fire and desire. Once they get in the game they have something to prove, so they must play with abandon. Whether it be 10 minutes or 1 minute, whatever amount of time they're on the court is going to be hell-bent. Walter McCarty of the Celtics, Michael Stewart of the Kings—they want to show what they can do and earn more playing time, so they give everything they have.

Look at Bo Outlaw—he hustled his way off the bench and into a starting role, first with the Clippers and then with Orlando, because he was such a gung-ho player. He comes into a game and creates havoc. He makes things happen—he's relentless. No wonder his coaches love him.

Clyde's Tip

It's a thin line between a seat at the end of an NBA team's bench and a place in the CBA, in Europe, or a seat in the stands. And the players who have been around know how thin that line is.

Watching Bench Players

Watch the energy level a player brings to the game when he comes off the bench. Does the team seem to sag or does it take on a new spark? Does he get right into the flow of the game or does he need some time to get his feet wet? Does the crowd respond to him the moment he rises from his seat and goes to the scorer's table to check into the game? Savvy fans watch for players like Starks or Bryant to enter the game because they know something exciting's about to happen.

135

If the guy coming in is a shooter, see how long it takes him to get his first shot off. Chances are you won't have to wait long. If he misses, watch for any sign of hesitation the next time he gets a shot opportunity. Chances are you won't see any. Remember, audacity and tenacity are the hallmarks of an effective "instant offense" guy.

Notice the pace of the game, and whether it changes when substitutions are made. This isn't necessarily bad. Some teams can play effectively at either a fast pace or a slow pace. But others are only comfortable one way, and if a substitution knocks a team off the tempo at which it is comfortable, that's bad.

Most of all, look for impact in one way or another. Does a substitute have an effect on the game by hitting a few shots, crashing the boards, making a steal, running a fast break, blocking some shots, making some hustle plays? This is what a coach wants.

Finally, if a substitute comes in for a star player, look at the score when he checks into the game and again when he checks out. Did the team lose much ground with its star on the bench? If not, that in itself is a net gain because your star can come back well-rested, bright-eyed, and bushy-tailed.

My Favorite Bench Players

Hondo, John Havlicek, set the standard for bench players and went on to a great career as a starter with the Boston Celtics. He was a perpetual motion machine, legendary for wearing out opponents.

Hondo was awesome as a sixth man because besides providing motion and scoring on offense, he also was a defensive stopper. He could shut down the other team's top scorer at one end and give a boost to Boston's offense at the other. He was unusual because he was a complete player, which is why he went on to become a long-time starter.

Quote...Unquote

"Guarding John Havlicek is the most difficult job I have. His every movement has a purpose."—*Bill Bradley of the New York Knicks, who played against Havlicek in the late `60s and `70s.*

Kevin McHale was the same way. Early in his career the Celtics used him as a sixth man, basically looking for instant offense. But he also was a good rebounder and defender, and he quickly became a valuable starter on one of the all-time great front lines, along with Larry Bird and Robert Parish.

I mentioned John Starks before. He's typical of today's sixth men, a shooter without a conscience. He can shoot you into games or shoot you out of them, depending on whether they're dropping. But one thing you can count on with Starksie is that he'll keep on shooting.

John Starks of the New York Knicks (taking the shot) has the ideal temperament for a sixth man, a shooter with absolutely no conscience. Associated Press

Cazzie Russell played the sixth man role on the Knicks teams I played with, and he was an instant offense guy. World B. Free, Vinnie Johnson, Ricky Pierce, Dale Ellis (who played for Seattle and San Antonio, among others), and Dell Curry were other instant offense guys who came off the bench and gave you points in a hurry.

137

Clyde's Record Book

Not every player has the type of game to be a sixth man. On our Knicks teams, Cazzie Russell had it but Bill Bradley didn't, which is why Red Holzman quickly worked Bradley into the starting lineup and brought Russell off the bench. Russell's game was more self-contained, while Bradley benefited from playing with the other starters, who knew how to get him his shots.

Michael Cooper of the Lakers was an energizer as a sixth man. He was perfect to run with Magic, because he picked up the pace from the starters and kicked it up a notch. He became a better shooter over the course of his career, but he was best known for his terrific defense and the way he ran the floor.

Bobby Jones of the 76ers was another player like that. He would come off the bench and give that Philadelphia team of the early '80s a boost at both ends of the floor.

Today, Kobe Bryant of the Lakers is Mr. Excitement, a force as a sixth man. It's not just that he gives them scoring, he does it with energy and flair. He's so popular with the fans that they voted him a starter for the 1998 All-Star Game—even though he wasn't even starting for the Lakers. He's lucky to be on a team that can afford to keep him on the bench and bring him along slowly, since he didn't play college ball. But he's playing so well that they're not going to be able to keep him on the bench much longer. Even the Lakers don't have that luxury.

The Least You Need to Know

➤ Since starters can't play 48 minutes and injuries inevitably crop up, a team needs a strong bench to be a winner.

➤ Unlike starters, who can ease into the flow of a game, a good bench player must be able to make an immediate impact—such as by hitting a few shots right away or applying some intense defensive pressure.

➤ A good bench player can't have a conscience—if he has second thoughts about the kinds of shots he's taking, he won't be effective.

Part 3
Beyond the Players

There are about 350 players in the NBA, but thousands of other people help make the league and its teams run. In this part I'll discuss what they do and show how they help you enjoy the game by doing their jobs.

Each team has a head coach, anywhere from two to five assistant coaches, a trainer, an equipment manager, and several scouts. It may have a video coordinator to compile scouting tapes, a strength and conditioning coach to help keep players' bodies from breaking down, and a team of doctors to mend those bodies when they do break down.

Referees keep order on the court and allow the players to display their skills within the rules of the NBA. The official scorer keeps the scorebook that records all points and fouls that are committed in the game, while statisticians use courtside computers to keep track of an assortment of numbers that reflect what's happening on the court. There also are two timers, one for the game clock and one for the 24-second clock.

Players can't communicate directly with all the fans who follow a team, so the media serves as an intermediary, explaining what goes on both on-court and behind the scenes and asking players questions they think fans would ask if they had the chance.

Finally, a huge business structure provides the framework for the teams. The NBA's league office, headed by Commissioner David Stern, employs more than 800 people in departments ranging from public relations to marketing to legal to operations. Each team has its own front office, with people serving similar functions on a local level.

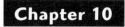

Chapter 10

Coaches Call the Shots

In This Chapter

➤ A head coach is like an orchestra leader, communicating and motivating to create harmony

➤ Assistant coaches are the mid-level managers, teaching, scouting, and handling a myriad of details

➤ Trainers and equipment managers keep a team running

➤ My favorite coaches

Think of an NBA coach as an orchestra leader, with each player on his team playing an individual instrument. Just as the orchestra leader must blend the sounds of each instrument into a melodious piece of music, the coach must blend the talents of each player into a cohesive team performance.

Coaching at the NBA level is far different from college, high school, or youth group coaching. By the time a player reaches the NBA he's expected to know the fundamentals of the game—how to shoot, pass, dribble, and so forth. I say expected because, unfortunately, this isn't always the case, especially with some players turning pro today at younger ages than ever before. In any case, NBA coaches don't have time to teach fundamentals; instead, they focus on getting the most out of the players' skills and preparing and motivating the team for competition.

Coaching overall makes more of an impact in college than the pros. In college a coach can dominate the game. Look at Bobby Knight; he outcoaches everyone in the Big Ten. He doesn't always have the best talent, but he wins because he's a great coach. Rick Pitino, who is now the coach of the Celtics, didn't have great teams early in his college career, but he won because of his coaching prowess.

Once you get to the pro level, it's a different story. It's very rare that you're really going to outcoach anybody. You've got to have the talent to win.

The role of the NBA coach has evolved over the years. As recently as the mid-1960s, an NBA team's coach often also served as trainer, equipment manager, and travel coordinator. No team had assistant coaches. Today some teams have as many as five, plus video coordinators and strength coaches and conditioning gurus, and who knows what else.

This extends off the court as well. When the Charlotte Hornets entered the NBA in 1988, they enlisted fashion designer Alexander Julian to create a look for the team, and his pinstriped teal uniform was a huge hit with fans and consumers. And the Indiana Pacers asked track star Florence Griffith-Joyner to help redesign their team uniforms a few years ago, which got them not only a new look, but a lot of publicity on and off the sports pages.

For many years NBA coaches were paid less than most of the players on the team, and far less than the team's stars. This is beginning to change, with so-called "franchise coaches" like Pat Riley of Miami and Rick Pitino of Boston—empowered by their teams' owners to make all the basketball decisions and run the team as they see fit— who are paid millions.

When there's friction between players and coaches, it's often the coaches who must modify their stance, since fans pay to see players play and owners know it. But the coach does hold one trump card: He decides how much each player plays in a game. Players value their playing time dearly, because they can't display their skills and compile statistics that lead to stardom if they're sitting on the bench. Smart coaches learn to play this powerful card judiciously if they wish to survive and thrive.

What Makes a Good Head Coach?

There are 29 head coaches in the NBA and they have 29 different personalities. All are leaders and all know the game of basketball inside-out, but that's about where the similarities end.

Some are former pro players, whether stars like Lenny Wilkens (Atlanta Hawks) and Larry Bird (Indiana Pacers), or a lesser player like Pat Riley (Miami Heat). Others never played the game beyond the high school or college level, such as Jeff Van Gundy (New York Knicks) or Chuck Daly (Orlando Magic).

Some are screamers and control freaks. Others are laid-back and seemingly content to let things swirl around them. Some drive their players hard but know when to ease up. Others keep a lighter touch on the reins but recognize when to be demanding.

Teams often reflect the personality of their coaches, which makes sense. If a coach is loose and relaxed, his players play that way. If a coach is uptight, you'll be able to see it and feel it in his players when they're on the court.

Communication Is Key

Communication is the most important part of coaching in the NBA today. A coach must be able to communicate with his players. This always has been the case, but it is more so today than ever because teams live in a fishbowl surrounded by the media.

A coach must be more democratic than autocratic. This may not be true in high school or even in college, where a coach can say it's his way or the highway. Say that in the NBA and often the coach will be the one headed for the highway because the players are still the game.

For a while the NBA had many autocratic coaches. I believe that started with the influx of college coaches into the league in the 1970s. They were used to controlling their players, but in the pros that doesn't work. Today's coaches are smarter than that.

Clyde's Record Book

Pat Riley is one of the NBA's most successful coaches, but he's something of a dinosaur. Not many can do what he does—impose his austerity, his work ethic, and other pressures he puts on the players. The bottom line is that he gets tangible results, so he can operate that way. But I can't name another coach in the NBA who has that persona. Riley's a marquee coach who overshawdows his team. He's a coaching icon, the man who made it possible for the astronomical salaries coaches receive today. He's the superstar.

Sometimes you'll hear a coach described as a players' coach. That's because he listens. He can see their point of view. As a player, you feel you can talk to him. If he says something you disagree with, you can say, "That's not true" and explain why, and he'll hear you out.

Red Holzman, my coach with the Knicks, was a players' coach. He'd listen to us. He'd even let us come up with our own plays. I remember Golden State had a play they used to run for Rick Barry, where he'd come back along the baseline to get the ball and get his shot off. I said to myself, this play shouldn't work, but it did. So we put it in and it became one of our more effective plays. We called it the Barry. We copied other effective plays from other teams, too.

Flexibility Is a Virtue

A coach must be flexible, and not just in adjusting his style to the skills of his players, as I mentioned before. He must also be flexible in dealing with his players as 12 individuals and recognizing that their personalities and characters aren't all the same.

That kind of flexibility was one of Red Holzman's strong points. He knew that a coach can't treat every player the same way. He'd yell at me because I was oblivious to it and could take it. But he knew he couldn't yell at Bill Bradley because if he did he'd only play worse. Like Red said, as coach, you also have to be a psychiatrist and know the 12 different personalities you're dealing with.

Here's another example of Red's flexibility. Let's say we were on the road and he wanted to practice from 6 to 8. We might not like that because we wanted to go out and relax and have dinner. So we'd suggest practicing earlier, say 4 to 6 or 5 to 7, and he'd go along with it. He'd change the schedule.

Quote...Unquote

"The best thing about Phil is he allows players freedom on the court. You need to be able to go out there and give yourself a lot of rope and see how far you can go just before you hang yourself."—*Scottie Pippen of the Chicago Bulls on coach Phil Jackson.*

Quote...Unquote

"Red has so much to offer as far as handling men goes. He was always a step ahead of everybody. About the time you thought he was going to give you hell, he patted you on the butt. And about the time you thought you just played your best game, he would ream you out for some little thing you didn't do defensively."—*Don Nelson on Red Auerbach, for whom he played on the Boston Celtics.*

Phil Jackson, my former teammate who coached the Chicago Bulls' championship teams in the 1990s, is like that. Back in 1992, when Michael Jordan and Scottie Pippen came back after playing for the Dream Team in the Olympics, he recognized that they'd been playing basketball almost continuously for a full year. So in training camp that fall he lightened up on them and let them get in shape at their own pace. A couple of the other players didn't like that, but they were too self-centered to understand his reasoning. Phil was bending the rules for the good of the team.

Coaches like Pat Riley, Chuck Daly, and Rick Pitino have become popular figures on the speaking circuit. Many corporations will bring them in to give inspirational pep talks to their key employees or motivational tips to their sales force. Riley, for one, put some of his thoughts into words in a best-selling book, *The Winner Within*. Reading this book, or others authored by Jackson or Pitino, can give a fan valuable insight into the coach's thought process.

Red Auerbach, the long-time coach of the Boston Celtics, was like Holzman in adjusting his approach to different players. He knew he could yell at Bob Cousy and it wouldn't bother him, or he could get on Tommy Heinsohn's case. But he also knew that wouldn't work with Bill Russell, and that he had to take a different approach with his introspective center.

Is that a double standard? No, because Auerbach and Holzman and Jackson and many coaches like them had 12 standards, one for each player on the team.

But don't mistake flexibility for weakness. Red Holzman could be a tyrant when we were losing. Then he cracked down and became all business. As long as we did our jobs and played well and won, he'd be flexible. But when we were losing we weren't keeping our part of the bargain, so he'd get tougher.

By treating each of his players as an individual, Phil Jackson helped mold the Chicago Bulls into an NBA dynasty.
Associated Press

Putting the Intangibles to Work

The Xs and Os of coaching, knowing how to diagram new plays and make strategic changes, is a given at the NBA level. Every coach on every team is going to be prepared. That's taken for granted.

It's not the Xs and Os but the intangibles that a coach must have in order to get the respect of his players and to get his players to give 100 percent. And by intangibles I mean communication and flexibility.

145

Players may have talent but not be successful because they succumb to all the distractions. They need tunnel-vision. Once they're on the court, for 48 minutes they must think nothing but basketball. It's the coach's job to shield them from the distractions and get them to focus on the job at hand, and the players are more likely to be responsive if they feel they can communicate with their coach.

Players today want instant credibility in their coach. It's not sufficient to bring in a guy they don't know. If you're not somebody with a proven record, players will disregard you. So today the focus is on name, marquee coaches, guys with a winning track record. That's instant credibility.

But I don't care how big a name the coach is, he's not going to be successful if he doesn't communicate and have flexibility. The coach may want to play a running game, but if his players are slow-footed and have trouble getting up and down the court in a hurry, he'd better adjust his thinking and play at a slower tempo.

Mike Fratello did just that. He was successful in Atlanta with an up-tempo game built around high-flying Dominique Wilkins, but when he got to Cleveland he didn't see any Wilkins around and knew he'd better change his strategy pronto. By preaching patience and playing at a slower pace, he managed to get a very ordinary Cavaliers team into the playoffs.

Why must the coach change? Because it's a lot easier to replace one coach than 12 players.

Quote...Unquote

"You have to look at your personnel and see what they are able to do offensively and defensively. That's No. 1 on the professional level. Systems are nice, but I think it's better to suit systems to personnel rather than vice versa. You have to learn to take advantage of the personnel that you are given."—*Hall of Fame coach Chuck Daly, currently of the Orlando Magic.*

Clyde's Chalk Talk

An *expansion* team is one that is added to the existing teams in the league. The NBA, which had as few as eight teams in 1960–61, has steadily added expansion teams as the sport's popularity has grown, moving into new markets where fans indicate an interest in supporting a team of their own.

Assistants Provide Assistance in Many Ways

The NBA's first full-time assistant coach was Al Bianchi, who aided Johnny Kerr on the expansion Chicago Bulls in 1966–67. That team made the playoffs and won 33 games, the most ever for an expansion team. Coincidence or not, assistant coaches were here to stay.

Bianchi served as the yang to Kerr's yin. Kerr was the easy-going Chicagoan who always had a quip for the media and kept things loose, while Bianchi was intense and driven. They complemented each other well, setting a pattern for coach/assistant coach relationships to come.

In the early years assistant coaches were jacks of all trades. They would help the head coach run practice, work on specific areas or with individual players, offer advice on the bench, and occasionally scout upcoming opponents or college prospects.

As time has gone by and the NBA has grown, assistant coaches—like everyone else involved in the league—have become specialists rather than generalists. Some assistant coaches are offensive experts, some are defensive gurus. Some serve as a liaison between the players and the head coach, to whom the players may be reluctant to bring issues or complaints.

Look at the Chicago Bulls' coaching staff in the early 1990s under Phil Jackson. Tex Winter was in charge of the offense and put in the triangle system (where players work in units of three, setting up, passing the ball and running in predetermined patterns) he had developed in his 30 years of coaching. Johnny Bach, another veteran college and pro coach, was in charge of the defense. And Jim Cleamons, an ex-player only a few years older than the Bulls' players, served as a link in case the players didn't want to bring something to Jackson or one of the older coaches.

When Larry Bird was named coach of the Indiana Pacers, the first thing he did was go out and hire long-time college and NBA coach Dick Harter to be his top assistant and to run the Pacers' defense. Bird knew that Xs and Os weren't his strength, but he also knew he could find someone who would fill that role while he concentrated on providing leadership and setting a tone for the team.

Assistant coaches often fall into two categories. There are the coaching lifers with vast knowledge of the game who may have been head coaches in the past, either in the NBA or in college. And there are the youngsters, many of whom are former players, who are looking to establish themselves in the NBA and hopefully get a shot at a head coaching job someday.

On Bird's Indiana staff, Harter falls into the first category and the other assistant, Rick Carlisle, goes into the second.

Quote...Unquote

"General managers realize that you can hire assistant coaches that have been around basketball for 20 or 30 years to take teams through practices or teach skills. It's really how you can motivate players and keep them interested in basketball that counts (for a head coach) at this point."— *Phil Jackson, Chicago Bulls coach from 1989–90 to 1997–98.*

Clyde's Tip

Being an assistant coach can be one of the best jobs in the NBA. You have all the excitement of competition and striving to win without the headaches and responsibilities that go with being the head coach. And you can be well-paid. Some long-time assistants make $250,000, $300,000, or more, which is a lot more than head coaches (or most players) made back in my playing days.

Perhaps the most extreme example of coaching specialization is the Miami Heat under Pat Riley. The Heat have five assistant coaches, each of whom has specific game, practice, and/or scouting responsibilities. They also have a video coordinator, a trainer who doubles as travel coordinator, a strength and conditioning coach, an assistant trainer who doubles as assistant strength and conditioning coach, and a scout. Finally, there's a VP of team operations to coordinate it all.

Video and strength/conditioning are coaching areas that have come into vogue in the past decade. Many coaches have the video coordinator prepare individual tapes for each player, focusing on an upcoming opponent's strengths and weaknesses, to help the player prepare for each game. This type of preparation used to be limited to the playoffs, but now is often done in the regular season as well. Strength and coordinating coaches have become valued for their ability to help players avoid injury and build their bodies during the season and offseason.

The Unsung Heroes

Trainers, who help the players stay healthy and deal with injuries, are among the unsung heroes on a basketball team. They're rarely in the spotlight, yet unless they do their jobs properly, it will cost their teams in the standings.

In the early days of the NBA, trainers didn't exist. Players taped their own ankles and played through minor injuries and illnesses. Teams gave little thought to preventive measures such as diet, stretching, or other exercises that might lessen the severity of injuries or ward them off altogether.

Today, with players earning millions of dollars a year, trainers have become VIPs. Many have significant medical training, which they put to use by trying to keep their players in top playing condition. Help a star like Shaquille O'Neal prevent an injury or come back from one earlier than expected and a trainer earns his paycheck, and then some.

Many trainers double as their team's travel coordinator, whether they carry the title or not. Because the trainer travels with the team and is familiar with the likes and dislikes of the coaches and players, it's often the trainer who books what hotels the team will stay in and makes travel arrangements. The latter has become much easier in recent years now that NBA teams fly on chartered planes most of the time.

Another important person who operates even further behind the scenes is the team's equipment manager. His job is to make sure all the "stuff" gets from point A to point B, even if those points are on opposite sides of the country. And that "stuff" consists of everything from uniforms to special exercise or medical equipment a player might need to keep his body from stiffening up during or after games.

Most teams also have begun traveling with a member of their public relations staff, whose job is to coordinate media interview requests for players and coaches. Back when I was playing this wasn't an issue, because most teams didn't get much media coverage. That's why players liked coming to New York; if they had something to say or some gripe to air, they knew they'd get a big audience in New York. Today it has changed so much that some players hire their own bodyguards for privacy when they travel.

My Favorite Coaches

Growing up, I liked Bud Grant of the NFL's Minnesota Vikings (who played briefly in the early years of the NBA, by the way), Tom Landry of the NFL's Dallas Cowboys, and John Wooden of UCLA. They would win or lose with dignity. When they lost they never made excuses and when they won they didn't flaunt it.

In high school my coaches were that way, too. We won or lost with dignity. We had no problem saying a team was better than us.

Today I think Lenny Wilkens epitomizes that. Phil Jackson, too. I see much of Red Holzman in Phil's coaching style, the way he relates to players. Often a player who becomes a coach adopts some of the characteristics of his favorite coaches like that. K.C. Jones of the Boston Celtics was a real players' coach, and Larry Bird seems to be like K.C. was, perhaps because he played under K.C.

My philosophy is that the players know what to do. I like the low-key coaches who don't think they created the game. They know it's a players' game. Talk to Chuck Daly—he'll tell you that it's a players' game. Without Isiah Thomas and Joe Dumars, he wouldn't have won in Detroit and he'll be the first to say so. At this level, it's talent that wins games.

As part of the NBA's 50th anniversary celebration in 1996–97, a panel of media members selected the top 10 coaches in NBA history, and I thought they did a good job. Here's the list, in alphabetical order:

Red Auerbach (Washington Capitals, Tri-Cities Blackhawks, Boston Celtics)

Chuck Daly (Cleveland Cavaliers, Detroit Pistons, New Jersey Nets, Orlando Magic)

Quote...Unquote

"Sometimes you've got to give the horse its reins and let it go. It knows how to run better than the rider—it's got its feet on the ground and you're just on its back. I like to bring a player to a place where he can see things for himself, to guide him there rather than have a direct confrontation. I don't like to hit people over the head with a hammer."—*Phil Jackson, Chicago Bulls coach from 1989–90 to 1997–98.*

Quote...Unquote

"In this day and age, the people aspect of coaching is paramount. A coach, to a great degree, has to be a people person. To be a successful coach in the NBA, you must understand the mentality of the players."—*Chuck Daly, who coached the Detroit Pistons to NBA titles in 1989 and 1990.*

Bill Fitch (Cleveland Cavaliers, Boston Celtics, Houston Rockets, New Jersey Nets, Los Angeles Clippers)

Red Holzman (Milwaukee Bucks, St. Louis Hawks, New York Knicks)

Phil Jackson (Chicago Bulls)

John Kundla (Minneapolis Lakers)

Don Nelson (Milwaukee Bucks, Golden State Warriors, New York Knicks, Dallas Mavericks)

Jack Ramsay (Philadelphia 76ers, Buffalo Braves, Portland Trail Blazers, Indiana Pacers)

Pat Riley (Los Angeles Lakers, New York Knicks, Miami Heat)

Lenny Wilkens (Seattle SuperSonics, Portland Trail Blazers, Cleveland Cavaliers, Atlanta Hawks)

Quote...Unquote

"You have to communicate to your players and to yourself. I tell the players that all the time. What is important is how you communicate what we are and who we are to yourself. Then you can communicate it to everybody else."—*Pat Riley, Miami Heat president and head coach.*

Among them they have won 31 of 51 NBA Championships (through 1997–98), which I'd say is a pretty good success ratio. They all knew it was a players' game, they were excellent communicators and had the flexibility you need to succeed.

You think of Riley as being very tough and demanding, but he's proven his flexibility. He was showtime in L.A., run-and-gun, razzle-dazzle, but when he left the Lakers and came to New York all of a sudden he became defense-oriented and was coaching a slower, more physical, pound-it-out style of play. Why? He saw he didn't have Magic anymore and he didn't have Abdul-Jabbar anymore; instead he had Patrick Ewing and Charles Oakley and Anthony Mason. He realized he wasn't going to win in New York if he didn't change his style.

That's flexibility, and that's a sign of a great coach.

Pat Riley won four championships as coach of the Los Angeles Lakers, then helped New York and Miami become title contenders.
Associated Press

The Least You Need to Know

➤ Communication and flexibility are vital to being a successful coach in the NBA, where motivation is more important than preparation.

➤ The NBA is a players' league; the coach's job is to get the players to play their best, which is what motivation is all about.

➤ Assistant coaches come in all shapes and sizes and with a variety of job responsibilities, from teaching to scouting to working with players on individual problems that require special attention.

➤ A trainer who knows what he's doing can win games for his team by keeping his players hale and hearty.

Chapter 11

Referees, Fouls, and Violations

In This Chapter

➤ Referees maintain law and order

➤ Fouls and violations

➤ What are the hardest calls to make?

➤ My favorite referees

I've said it before and I'll say it again: Referees should be like children. They should be seen but not heard.

If you're watching a game and focusing on the referees, then something is wrong. You should be watching the players and thinking about moves made by the coaches. The referees are there to let the players play, not keep them from playing. If the referee is the center of attention, he's not doing his job properly.

Good games have a pace to them, a rhythm that comes only when play isn't constantly interrupted by whistles. Fans get caught up in those kinds of games just like players do, and that's what we all hope to see when we come to the arena. Referees must exercise judgment in deciding what fouls to call and what not to call, so the game can develop that special flow.

The highest compliment a coach or player can pay to a referee is that he never noticed him out on the court.

In this chapter I'll explain why control and consistency are essential for good refereeing. I'll also go over the most common fouls and violations committed in an NBA game, so when a whistle blows you'll understand why.

What Makes a Good Referee?

Clyde's Chalk Talk

The terms *referees* and *officials* are interchangeable in the NBA. Each of the three referees on the court has the same responsibilities and is empowered to make all calls.

The referees maintain order on the court and enforce the rules of the game so the players can put on an exciting and entertaining show for the fans. It's the players who are the show, not the referees, which is why I say good referees are seen but not heard.

Referees have a hard job and it's getting harder all the time, because NBA players are getting bigger, stronger, and faster with every generation. I always pay homage to the officials and extol their virtues because I think basketball is the most difficult game to officiate, but a good official is one who somehow makes it look easy.

Control and consistency are vital for referees. They must maintain control of the game and they must be consistent with their calls.

Confidence Leads to Control

The important thing to remember, and one of the hard things for young officials to learn, is that a referee does not have to blow his whistle all the time to be in control of a game. Control comes from self-confidence, an attitude that good referees project the moment they step onto the court.

When I think of referees, I see Mendy Rudolph, one of the all-time great officials who worked when I was playing. He was one of the few refs I knew. As I mentioned earlier, I

Clyde's Record Book

Throughout this chapter I'll refer to referees as "he" to keep things simple, even though in 1997–98 the NBA added two female referees to its staff for the first time. Dee Kantner and Violet Palmer were the pioneers who became the first women to referee in the NBA.

really didn't pay any attention to who was refereeing the game. But Mendy was one referee you couldn't ignore.

Mendy thought everyone came to watch him. He was cocky, he was arrogant, he just knew the crowd was there to watch him—at least that's what he thought. But he talked the talk and he walked the walk. He had flair, but because he also had good judgment and was consistent with his calls, players and coaches respected him and fans loved him. He had control of the game the moment he walked onto the floor, and he let you know it.

Mendy went against the rule that referees should be seen and not heard. In fact, many of the officials in the league's early years were that way. The NBA was struggling for attention and so it didn't mind if its referees played up to the fans and did a little showboating. Back then the thinking was anything that made the fans happy and brought them to the arena was good for the league.

That thinking has changed dramatically in recent years, when the NBA has made a conscious effort to make its referees as anonymous as possible. That's why you only see numbers on their shirts, not names, and why referees are forbidden to give interviews to the media without permission from the league office—permission that's rarely granted.

NBA referee Bennie Adams (47) tries to separate the bodies in this 1996 brawl between the Miami Heat and Washington Bullets. Associated Press

Another thing that has changed is the relationships between players and referees. In the old days, teams and referees used to travel together, so we'd stay in the same hotels, hang out together, and fraternize all the time. Now referees must take different flights and stay at different hotels. The theory is that the authenticity of the game

Clyde's Chalk Talk

The term *foul trouble* refers to how close a player is to fouling out of a game. In the NBA, a player is allowed five fouls; when he commits his sixth, he is disqualified and cannot return. In college ball, where games are shorter (40 minutes instead of the NBA's 48), a player is disqualified on his fifth foul. And keep in mind that a player can get into foul trouble at any point in a game. If he commits two or three fouls in the first quarter, he is said to be in early foul trouble and usually will spend the rest of the first half on the bench rather than risk picking up additional fouls.

Clyde's Chalk Talk

If a game is called *loosely*, that means the referees are allowing a certain amount of contact without calling fouls, and play tends to get more physical. Another phrase for this is "letting them play." If a game is called *tightly*, or *closely*, that means a foul is called on just about any contact.

must be above reproach, and the league wants it to be unequivocal that these guys aren't associated with any shenanigans—or the appearance of any.

But to get back to control, the toughest thing a referee must learn is when to blow his whistle and when to swallow it. There's contact on every play, so if they wanted to, referees could call a foul on every trip downcourt. And wouldn't that be boring!

All Players Ask of Referees Is Consistency

The thing that bothers players most about referees is when they aren't consistent with their calls. You can accept a referee who you think misses a call once in a while, because he's going to miss it at both ends of the floor. But if a referee calls a play one way one minute and another way the next, that drives players crazy. That's also when players tend to get into foul trouble, since they don't know what to expect from the officials.

As a player, you need to know what to expect. Is the game going to be called loosely or tightly? Referees must let the players know right away how much contact they'll allow before a foul is called, and must stick with that standard throughout the game. Players can and will adjust to anything, as long as they know what to expect.

Consistency is the hallmark of a good referee. He calls plays the same way night after night, whether it's the first quarter or the fourth quarter and no matter who's playing.

Rules Changes Have Helped the Game

One thing the NBA has done well is tinker with the rules to make the game better and the referees' job easier. The league is on top of it.

Most dramatically, the NBA went to three referees instead of two for better control of the game. There's no doubt that three sets of eyes, from three different angles, can see what's going on better than two.

When we played, guys got away with a lot. Players had all sorts of little tricks they'd try to get away with, and often they did. They'd hit you on the elbow when you were shooting, stand on your foot while you're going for a rebound, grab your shorts, jump into you and pull you down so it looked as if you initiated the contact. With two officials you could get away with a lot, but you can't rely on trickery with three officials.

A little thing like putting the shot clocks and the game clocks above the baskets was a big help for players. When I played, the 24-second clocks were on the floor in two corners of the court and the game clock was on the scoreboard, so if you were racing upcourt with the ball you had to look in all sorts of directions to know the time situation. Now all you have to do is look toward the basket and you can see all you need to know.

This year they added a dotted line under each basket to help referees decide whether or not to call a charging foul (more on this type of foul in a moment). Before there used to be an imaginary area under the basket where, even if there was contact, a referee wouldn't call a charging foul on the offensive player. But why leave it to the imagination? So they drew a line on the floor to give the referee something clear to go by and make his job easier. The game is so fast, it makes sense to give the referees more visual cues to go by.

What's a Foul? What's a Violation?

A personal foul is when a player makes illegal physical contact with an opponent. The NBA rule book spends several pages discussing what type of contact is illegal, starting with, "A player shall not hold, push, charge into or impede the progress of an opponent by extending an arm, leg or knee or by bending the body into a position that is not normal."

In the end, it becomes a matter of the referee using his judgment to decide what contact he should allow and what should result in a personal foul. The judgment often hinges on whether the contact impeded the progress of the other player or whether it was incidental, although in the case of a shooter virtually any contact made by a defender while he's in the act of shooting will be called a foul.

The penalty for a personal foul on the defensive team is two free throws if the fouled player was in

Clyde's Record Book

Norm Drucker, a former NBA referee and Supervisor of Officials, tells a story about Hall of Famer Walt Bellamy, who liked to talk about himself in the third person. "Why is that a foul on Walter?" he'd say. Or, "Bill Russell wouldn't get called for a foul on that." Relates Drucker, "I'd call one on him and he'd say, ʻSure, Walter doesn't get that call.' When I'd heard enough, I'd tell him to keep quiet. And one time, when he didn't, I said, ʻBellamy, tell Walter he just got a technical.'"

the act of shooting, and three if he was in the act of shooting a three-pointer. If the player who was fouled wasn't in the act of shooting, his team receives possession of the ball out of bounds. If the fouling team is over the limit of four fouls allowed in each quarter (or one in the last two minutes of a quarter), the player who was fouled receives two free throws.

The penalty for an offensive foul, a personal foul committed by a member of the team with the ball, is loss of ball possession. The other team takes possession of the ball out of bounds.

A technical foul is assessed for unsportsmanlike conduct, whether verbal or physical, by a player on the court or anyone seated on the team bench. It's also assessed for playing an illegal defense, after a warning has been issued. The penalty is a free throw for the other team.

His tie flying as he races along the sideline, Rick Pitino gets whistled for a technical foul by referee Andre Patillo in this 1997 game between Pitino's Kentucky Wildcats and the South Carolina Gamecocks. Pitino now coaches the Boston Celtics. Associated Press

Fines also are automatic for technical fouls called for unsportsmanlike conduct, and a player or coach is ejected from the game if he receives two such technical fouls. More severe penalties may be levied for fighting or flagrant fouls, those which, in the opinion of the referee, involve excessive force or intent to harm.

While a personal foul involves contact between two players, a violation is when a player doesn't abide by a rule. For example, taking two steps with the ball without dribbling is a traveling violation. Generally the penalty for a violation is loss of ball possession.

Give Me a Signal

Table 11.1 gives you a guide to the signals that referees use to control the game. There is a different signal for each foul, violation, or other stoppage of play.

Table 11.1 Fouls, violations, and referee signals.

Signal	Description
	The TIMEIN signal restarts play after a time out.
	The TIMEOUT signal stops play.
	A raised fist signals a PERSONAL FOUL against a player.
	When a referee makes a "T" with his hands, he's signaling a TECHNICAL FOUL, usually for unsportsmanlike conduct.

continues

159

Table 11.1   Continued

Signal	Description
	To show that something doesn't count, the referee uses the CANCEL SCORE, CANCEL PLAY signal.
	Raising three fingers signals a 3-SECOND RULE INFRACTION—a player was in the lane for too long.
	CHARGING is when an offensive player initiates contact with a defender who has established position.
	If a referee feels both players were at fault, he can signal a DOUBLE-FOUL.
	An ILLEGAL SCREEN is when the offensive player does not remain still, but moves into the path of the defender.
	If a team fails to get a shot off in time, the referee taps his head to signal a 24-SECOND VIOLATION.
	Upon a 3-PT. FIELD GOAL attempt, a referee raises one hand; if the shot is good, the second hand goes up as well (BOTH SIGNALS)
	In addition to regular timeouts, each team is allowed one 20-SECOND TIMEOUT per half.

Signal	Description
	PUSHING is when a defender knocks an offensive player off balance, or an offensive player uses his hands to get away from a defender.
	BLOCKING is when a defender gets in the way of an offensive player without getting into a set position (opposite of charging).
	BASKET INTERFERENCE is when a player from either team touches the ball when it's in the imaginary cylinder above the rim.
	If a player takes two steps without dribbling, passing, or shooting the ball, he's guilty of TRAVELING.
	A JUMP BALL is when players from opposite teams both have possession of the ball. It also is used to start the game.
	GOALTENDING is when a player from either team interferes with a shot on its way up toward the basket.
	An ILLEGAL DRIBBLE is when a player interrupts and then resumes his dribble, or dribbles the ball with both hands.
	DIRECTION OF PLAY—You'll see this after a change in possession, because sometimes everybody needs a reminder which way to go.

continues

Table 11.1   Continued

Signal	Description
	A referee calling a foul or violation will use his fingers to represent the player's uniform number in order TO DESIGNATE THE OFFENDER to the coaches and the official scorer.
	To promote movement, the NBA has instituted rules against ISOLATION plays in which several offensive players stand far away from the ball, to give a teammate more space in which to operate.
	If a player guards an area of the floor instead of a man, or if a player without the ball is double-teamed, that's an ILLEGAL DEFENSE violation.
	A player may not impede another's progress by HOLDING onto him.
	LOOSE BALL FOUL is one that is committed when neither team is in possession of the ball.
	ILLEGAL USE OF HANDS is a foul such as holding, hitting, or otherwise making contact with an opponent.

Tough Calls

The toughest call in basketball for a referee is to decide between charging and blocking. This occurs when a player with the ball is driving to the basket and a defender gets in his way. When the two collide, it's a foul—but on whom?

If the defensive player establishes his position on the court and doesn't move before the contact occurs, a charging foul is called on the player with the ball. This is an offensive foul and his team loses ball possession.

If the defensive player is moving in any way when the contact occurs, it is almost always called as a blocking foul against the defender for impeding the dribbler's path to the basket. Moving doesn't only mean feet, either—a defensive player may be planted on the floor, but if he leans his body into the dribbler's path and causes contact, it's a blocking foul. An exception is when both players are moving and the offensive player leans into the defender, thus initiating the contact—this may be called as a charging foul against the dribbler.

What makes this call so tough for referees is that in the midst of bang-bang action, he must determine whether the defender had established his position on the court, whether he had moved in any way, and whether the dribbler had initiated the contact by leaning into the defender. Those are all judgment calls that call for split-second decision-making by the referee.

There's another thing the referee has to look for on that play, and that's flopping. A defender, in order to make it look like the offensive player made more contact than he really did, will sometimes fall to the floor in dramatic fashion. Bill Laimbeer, who used to play for the Detroit Pistons, was 6'10" and weighed more than 250 pounds, yet he was constantly flopping to the floor at the slightest contact, even if it was from a guard who was 80 pounds lighter and couldn't possibly knock Laimbeer down unless he was driving a truck.

Clyde's Record Book

One of my favorite moves when I had the ball, and one you don't see very often anymore, was to fake a shot in order to get my defender to jump. Then, when he was in the air and unable to change direction, I would go up and take my jumper, knowing there would be contact. As long as I jumped relatively straight and didn't lean too far into the defender, the call would invariably go my way since we were both in motion. I'd either get two free throws or, if my shot went in, a basket plus one free throw.

Clyde's Rules

Remember that every player has an equal right to space on the court. Don't assume that because a player has the ball and is headed toward the basket, defenders must get out of his way. The NBA rule book states, "If a defender is able to establish a legal position in the straight path of the dribbler, the dribbler must avoid contact by changing direction or ending his dribble."

It doesn't take long before the referees catch on to this tactic, so Laimbeer had to learn to pick his spots. He became a much more effective flopper when he used some

Clyde's Chalk Talk

You may hear about something referred to as a *makeup call*. That's when, after a controversial call against one team, a call is made against the other team shortly thereafter, as if to even things out (and "make up" for the first call). Referees adamantly deny the practice, but players and coaches insist makeup calls occur.

Clyde's Tip

Many people believe stars get special treatment from referees, who give them the benefit of the doubt on violations and don't call fouls against them in order to keep them in the game. Referees deny it and it's certainly hard to prove. When a player of lesser stature complained about this alleged star treatment to the late Earl Strom, one of the NBA's all-time great officials, Strom shot back: "Sure we do, so why don't you become a star?"

discretion, didn't fall down on every play, and instead saved his Hollywood act for crucial times in a game. That's a lesson for all floppers: If you stay on your feet through the first 47 minutes of the game, you're much more likely to get the benefit of the doubt in the final minute than if you're constantly falling to the floor. Of course, by the time Laimbeer learned this lesson, he had to overcome his league-wide reputation for flopping as well.

Another tough call for referees is goaltending, whether by an offensive or defensive player. This is a matter of geometry: It's hard for a 6-foot referee to see exactly what's happening above a 10-foot basket.

For a violation to be offensive goaltending, the ball must be touched while it's in an imaginary cylinder directly above the basket. But often a ball is tipped by a player when it's just bouncing off the rim, and the referee must somehow determine whether the ball was in that imaginary cylinder or not.

On defensive goaltending, a referee must decide if the shot attempt was still on its upward flight toward the goal, when a block would be legal, or whether it had already reached its peak and was on its way down, when a block would be goaltending. He must also decide if a shot had a chance to go in the basket, because if it didn't, no goaltending can be called.

Three-second violations also become difficult to call unless a referee is careful to remain consistent. Most referees tend to ignore them unless they become blatant—unless a player sets up camp and does everything but pitch a tent in the lane. Once a referee calls a violation, he must use the same standard for the remainder of the game to avoid sending mixed signals to the players.

The most confusing call to fans has got to be the illegal defense violation, because this is the most complicated and least understood rule in the NBA. What's more, it's constantly being tweaked by the rules committee, so once you think you understand it, you have to go back and learn the new guidelines. This rule isn't only confusing to fans. Many players and even some coaches have trouble with its nuances.

Basically, as a fan you should watch whether a team double-teams a player when he doesn't have the ball, which is illegal. A defensive team can't assign two players to guard Shaquille O'Neal to prevent him from catching the ball, it can only double-team him once he touches it. There are other ways a defense may be illegal, but this is the simplest problem to watch for.

Why Bother Arguing?

As I mentioned earlier, I never knew who the referees were when I was playing—I still don't know who most of them are—and I never bothered to argue their calls. That's why I was never called for a technical foul in my entire career. I learned the game under coaches who told us not to get distracted by talking to the referees, so that's the way I always played. I never contested the refs' calls. If a ref made a call I disagreed with, I just went back the other way and played that much harder.

The first pro game I ever saw was the first one I played in, and I was appalled at all the talk that went on between coaches and refs, and players and refs. Back then they all knew each other and hung out together, so they were constantly talking on the court. I didn't know what to make of it because that wasn't the way I was taught to approach the game.

I never talked to referees. I figured, why waste my breath? They're not going to change their calls because of my complaining. Plus, I'm a pragmatist. Sometimes a guy would be guarding me and would try to block my shot and a foul would be called even though there really was no contact. I can't be a hypocrite and then complain when it happens the other way around.

I've got to believe my approach to referees helped me get some calls during my career. Again, it's human nature to give someone who is nice to you the benefit of the doubt. I remember once Richie Powers, one of the better referees, came up to me just before the tipoff and said, "Clyde, I'm glad you're out here. At least there are only nine guys against us."

Clyde's Tip

Do referees carry grudges against players who constantly complain? "All pro referees try not to let this dimension come into the game," said former NBA referee Norm Drucker, who is more candid than most, "but I rather doubt that it can be eliminated from your mind." Most players and coaches would agree. After all, it's only human nature. That's another reason why I chose not to argue referees' calls.

Quote...Unquote

"There's no use in my being on those guys all the time. If they make two or three calls in a row that I think are bad, yeah, I'll challenge them. But if you go back and watch the tape, a lot of the stuff that we're complaining about, they usually make the right calls. Sure they miss some calls here and there, but overall, I think they do an excellent job."—*Larry Bird, former Boston Celtics star and current Indiana Pacers coach, on his approach to referees.*

Referees, Like Coaches, Should Be Flexible

Good officials demonstrate flexibility, just as good coaches do.

One thing that impresses me is that today's NBA officials will change a call. If a guy doesn't see a play clearly, he'll ask one of the other referees for help. If they're not sure about something or disagree about what happened, they'll confer. They'll huddle and change a call if they feel the wrong call was made.

In the old days referees were adamant. They made a call and they stuck to it. Any wavering was considered a sign of weakness, a lack of confidence and control.

Clyde's Tip

When a player complains, most of the time, he's having a bad game anyway. He doesn't want to blame himself and he's afraid to talk back to his coach, so he complains to the refs when he thinks he's not getting a call.

Today they want to make the right call above all else, so if there's doubt they'll confer and consider changing it. That's all a player can ask for, that and consistency.

My Favorite Referees

As I said, I didn't pay much attention to the referees, but a few do stick out in my mind.

Mendy Rudolph was special because he brought so much to the game. He was a showman, an entertainer, but he was also a terrific referee. He had great judgment, he was consistent with his calls, and he maintained control of the game, so how could anybody complain if he liked to grab the spotlight?

Clyde's Record Book

Whenever I was on the road, I used to love to walk onto the court and see that Earl Strom was one of the referees. He could tune out a rambunctious crowd better than any referee I've seen and would bend over backwards to make sure the visiting team got a fair shake. When we were in a place like Boston Garden, I appreciated that.

Sid Borgia was another referee like that. He was one of the pioneers of NBA officiating and I heard all sorts of stories about him. He was a showman who put maintaining control of the game above all else, to the point where sometimes he wouldn't call everything by the rule book if it interrupted the flow of the game. The story goes that players had to ask him before a game, "Who's rules are we playing by tonight, the NBA's rules or Sid's rules?" But he was consistent with his calls and kept the game under control so the players could do their thing.

Some other referees I respected were old-timers like Richie Powers, Manny Sokol, Joe Gushue, Don Murphy, Jack Madden, Jake O'Donnell, and Earl Strom. They all exercised good judgment and kept the game under control.

The Least You Need to Know

➤ Consistency and control are the hallmarks of a good referee, because players can't play their best if they don't know how the refs are going to call the game.

➤ Because of its non-stop action and the size and speed of its athletes, basketball is the toughest game of all to officiate, and NBA referees do a remarkably good job of it.

➤ Among the toughest calls for a referee to make are goaltending and the choice between charging and blocking fouls.

➤ Don't think it's a foul every time a player drops to the floor—beware of floppers.

➤ Today's referees will confer and change their call for the sake of getting it right. That's not weakness or lack of control, that's flexibility.

Chapter 12

Keeping Track of All Those Numbers

Read a story about an NBA game, watch a game on television, or listen on the radio and you'll be hit with a blizzard of numbers, some of which are revealing while others are deceiving. Where do all these numbers come from and how do people like me throw them at you so fast?

I'll let you in on a secret if you promise not to pass it on: They don't all come from my head.

When I'm broadcasting a game, I've got a computer terminal nearby that provides a continuously updated boxscore of the game, summarizing each player's individual statistics as well as team statistics. This information is compiled by a stats crew that works in each arena, entering their data into both an official scorer's book and a courtside computer system. This information is provided instantly to broadcasters or writers on deadline, so we can give you a more complete picture of what's going on and try to explain why.

I'm also seated next to a statistician who keeps track of scoring streaks ("Chicago is now on an 11-2 run") and other data not on the standardized computer program. He feeds me the information whenever he comes up with something good. And in front of me I'll have my notes, which come from reading reams of information provided by the competing teams and the NBA as well as stories in the papers and from speaking with players, coaches, and other members of the media.

In this chapter I'll take you behind the scenes for a look at how game statistics are compiled. I'll explain what they mean and which statistics are worthy of special attention. And I'll explain how the NBA standings are compiled and presented and how the NBA Playoff system works, so you can keep tabs on your favorite team's status each day.

The Key Numbers: Score and Time

In the beginning, when life was simpler, there was a guy sitting by the side of the court with a big notebook in which he kept track of all points scored and fouls committed. Next to him was another guy with his hand on a button, starting and stopping the game clock at the referees' signals. And that was it.

What more do you need? One guy keeps score and tells who is in foul trouble, while another operates the clock. Score and time—the basic elements of any sport.

Soon additional statisticians were added to keep track of rebounds and assists, but things really started to get complicated in 1954–55 when the NBA added the 24-second shot clock. This meant a second clock operator was needed, and he had to work in synch with the game clock operator (the person tracking time left in the quarter or game). You couldn't very well have one clock moving and the other standing still, right?

Clyde's Rules

While referees are hired and paid by the league, the scorers and timers in each arena are hired and paid by the home team (although they're tested and certified by the league). So don't be surprised if, in a close game, the clock seems to work in favor of the home team. Maybe a friendly clock operator will start the clock a little late to give the home team more time to get a shot off. Hey, it's only human nature—chalk it up to the home-court advantage.

Here are some basics to keep in mind on timing. An NBA game is 48 minutes long, divided into four 12-minute quarters. If the score is tied after 48 minutes, 5-minute overtime periods are played until a winner is determined.

The reason a 48-minute game takes about two hours, 15 minutes to complete is because there are numerous play stoppages. The clock is stopped whenever the ball goes out of bounds or a player shoots free throws. It also stops after each made basket in the final two minutes of each quarter. Each team is allowed up to seven timeouts, lasting 1:40 apiece, plus two 20-second timeouts during the course of a game. And there are the breaks between periods, lasting 15 minutes at halftime and 2:10 at the other quarter breaks.

The Stats Crew

Over the years, more statistical categories were introduced to give fans, as well as players and coaches, more insight into the game—blocked shots, turnovers, steals, three-point field goals. Rebounds were broken down into offensive and defensive categories. A play-by-play sheet was kept, rudimentary at first but increasingly complete and complex as years went by, detailing each play that took place in the game. Since the pace of the game makes it difficult to type play-by-play and watch the game at the same time, a spotter was needed to make sure the typist didn't miss a play.

Clyde's Chalk Talk

The *play-by-play sheet* records virtually everything that takes place in the game—each score, shot type, assist, foul, turnover, and substitution, with the time remaining in the period and score of the game at that point. It's invaluable to members of the media covering a game, since it provides an official record of events, and provides the raw data coaches need for their post-game analyses.

Before long, you had as many as a dozen people sitting courtside (or elsewhere in the arena, once owners like Jerry Buss of the Lakers realized those courtside seats could be sold for big bucks), writing, typing, and calling out numbers at a pace as fast as the game itself.

And then (drumroll, please) came the computer. The play-by-play typist gave way to a keyboard operator, who then gave way to a guy with a magic pen who touches boxes on a screen to describe each play. The stats crew that had grown in size began to shrink again, because statistics were now generated by computer off the play-by-play input data.

Members of the Houston Rockets stats crew have a tough time following the action when Charles Barkley decides the scorer's table is a nice place to stretch out while he waits to enter the game.
Associated Press

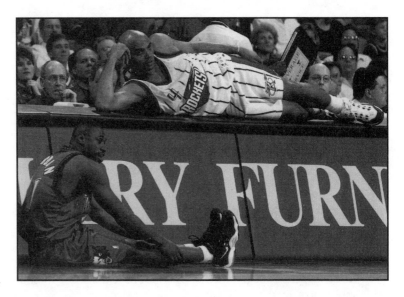

Let's take a look at the information contained in a play-by-play sheet. Here are the first few lines you might see for a fictional game:

Time	Cowboys	Score	Lead	Indians
12:00	Jump ball, Smith vs. Jones.			Tip to Jones
11:27	Monteleone layup	2-0	+2	
11:01	Voorhees 2FT (xo)	3-0	+3	Burke foul (P1, T1)
10:43		3-2	+1	Gola 16' jumper
10:01		3-4	-1	Grant dunk
09:53	Smith bad pass TO #1			
09:38				Jones traveling TO #1
09:15	Kaufman scoop	5-4	+1	

The game, date, and site generally are listed at the top of the page, along with the starting lineups. The far left column lists the time remaining in the quarter, while the middle columns provide a running score and lead. The main columns on the left and right show who scored or committed fouls or violations for each team. Substitutions are noted as they occur, and a summary of highlights such as leading scorers usually appears at the bottom.

For example, "11:01 Voorhees 2FT (xo) 3-0 +3 Burke foul (P1, T1)" means that with 11:01 remaining in the period, Voorhees was fouled by Burke and attempted two free throws, making the first and missing the second. That made the score 3-0, which gave Voorhees' team a three-point lead (+3). It was the first personal foul on Burke and also the first team foul called against Burke's team in this period.

Another example: "09:53 Smith bad pass TO #1" means that with 9:53 remaining in the period, Smith threw a bad pass that resulted in a turnover, the first by his team in this period.

The Boxscore: The Individual Tally

Based on the play-by-play sheets, an official boxscore (a statistical compilation of everything that happened in the game) is generated by computer immediately after the game ends and distributed to the media right away, so they can include exactly how many points Karl Malone scored or assists John Stockton handed out in their stories—and still meet their deadlines. What's more, in addition to the final boxscore, media members are provided with boxscores summarizing the first quarter, the first half, and the third quarter as well.

If you're at a game and you see people scurrying about the press tables handing out sheets of paper, chances are they're distributing printouts of either a play-by-play sheet or a boxscore for the quarter that just ended.

In the beginning, back in those good old days, boxscores simply listed the name of each team and its score, along with each player, his field goals made, free throws made, and total points, like this:

Cowboys (85)				**Indians (69)**			
Jones	3	2	8	Smith	9	1	19
Monteleone	7	8	22	Voorhees	6	7	19
Kaufman	12	6	30	Burke	4	1	9
Hopkins	7	2	16	Terrell	3	5	11
Downs	3	3	9	Sherman	2	7	11
Totals	32	21	85	Totals	24	21	69

Soon, free throw attempts were added. For example, "2-3" means the player completed two out of three attempted free throws. With free throw attempts added, the box score looks like this:

Cowboys (85)				Indians (69)			
Jones	3	2-3	8	Smith	9	1-1	19
Monteleone	7	8-9	22	Voorhees	6	7-13	19
Kaufman	12	6-6	30	Burke	4	1-2	9
Hopkins	7	2-5	16	Terrell	3	5-5	11
Downs	3	3-3	9	Sherman	2	7-9	11
Totals	32	21-26	85	Totals	24	21-30	69

To this day, you'll find many boxscores printed as shown and followed by the score made in each quarter, along with additional information in paragraph form, like this:

Cowboys	16	20	22	27	—	85
Indians	22	11	23	13	—	69

Fouled out: None. Total fouls: Cowboys 21, Indians 14. Technicals: Monteleone, Voorhees. Referees: Garretson, Strom, O'Donnell. A: 19,694.

To save space, some newspapers take the individual players' statistics and condense them in a paragraph format like this:

Cowboys (85)

Jones 3 2-3 8, Monteleone 7 8-9 22, Kaufman 12 6-6 30, Hopkins 7 2-5 16, Downs 3 3-3 9. Totals: 32 21-26 85.

Indians (69)

Smith 9 1-1 19, Voorhees 6 7-13 19, Burke 4 1-2 9, Terrell 3 5-5 11, Sherman 2 7-9 11. Totals: 24 21-30 69.

It's the same information, just in different packaging.

Over the years, however, things got complicated. More and more statistical categories were devised and compiled, such as rebounds, assists, steals, and blocks. Computers were introduced to keep track of everything and spit it out instantly so broadcasters like me can relay the information to fans watching or listening at home, or so newspapermen (and women) can use them in their game stories.

Today's NBA boxscore includes a total of 16 statistical categories for every player: minutes played, field goals made and attempted, three-point field goals made and attempted, free throws made and attempted, offensive rebounds, defensive rebounds, total rebounds, assists, personal fouls, steals, turnovers, blocked shots, and points. It also includes team information such as shooting percentages and total fouls, and additional information like the attendance and the names of the referees.

Newspapers rarely print complete boxscores, although you might see one for the All-Star Game or the NBA Finals. Most papers pick and choose a number of categories, balancing a large amount of information against a limited amount of space. That's why the boxscore formats you see vary slightly from one paper to the next—each editor has to make his own calls about what to run.

In addition to each game's boxscore, you may also find cumulative league leaders (top 10 or 20 in each category) in your local newspaper, often on a weekly basis. If you're like me and don't want to wait that long, log on to one of the many sports sites that are so popular on the World Wide Web, such as ESPN.SportsZone.com, cnnsi.com, cbs.sportsline.com, sportingnews.com, or the NBA's own NBA.com, among others. All of them carry stories and boxscores after every game plus updated statistics, features, and much more. I'll talk more about Web sites in Chapter 26.

The Standings: The Team Tally

How's your favorite team doing? You can get the answer each morning in the NBA Standings, which list each team's won-lost record, printed in your local paper (or available on any of the Web sites listed above). As with boxscores, these may appear in different formats, from the most basic listing of wins, losses, winning percentage, and games behind the division leader to jazzier versions that include current winning or losing streaks and each team's record broken down into home and road games or conference and non-conference games.

These standings are generally accompanied by the scores of the most recent day's games and a schedule of upcoming games for the next day or two.

Clyde's Chalk Talk

An *assist* is a pass that leads directly to a basket. There's some subjectivity involved in how people interpret "directly," which makes it an imprecise stat. Today's scoring crews seem to distribute assists more liberally than they did when I was playing, which makes it hard to compare players from different time periods.

Clyde's Tip

Basketball moves too fast for fans to try to keep a full boxscore. Instead, keep track of the statistics that interest you to get more involved in the game. You may want to keep each player's scoring or tally as many statistics as possible for a favorite player. Compare your numbers with what appears in the next day's paper and see how close you came (remember that while points are cut and dried, a category like assists is somewhat subjective).

The regular season standings determine which teams qualify for the postseason play-offs and a shot at the league championship.

The NBA divides its 29 teams into two conferences, with two divisions in each. The Eastern Conference consists of the Atlantic and Central Divisions, and the Western Conference consists of the Midwest and Pacific Divisions.

A total of 16 teams qualify for the NBA Playoffs, eight in each conference—the four division champions and the next six in each conference based on winning percentage. The first round of the playoffs is best-of-5, all remaining rounds best-of-7, and in each series the team with the better regular-season record gets the home-court advantage in the extra game.

The qualifiers in each conference are seeded Nos. 1 through 8, with the division winner with the better record being placed No. 1 and the other division winner slotted at No. 2. The remaining six teams are seeded (ranked) 3 through 8 according to their records. The pairings for the first round of the playoffs are teams 1-8, 2-7, 3-6, and 4-5.

Most newspapers like to give a graphic treatment to this information, in the form of brackets like this:

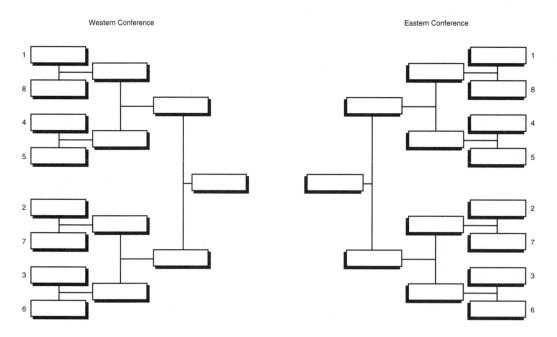

The NBA plugs the eight qualifying teams from each conference into playoff brackets, so you'll know how teams are seeded and which teams play each other in each round.

Numbers That Are Really Important

As a former guard, I like to look at the assists and turnovers for a team's guards, especially its point guards. A top point guard should have an assist-to-turnover ratio of 3:1 or better, meaning at least three assists for each turnover.

It's important to look at those two statistics together. Just because a point guard has a lot of turnovers doesn't mean he isn't playing well. Some guards are more creative and more daring, trying to make things happen for their team. As a result they may commit some turnovers, but you have to be willing to take risks to rise above the ordinary.

Not many statistics reflect defense, which is unfortunate. And even those that do, steals and blocked shots, don't tell the full story. A player may get steals or blocks because he gambles a lot, and by leaving his man alone he gives up some easy baskets and hurts his team. Good defense must be played as a team, and there's no way to measure or reflect this in individual player statistics.

I do like to look at a so-called "effort statistic" like offensive rebounds. Hustle is something that isn't measured in a boxscore, but about the closest you can come is offensive rebounds. You have to constantly be working for position and hustling if you want to grab offensive rebounds. Second-chance points, compiled in boxscores for each team but not for individual players, is another effort statistic.

The most important statistic, however, is the one after the team's name in the standings: wins and losses.

Clyde's Record Book

Don't get hung up on turnovers. Creative guards who take risks are going to turn the ball over on occasion, but if they're good the rewards outweigh the risks. Three of the greatest point guards of all time, Isiah Thomas, Magic Johnson, and John Stockton, rank among the top five in career turnovers.

The Least You Need to Know

➤ Each team has a stats crew that keeps track of a myriad of numbers, making the lives of writers and broadcasters (like me) much easier.

➤ The boxscore is a numerical record of which team won and what each player did in an individual game.

➤ The standings tell you how your favorite team is doing.

➤ Of the 29 teams in the NBA, 16 qualify for the post season playoffs, which can last nearly two months.

Chapter 13

The Media Links Fans to the Game

In This Chapter

➤ Print and electronic journalism

➤ The impact of television

➤ Attitudes have changed among players and the media

➤ The "play of the day" syndrome

➤ National and team broadcasters

➤ How I got into broadcasting

➤ My favorite broadcasters

The media plays a major role in shaping how you feel about your favorite team. It serves as your window to what's really going on in the locker room, the front office, and behind the scenes. Like all windows, it can be clear and provide a true picture, or it can be dirty and give a distorted view.

It's important that you, the fan, keep this in mind when you read an article about a team or a profile of a player, or when you listen to broadcasters describe a game or give you the highlights on the nightly news or the sports wrap-up shows.

Fans can be gullible, often believing everything they read. I would be that way, too, if I wasn't behind the scenes. If I hadn't been exposed to it all and didn't know the nuances, I would believe it all, too.

My advice is don't absorb everything 100 percent. Use some discretion, as you would in dealing with anything else. Remember that papers are in business to sell papers and TV success is predicated on ratings, so those media sometimes go for the sensational. The bottom line is you can't believe everything 100 percent of the time.

Clyde's Record Book

The NBA and many of its teams run seminars for players to inform them about the media and introduce them to the roles played by various media members. The league office has prepared a videotape in which former players and members of the media give tips on how to develop a mutually productive relationship.

Clyde's Tip

Remember that columnists are giving their opinions, and that the objectivity that is the standard for the rest of the newspaper does not apply to columnists. They are paid to give their viewpoint. Also remember that just because their opinions appear in print doesn't make them any more correct than your own. Read columns with a skeptical eye. Think for yourself!

In the best of all possible worlds, media members are objective and unbiased. They answer the basic questions of journalism: who, what, where, when, why, and how. They uncover what you want to know, asking the questions you would ask if you had their access to players, coaches, and executives.

In the real world, media members carry some biases. We all do—everyone carries his background with him wherever he goes. Media members are no different. They approach every game, every assignment, every interview with opinions and attitudes formed over a lifetime. And they're only human—if a player is consistently rude, uncooperative, and downright boorish to a writer, how likely is it that this writer is going to give this player the benefit of the doubt in an article about him?

Add to this the biases of their employers, who often have their own reasons for promoting a certain point of view, and you can see why I feel so strongly that fans must take everything you see in the media with a healthy measure of skepticism.

I'm not saying don't believe everything you see, hear, and read; I am saying be skeptical and form your own opinions.

Sports Media 101

It helps to understand various forms of media to get an idea of who does what.

Print journalism refers to newspapers, magazines, and news services. Electronic journalism refers to radio, TV, and the most recent addition to the field, the Internet.

Daily newspapers in NBA cities generally assign one writer to cover the team all season, known as a beat writer. There's usually a backup beat writer as well, and the larger papers also assign a writer to cover the NBA on a league-wide basis (as opposed to the home team). These papers also have columnists, generally more experienced writers who are paid to give opinions rather than report news.

Daily papers contain a mix of game stories and other news about the team plus feature articles and columns. Weekly newspapers and weekly or monthly magazines are built around features—interviews, profiles, and trend stories—rather than day-to-day news or game stories.

Electronic journalism is divided between reporters who cover games and produce features for radio and TV stations or for Internet services, and broadcasters who do the actually play-by-play and commentary on game broadcasts, whether on radio or television, local or national.

Basketball News on TV

The TV boom has changed the nature of print game reporting. In the old days, most fans didn't know what happened in a game played by the home team the previous night until they picked up their papers the next morning. So writers spent the bulk of their stories describing the game action, with little time used for analysis or quotes from the participants.

Now most fans already know the final score before they go to sleep, thanks to the sports segments on local news programs and national sportscasts on networks like ESPN, CNN/SI, and Fox, which show highlights from each night's games. And because virtually every game is televised in some form or another, many fans have watched all or part of the game itself.

A newspaper writer can't just tell what happened. He must provide something more, explaining why the team won rather than just describing the win. So as soon as the game ends he heads to the locker room to interview coaches and players from both teams, gathering quotes that hopefully tell you something you didn't know about the game. Thus the beat writer takes you behind the scenes and gives you a chance to read what coaches and players have to say about key plays or strategic moves.

Clyde's Tip

If you see a blaring headline and the story doesn't really back it up, don't blame the writer whose byline is on the story. Headlines usually are written by copy editors back at the newspaper office, who try to make them as eye-catching as possible. Remember, a snappy headline can sell newspapers. I remember once the front page of the *New York Daily News* had a picture of President Gerald Ford and a huge headline: "Ford To NY: Drop Dead!" I'm sure that sold some papers!

Clyde's Record Book

The term "sound bite" refers to a 10- or 15-second comment that appears on TV or radio. It's cut from a longer interview done by a reporter who knows that because news programs are so fast-paced, the point needs to be made as quickly as possible. So he looks for that one snappy sentence that summarizes what the person he interviewed was trying to say. All electronic journalists quickly learn who gives good sound bites and who doesn't, which is why some athletes are seen and heard on the air far more than others.

Mark Jackson of the Indiana Pacers plays meet the press in the locker room after a game. Associated Press

Attitudes Have Changed on Both Sides

Perhaps a more subtle change, but equally important, is in the way both print and electronic reporters approach their jobs today, and the way athletes view the media.

In the old days, writers seemed happy to be involved in the sports business. They considered themselves lucky to write about a team and get paid for it. You'd never see anything negative printed in those days unless there was absolutely no way to keep it quiet. If you were involved in something, the coach would come to you with the reporter and you'd discuss how you all should deal with it. Reporters didn't look for sensationalism like they do today.

Clyde's Tip

Every New York writer thinks he knows everything about the game and can do a better job than the coach. It's like it's a prerequisite for working there.

I hated writers using their thoughts instead of what we players and coaches actually said. I actually stopped talking to the press for a while. Too many of them were really out for negative comments, for anything that would make a provocative headline. If the story didn't back it up it didn't matter, because all people saw were the headlines, few bothered to read the whole story. Finally I said, "You guys are writing what you want, you don't need me." So I stopped talking to most of them for my last two years with the Knicks—I would still talk to the older guys, because they'd essentially print what I said.

The press can make or break you. It's that simple, man. They can make or break you. Look at Rod Strickland, the point guard who has played for several NBA teams including New York, San Antonio, and Washington. He's a guy they're breaking. He should be an All-Star the way he's playing, but because of his media image, he's never made the team. How does a guy get in that spot? Maybe at some time he wouldn't give an interview or maybe he did something the writer never forgot. Who knows?

Some players are naturally more comfortable dealing with the media. Whether it's their backgrounds, their education, or their personalities, they understand what the media is looking for and can maintain a positive relationship that works to their benefit. Others, whether out of a lack of self-confidence, a general mistrust of strangers, or some prior bad experience, choose to be curt with media members or cut them off entirely.

I think the big difference between then and now is that we, as players, coveted writers back then. We wanted articles written about us. Everyone wanted to play in New York because you got the media attention that would make you famous. There was virtually no media coverage in other cities because the league was struggling.

Today it's the other way around. Writers are clamoring for access to players and many players do all they can to avoid them. Now players just want privacy. They don't know what it's like not to have the publicity and interview requests.

One healthy change in the media in recent years is the arrival of female sports writers, editors, broadcasters, and producers. In my day there were virtually no women in the media, but today you see them all over. It's good because they bring a different perspective and have helped change some (but not enough) old attitudes that needed changing.

Clyde's Record Book

There was a changing of the guard in the media in the '70s. Older newspaper guys like Lenny Lewin and Sam Goldaper in New York were on the way out, and young turks came in, looking to make names for themselves. One young guy who is now a columnist made a name for himself by bashing me. I was famous, so he went about bashing me. I used to like reading the papers in New York because some of the stories were so hilarious. But when they were about me, they weren't so funny anymore. So I stopped reading.

Clyde's Record Book

I always enjoyed talking with writers if I felt they were fair to me and would write what I said, not what they were thinking. Guys like Leonard Koppett, the late Dick Young—I'd talk to these guys any time. After a game they would interview others first and then get around to me, knowing Clyde would be there waiting for them. So it was disappointing to me when they left the scene.

183

The growth of the league, the increased media coverage, the presence of television—it's all connected. With us there was no growth and little media or TV. Now you have it all.

The "Play of the Day" Syndrome

Television has had its impact on players, too. When I played it was a kick to see my picture in the newspaper, but that was something that just happened. I couldn't make a special play just for the benefit of the photographer because there was no guarantee he was focused on me.

But the TV camera misses nothing, and today's players know it and play to it.

So when they're ahead of the field and going in toward the basket, they all seem to think, "What can I do that will get me on TV?" There are no layups anymore, because layups don't get on the highlight reels. Spectacular slams and 360-degree dunks make the "Play of the Day," so that's what today's players try for.

Don't get me wrong—I have nothing against the spectacular. Hey, I was known for my flair on and off the court. There was nothing conservative about Clyde.

But where I see a problem, and where I think TV has had a negative influence, is that today's players focus so much on the flair that they neglect the fundamentals. It's particularly true among today's young players—and players are coming into the NBA at a younger age every year.

Why can't anybody shoot free throws anymore? Why don't players box out for rebounds instead of just leaping into the air? Why has crisp passing become a lost art? It may not be totally the fault of television, but if they showed something besides dunks and razzle-dazzle, perhaps today's players would be inspired to develop some substance to go with the sizzle.

Clyde's Record Book

Kobe Bryant of the Los Angeles Lakers, the youngest NBA participant ever at 19, got a lot of attention in the 1998 All-Star Game with his flashy moves. Did he really have to do a 360 when he was going in alone for a dunk? Did he have to dribble behind his back to himself? No, but he did—and those are the plays we all remember from that game. Kobe is truly a product of television, with a game made for television, and we'll be seeing a lot of him in the highlights.

Where National and Team Broadcasters Fit In

Announcers on game telecasts and radio broadcasts, whether for the national media like NBC, Turner, or ESPN, or for individual teams and local stations, have different roles from the print reporters and electronic journalists who cover the NBA. They're like throwbacks to the old-time newspaper reporters in that they're supposed to tell what's happening by getting back to the basics of reporting—who, what, where, when, why, and how.

This applies both to the play-by-play man, who calls the action (who, what, where, when), and the color commentator, who provides the analysis (why, how).

They must work together as a team, blending smoothly so that one's words complement the other's.

Radio vs. TV

There's a big difference between broadcasting a game on radio and on television—a huge difference from a broadcaster's standpoint.

TV is much easier because the audience can see what's going on. There's enough time for an analyst to explain a point because you don't have to describe so much of the play itself. You have plenty of time to express yourself. On radio, the announcers must spend more time just describing the action, so there is less time left for anecdotes and stories.

When you're doing radio you're like a catcher in baseball. You're always in the action. When I go from doing a game on radio to doing one on TV, it's like I'm hardly working. It's difficult to get momentum. With radio you're always in the game.

National vs. Team Broadcasters

Good play-by-play is good play-by-play whether it's on a national broadcast or a team broadcast on a local radio or television station. Marv Albert proved that with his superb work for the Knicks and for NBC. The same is true for color commentary—good analysis is good analysis.

However, national broadcasters must take a different approach to a game from team broadcasters, because their audience includes fans of both teams as well as people with no rooting interest at all. A national broadcaster has to call the game down the middle, from a neutral perspective.

The national audience also probably has a greater number of casual fans, who may not be as knowledgeable about the game of basketball and its nuances. When you're a team broadcaster, you can be certain that just about all your listeners are fans of that team and are pretty well versed in the sport.

As a team broadcaster on a local station, you describe a game from your team's standpoint. That's what your listeners want to hear. You don't have to worry about giving each team equal coverage, as a national broadcaster might. When I'm doing a game I'm doing a Knicks game, not a Knicks-Cavaliers game. And Joe Tait, the long-time Cleveland broadcaster, is doing a Cavaliers game.

185

So How Did I Get into This Racket?

What's a nice guy like me doing in broadcasting?

It was serendipitous, to use one of my favorite words.

When I was inducted into the Hall of Fame in 1987, I was interviewed by a number of print and electronic journalists, including Marv Albert at Madison Square Garden Network, the cable network that televises Knicks games. One of the producers liked my comments and thought I might be good for TV. They approached me to see if I would be interested.

At the time I wasn't doing anything very exciting so I said I'd like to try it. I'd been out of the game for a number of years and the idea of getting back in was appealing. They hired me to work 15 games, doing pregame, halftime and postgame analysis with Greg Gumbel, who is now with CBS but then was with the MSG Network.

I was up in the studio, which was a very calm and controlled environment, for the pregame show. But we went down onto the court to do halftime and that was like a three-ring circus. There was loud music, and people were yelling and coming over to say hello, especially since they weren't used to seeing me at the Garden. It was intimidating, but somehow I survived.

Clyde's Record Book

When I began broadcasting, I always had the fear that I would try to answer something and wouldn't be able to get out of it. I would just keep talking and talking. We only had two or three minutes on our halftime segment so we had to make our points quickly. That taught me early-on that I would have to improve my vocabulary, so I began to read dictionaries and other books on language usage. I'd find a new word and try to work it into different sentences until I was comfortable enough to use it in my commentary. That was the genesis of Clyde the Wordman.

The guy who really helped me in terms of radio broadcasting was Marty Glickman, one of the true pioneers of this business who now does some work as a coach for broadcasters. He critiqued me for six or seven games and told me all the vital points I needed to know about radio.

For example, he told me that when I was working radio, I should assume the audience was blind. A guy doesn't have the ball on the baseline, he has it on the right baseline. He's not penetrating, but penetrating diagonally into the paint. You have to be descriptive when doing radio because the listeners don't have a picture to watch—you have to create it for them. That's how I try to be now. After about six or seven meetings I started to improve. I really saw what he was saying.

Another thing he told me was simplistic, but not so simple. He said, "Clyde, just be yourself. Everyone in New York knows you. They know your authority. You don't have to prove to them that you know the game. Just be yourself and tell them what you know." He reminded me of my mom, who was always telling me to just be myself.

It sounds simple, but when you're starting something new, it really isn't. I'd heard other announcers, I'd heard the clichés and sometimes I'd copy them. Then I'd say to myself, "Why did that come out?"

The best thing that happened to me was starting out in TV in a segment where you have a finite time to express yourself. That made it crucial to get in and out, to say something succinctly. That's a valuable skill for any commentator.

Another thing Marty taught me is that when the ball is in play, the play-by-play man talks. When the ball is dead, you (the color commentator) talk. There can't be any egos. If there's an ego problem in the booth, you can be sure the people will pick up on it.

I did 15 games that first year, 30 games the next. I also did commentary on some road games for the Atlanta Hawks, which furthered my career. The next season Ernie Grunfeld, who had been the Knicks' radio commentator, went into coaching and so I ended up on the game broadcasts, doing color commentary. Lately I've been doing color commentary on radio and also halftime reports on Knicks telecasts, which keeps me busy on game nights!

My first partner was Jim Karvellas, which was an interesting experience because he was used to working alone. When he worked with the Bullets he didn't have a broadcast partner, so he did all the talking.

When I worked with Jim, that's when I started rhyming. I knew he had to take a breath sometime and that would be my chance. I knew I had to get in and out and leave an impression in a short time, so I did the rhymes—swishing and dishing, bashing and dashing, wheeling and stealing, penetrating and devastating. That's how that whole rhyming thing evolved. That was all I could do, because Jim was doing play-by-play and color, too. I didn't have many chances to jump in so I had to make the most of it.

When Jim left and Mike Breen came in as the play-by-play man, things changed. I could do what I was supposed to do, which was give my analysis and explain how things happened. It became completely different for me. I was more relaxed. With Jim I was always tense because I felt such pressure to get in and out. Breen gave me time to say my piece.

Clyde's Record Book

My predecessor as analyst on Knicks broadcasts was Ernie Grunfeld, who is now the team's president. But Jim Karvellas was used to working alone, doing the play-by-play and color commentary all by himself. No one knew Ernie was doing the games because he never got a chance to say anything. Karvellas did all the talking.

My partner on the radio last year was Gus Johnson, who comes from a TV background. He's used to just sitting there, so I find I'm talking more. Gus is still making the transition. It's more difficult to go from TV to radio than vice versa, because you have to describe so much more. On TV you have pictures, but in radio you have to set up plays and he's still trying to develop that, to come up with a style.

My Favorite Broadcasters

Too many broadcasters act like coaches today; they want to be bigger than the game. That's not my style. People aren't listening to hear me talk, they're listening to find out how the Knicks are doing. You can't let your ego get in the way of serving your audience.

One guy I really liked was Ray Scott, who did pro football and other sports for NBC and other networks for so many years. He was so professional in the way he talked; the way he brought you into the game. I always enjoyed his work. Lindsay Nelson, who did a lot of college football and was one of the New York Mets' broadcasters when I was playing for the Knicks, was another guy like that.

I think among today's broadcasters, Dick Enberg of NBC Sports would be my idol because he just does the game cleanly, without all the shtick you get from some others. He's a professional. He reports the game.

I always like Al McGuire, too, even though he projects his personality into his college basketball broadcasts more than the others I mentioned. But he doesn't try to be bigger than the game. He's honest and he tells it like it is. He was one of those coaches who looked out for his players, and as a broadcaster he looked out for his audience.

The Least You Need to Know

➤ Don't automatically believe everything you see, hear, or read. Be skeptical and form your own opinions.

➤ Television has impacted the way sports writers do their job, because so many fans already know what happened before they pick up the paper.

➤ Another effect of the increased television coverage is that players seem to play for the camera, trying to make the spectacular play that will get them on the news.

➤ National and team broadcasters do the same job, but take a different approach to it; team broadcasters have to appease a more local audience with a definite rooting interest, while national broadcasters must treat both teams equally.

Chapter 14

The (Big) Business of Basketball

In This Chapter

➤ What goes on off the court matters, too

➤ Where does all the money come from?

➤ The salary cap: one size doesn't fit all

➤ Behind the scenes at the teams and the league

➤ Agents and the Players Association

➤ Getting caught in the draft

➤ Marketing brings in the Benjamins

Most fans aren't particularly interested in reading about the business of basketball. They care about what happens on the court, not in the conference room. They want to read about the people in uniforms, not in pinstripes.

I understand where they're coming from. I also get tired of reading about salary caps and labor disputes, sponsorships and marketing deals, agents and contracts.

But the fact is basketball has become big business. The NBA league office, which had about 35 employees as recently as 1980, now employs nearly 900 people in offices ranging from New York to Tokyo, from Paris to Melbourne. All those people, and several thousand more at the 29 team offices, work to bring in enough money so NBA teams can pay players an average salary that has soared to an estimated $2.2 million a year, with enough left over so the team owners can show a profit. NBA games are broadcast in more than 190 countries around the world and more than 150 companies have licensing deals with the NBA to produce official league merchandise and market it worldwide.

In this chapter I'll explain some of what goes on off the court and how it impacts what takes place on the court, which is why you should care about it in the first place.

Besides, some of these numbers are fun.

Players and Coaches Take Home Big Bucks

For playing basketball with the Chicago Bulls in the 1997–98 season, Michael Jordan was paid a reported salary of $33,140,000. That's $404,164.34 per game. Or $4,928.61 per minute, including time spent sitting on the bench.

Nice work if you can get it.

But no one is holding a gun to the head of Jerry Reinsdorf, the man who signs Jordan's paychecks. (Or at least authorizes them to be issued, since I doubt he signs them himself. Actually, there probably are no real paychecks—the money likely bounces from one account to another electronically.) "The best player should make the most money. Michael is in a league by himself," said Reinsdorf.

While Michael may be in a league by himself, the rest of the NBA players aren't doing too badly. One published survey listed 265 players slated to draw paychecks of $1 million or more in 1997–98, including 42 at the $5 million plateau and nine at the loftier level of $10 million.

Following are the 10 highest paid players in the NBA for the 1997–98 season, according to a report published early in the season that listed the money guaranteed to each player:

1. Michael Jordan, Chicago Bulls	$33,140,000
2. Patrick Ewing, New York Knicks	$20,500,000
3. Horace Grant, Orlando Magic	$14,285,714
4. Shaquille O'Neal, Los Angeles Lakers	$12,847,143
5. David Robinson, San Antonio Spurs	$12,397,440
6. Alonzo Mourning, Miami Heat	$11,254,800
7. Juwan Howard, Washington Wizards	$11,250,000
8. Hakeem Olajuwon, Houston Rockets	$11,156,000
9. Gary Payton, Seattle SuperSonics	$10,514,688
10. Reggie Miller, Indiana Pacers	$9,031,850

League-wide, it's estimated that the NBA paid out more than $400 million in player salaries in 1997–98.

Coaches didn't do too badly, either. Rick Pitino began a 10-year contract as president and head coach of the Boston Celtics that will pay him a reported $70 million. Phil Jackson was given an estimated $6 million to coach Chicago for one more season, while Larry Brown signed in Philadelphia for $25 million over five years and Chuck Daly signed for $15 million over three years to coach Orlando. Larry Bird was lured out of retirement to try his hand at coaching by the Indiana Pacers for a reported $4.5 million a year.

Meanwhile, in Miami, Pat Riley labored as coach and president for a mere $3 million—but he also owns a chunk of the franchise. Finally, several other coaches, including Rudy Tomjanovich of Houston, Mike Fratello of Cleveland, and Lenny Wilkens of Atlanta, were able to renegotiate their contracts based on the way the going rate was going through the roof.

David Stern has been the NBA's Commissioner since 1984, during the league's greatest period of prosperity.
Associated Press

And the man who oversees the whole party, Commissioner David Stern, has been amply rewarded for the league's success. His bosses, the NBA Board of Governors (the owners of the 29 teams), recently gave him a five-year contract worth a reported $40 million.

So Who Pays These Salaries?

The good news is the money doesn't all come from ticket prices, which go as high as $1,250 for Spike Lee's courtside seat at Madison Square Garden.

The bad news is that while the fan may not be paying it at the ticket window, he's paying it somewhere down the line. Here's an example of how the fan indirectly pays, in three easy steps:

1. NBC doubles the money it's paying the league in order to renew its TV contract.

2. NBC raises the rates it charges sponsors to advertise on those NBA telecasts.

3. Sponsors must make up for these increased advertising costs by earning more money with their product, which means either selling more of it (if they're lucky) or selling it at a higher price (more likely).

So if the product that used to cost you $2.59 now costs $2.79, that's how you're indirectly paying for players' salaries.

Ticket prices represent just a small portion of the money taken in by the NBA and its teams. Most of the money comes from companies who want to be business partners with the NBA, whether through sponsorship agreements or licensing deals to sell NBA-identified products, and from television networks who want to broadcast NBA games so they can attract advertisers.

I'm not going to go into detail about how this works. All you really need to know is that more than 150 companies have licensing deals with the NBA to sell everything from Spalding NBA basketballs to Mattel WNBA Barbie dolls. Every time you see an NBA logo, an NBA team logo, or a team uniform on anything, whether it's a replica jersey, a $2,500 leather jacket, or a garbage can, some company paid the NBA money for the right to use its trademarks. And this means a whole lot of money for the league.

The same goes for corporate sponsorship. Why would a company like Coca-Cola want to pay several million dollars to become "the official soft drink of the NBA?" In addition to being able to use that catchy phrase in their advertising, they can build upon their relationship with the league because they get first crack at advertising on NBA telecasts, they can sponsor NBA events, and they can use NBA players, in uniform, in their commercials

Clyde's Tip

Being associated with something that's considered hip, cool, and happening like the NBA is some-thing companies strive for, and pay for. That's what sponsorship deals are all about.

(providing they sign up the players; the sponsorship just gives them the right to use the uniforms).

Then there's television. NBC and the Turner networks will pay a combined $2.64 billion to televise NBA games for the next four years, through the 2001–2002 season. I'll save you the trouble of doing the math: That comes to roughly $22 million per team, per year. To put that in perspective, remember that Charlotte, Miami, Minnesota, and Orlando paid just $32.5 million to join the league as expansion teams less than a decade ago.

Some Basics About the Salary Cap

In the early 1980s, when today's prosperity was merely a gleam in David Stern's eye, team owners and leaders of the players' union agreed on a plan for a *salary cap*, a maximum that each team could spend on player salaries, along with a minimum that each team would be required to spend. The idea was to give owners a handle on labor costs so they could run their teams in a more business-like fashion, which would benefit everyone in the long run.

And it has. The salary cap, pegged at $3.6 million per team in 1984–85 when it was introduced, has climbed to $26.9 million in 1997–98. To put that another way, the salary cap today is seven and a half times what it was 14 years ago.

Here's a look at how the NBA Salary Cap has grown over the years:

Clyde's Chalk Talk

The *salary cap* is the maximum a team can spend on player salaries in a given season. Signing bonuses are pro-rated over the course of a long-term contract. Unlike the NFL, which has a "hard" cap that teams may not exceed, the NBA has a "soft" cap which teams may go beyond under specific conditions, such as to re-sign their own players.

Year	Cap in Millions
1984–85	$3.60
1985–86	$4.23
1986–87	$4.93
1987–88	$6.16
1988–89	$7.23
1989–90	$9.80
1990–91	$11.87
1991–92	$12.50
1992–93	$14.00
1993–94	$15.18

continues

Year	Cap in Millions
1994–95	$15.96
1995–96	$23.00
1996–97	$24.30
1997–98	$26.90
1998–99	?????

Is it working? Well, it worked for awhile. Franchises became stronger and grew, owners prospered, and players shared in the prosperity more so than ever before. But I'm not sure it's still working—and more importantly, neither are the owners and the players, which is why they reopened negotiations toward a new contract last spring, which should produce a tense summer.

For one thing, nearly all teams are over the cap thanks to the provision that a team may re-sign its own players for any amount once their contracts expire and they become free agents. Thus Michael Jordan can be paid more by the Chicago Bulls than the amount that's supposedly the maximum the team can spend on salaries for all its players.

What has happened has been a widening of the gap between the players at the top of the salary scale and those at the bottom, and a squeezing out of the middle. If teams have to pay their stars anywhere from $10 million to $20 million a year, they look to compensate by loading their rosters with as many players as possible at the league's minimum salary, which is currently $272,500. The mid-level player becomes a luxury owners feel they can't afford, and many solid pros either lose their jobs or are asked to play for the minimum.

Clyde's Record Book

The guru of the NBA salary cap was Gary Bettman, now the commissioner of the National Hockey League. Bettman was the NBA's head lawyer when the cap was introduced, and for years many around the league felt he was the only one who fully understood its workings. In his office at the NBA Bettman had a baseball cap with the words NBA SALARY CAP on the bill.

This is a growing concern among the players, who also wonder why a salary cap is needed at all anymore, in light of the rich TV contracts and the marketing money that seems to be pouring in.

But the league paints a different picture, contending that player salaries have escalated so fast that they more than exceed the money coming in. There were reports circulating at the 1998 All-Star Weekend that more than half of the NBA's teams may actually lose money for the 1997–98 season. So the owners not only want to keep the salary cap, but sew up some of its loopholes—perhaps instituting a hard cap similar to that used in pro football, which a team cannot exceed.

Inside the League:
Team Offices

Does it really take nearly 900 people to run a basketball league?

Of course not. The NBA managed with an office of three people (a president, a PR man, and a secretary) when it started and maybe a couple of dozen when I was playing. But the NBA is no mom-and-pop operation anymore, with annual revenues in the billions, and it does far more than run a basketball league.

All those sponsorship and licensing deals don't just happen—people have to go out and sell corporate America on getting involved with the NBA. TV deals have to be negotiated. Contracts must be drawn up. Publicity must be generated.

As the NBA grew, it became an event producer, a sports marketing organization, a logo designer, and a video production house, using its facilities and expertise not only for its basketball business but to bring in some extra money on the side. For example, the league has a state-of-the-art TV studio in Secaucus, NJ, where it not only produces its own shows and commercials but does contract work for others.

The NBA has offices in New York and Secaucus, NJ, with nearly 30 departments ranging from basketball operations to consumer products, from events and attractions to NBA Entertainment.

In many instances, the NBA office coordinates activities that take place at the team offices. Each team, for example, has its own public relations staff to deal with publicity in its local market, and national publicity for that team. Assisting in the latter is the league's PR staff, which also handles league-wide publicity for the NBA.

Team office staffs have grown rapidly in recent years, because they must fulfill many of the same functions as the league office personnel, only on a local level. The NBA sells sponsorships to companies that want to be involved on a league-wide

Clyde's Tip

The NBA is technically a Limited Partnership owned equally by its 29 teams. The league office is run by a commissioner who reports to the Board of Governors, the owners of those 29 teams. Think of it as a company with a headquarters and 29 branches, each operating independently but within the same business.

Clyde's Record Book

Under Stern's stewardship, the NBA has become a global enterprise, with offices in Tokyo, Taiwan, Singapore, Melbourne, Toronto, London, Paris, Barcelona, and Mexico City, plus a Miami office serving Latin America. With NBA teams playing to over 90 percent of capacity, TV revenues at a peak, and sponsorship and licensing markets saturated, the league sees its greatest growth area as being outside the United States. Basketball is booming worldwide, thanks in part to the 1992 Dream Team, and while the NBA has no plans to put expansion teams outside North America, it has every hope of building its television, sponsorship, and licensing presence around the world.

basis; each team sells additional sponsorships to companies that want to be involved with specific teams.

Generally, responsibilities at the team level are split between basketball and business sides. The coaching and PR staffs are on the basketball side while the marketing and ticket sales people are on the business side.

Agents, the Union, and the Draft

I've explained how things work from the league and team perspective. Now let's look at some things from the players' point of view.

Agents Aren't Necessarily Evil

One of the first thing a prospective NBA player does, before he shoots his first basket as a pro, is hire an agent—a person or persons to handle his business and legal affairs, including contract negotiations with his team. An agent is paid a fixed percentage of the salary he negotiates for his client, and usually has legal and business advisors working with him to help his client keep his money and make it grow.

Some agents are flashy, their names in the papers all the time. Others are quiet, working behind the scenes. That's a matter of style, and neither one is right or wrong. The only thing that matters is how effectively an agent represents his client, the player. And this can't be measured just in terms of dollars, because at a certain point, the dollars don't mean much—what's really the difference between $10 million and $15 million?

The way to measure the effectiveness of an agent is to take a look and see how happy his client is. Some players would rather play in a small market, while others crave the major media centers. Some players can flourish in supporting roles while others must be the centers of attention. Some players will do anything to play for a winner, while others would prefer to be the big fish in a smaller pond, putting up impressive numbers but playing on a losing team. A good agent will know his client, recognize his needs and wants, and work to get them for him.

The best-known agent in the NBA today is David Falk, thanks to the brilliant job he has done with Michael Jordan. With Falk calling the shots behind the scenes, Jordan has transcended not only basketball but all of sports and become a cultural icon, marketing his own line of cologne and starring in a movie with Bugs

Clyde's Tip

Owners and management often will portray agents as greedy and evil; agents will throw the same charges back in their face. Don't get caught up in the rhetoric and the posturing; some of it is done for effect, other as a result of the heat of argument. The fact is that everybody is out to make money here—owners, players, and agents alike. Try to figure out for yourself how happy your favorite player seems. If he looks happy on TV and seems happy when you read about him in the papers, his agent is doing a good job.

Bunny, among other endeavors. Since success breeds success, Falk has many other prominent NBA clients, including Patrick Ewing and Juwan Howard.

The Players Association

The National Basketball Players Association is the players' union, responsible for negotiating a collective bargaining agreement with the league that establishes working conditions such as salary standards, medical and pension benefits, expense money, and other such matters. Each player is automatically a member of the union.

Confused about the difference between a player's negotiations with his team and the union's negotiations with the league? Think of it this way: The Players Association establishes the framework under which all players work, then each player negotiates his specific salary with his team.

The Players Association was formed in the early 1960s, with Tom Heinsohn of the Boston Celtics playing an instrumental role along with the NBPA's first Executive Director, Larry Fleisher. In those days players were not well-paid, to the point where many had to work offseason jobs to make ends meet. In addition, they were bound to their teams by a reserve clause—there was no such thing as free agency, so a player had little recourse but to accept whatever he was offered by his team.

The reserve clause was later struck down by the courts as illegal, because it prevented a player from offering his services to the highest bidder on an open market. Under Fleisher's leadership the union gradually won true free agency, first under limited circumstances that gave a player's old team a chance to match any offer or receive compensation for a player it lost, and more recently with much less stringent restrictions under the salary cap system described above. Fleisher served as Executive Director of the NBPA for more than two decades; the union today is led by Billy Hunter.

The Draft: Trying to Strengthen the Weak

The NBA Draft is a system for allocating incoming players among the league's teams. It is held annually, with teams selecting in inverse order of their won-lost records from the previous season. The idea of having the weaker teams pick first is an attempt by the league to increase competitiveness and parity throughout the NBA.

At first the draft was open only to players whose entering college class had graduated— in other words, a player had to wait four years from the time he entered college in order to turn pro. The league set it up this way because it saw the colleges as a natural farm system feeding polished players to the pros, and wanted both to stay on good terms with the colleges and to avoid any appearance of raiding the colleges for talent and to avoid conflict with the colleges for players.

In 1969, a player named Spencer Haywood, who would not have been eligible for the draft until 1971, filed a lawsuit claiming restraint of trade. He argued that he ought to be able to go out and make a living at any time, just like people in other fields. The courts agreed, and in order to keep some sort of draft, the league negotiated new terms with the Players Association that opened the draft to everyone. At first young players had to show evidence of financial hardship in order to be included, but that restriction too was quickly dropped and now the draft is basically open to anyone who notifies the NBA that he wants to turn pro.

In recent years, more and more college underclassmen have gone pro early—even some high school players are jumping directly to the NBA. I see this as a very danger-ous trend. Many 18-, 19-, or 20-year-olds are not ready, physically or psychologically, for life as a pro. They would be much better served by spending time in college, where they could adjust to being away from home and also compete at a high level. A player often has just one shot to make it in the NBA, and it's in his own best interest to be as prepared as possible when he takes that shot.

The influx of young players also has caused a big drop in fundamental execution all around the NBA. Players can't make free throws the way they used to. They don't pass as well, they don't box out for rebounds as well, and they don't shoot the mid-range jumper as well. When players had four years of college ball, they were taught the fundamentals and worked on them until they became part of their games. Now they come to the NBA early, and pro coaches say they don't have time to teach these players the basics they should have learned earlier—but maybe they'll have to make the time.

The Mighty "M" Word: Marketing

I've already explained how the ticket prices you pay make up only a fraction of the revenues taken in by the NBA and distributed among players, coaches, owners, and staff. TV money makes up another large chunk that fans can readily understand—the NBA provides programming that national networks and local stations pay for the right to air.

Another significant source falls under the umbrella term of marketing. This includes efforts to boost ticket sales and increase TV revenues; licensing the team's name and logo for use on products; and the sale of sponsorships to companies who wish to be associated with the team. While some of this marketing is done at the team level, many NBA licensing and sponsorship deals are made at the league-wide level, benefit-ing all teams equally.

Marketing is why teams change their logos and colors and come out with new uni-forms every few years. Uniform shorts and jerseys have made the leap from clothing players wear to fashion items sold to the public, and as such their sales must reflect the hottest colors and design elements. It's no coincidence that so many teams are wearing black, silver, and teal these days—these are the colors that sell in the stores, so more and more teams are adopting them.

Today's Arena: More Than a Place to Play

In the old days, teams played in whatever building was available. A team owner would work out a deal with the local municipal arena or perhaps a privately owned building, pay some rent that often included a percentage of ticket sales, and that was that.

Not anymore. Today's arenas are luxurious sports palaces that often cost hundreds of millions of dollars to build and bring in millions in revenues from sports and non-sports events like concerts, circuses, and ice shows. They often are multi-media entertainment centers, including food courts, shopping malls, luxury accommodations, state-of-the-art broadcast facilities—and oh yes, a court on which to play some basketball.

Many municipalities have become reluctant to allocate public money for arena construction and operation. The idea of using tax dollars to help rich owners and highly paid athletes is not very popular, and politicians who support such plans run the risk of being voted out of office. So more and more arenas are privately financed in part or in whole, which is a better deal for the owner with deep pockets because he then gets to keep more of the revenue that comes in from things like parking and concessions.

Arenas provide companies with attractive advertising opportunities. Think about it—you sit in a building for at least $2^{1}/_{2}$ hours watching a game in which there are 48 minutes of action, but what do you do the rest of the time? You look around at the signs in the building, you watch promotional events like halftime fan shootouts (sponsored by so-and-so), you read a game program or a yearbook with ads—you get the picture. Those courtside signs, particularly the ones facing the TV cameras, bring in big bucks and there's no shortage of companies wanting in on the action, which is why you'll see those signs rotate every few trips downcourt.

Luxury suites also bring in big bucks, often biggest of all. Detroit Pistons owner Bill Davidson ushered in a new era in 1988 when he built the suburban Palace of Auburn Hills, which contained three rings of more than 200 luxury suites, the lowest ring of which is barely a dozen rows above the court. Instead of boxes situated high above the other seats in the arena, which afforded privacy and comfort but a lousy view of the game, luxury suites now were in prime viewing locations and owners could justify charging ever-higher rates for them, bringing in the kind of money they claim they need to compete in today's environment of skyrocketing player salaries. Even perfectly serviceable arenas like the Forum in Los Angeles and Market Square Arena in Indianapolis are being phased out because of a lack of luxury suites.

The Least You Need to Know

➤ Basketball has become a big business, one that extends around the world.

➤ While the sky is the limit for star players' salaries, some pros at the middle and lower levels are getting squeezed out of jobs as owners look to control labor costs.

➤ A good agent can play a key role in a player's success and happiness by taking care of off-court matters for him.

➤ The National Basketball Players Association is the players' union, negotiating a collective bargaining agreement with the league that determines overall working conditions.

➤ Companies that want to be associated with the NBA are willing to pay big bucks for the privilege, which helps keep ticket prices just below your monthly mortgage bill.

Part 4
Basketball Strategy

As I've said before, basketball can be as simple or as complicated as you want it to be. That's one of the beauties of the game. This especially applies to basketball strategy. Teams with thick playbooks full of complicated plays don't necessarily win. In fact, there's a point of diminishing returns where the more plays you add and call from the bench, the more you confuse your players, stifle their creativity, and inhibit their play.

The greatest dynasty in NBA history, the Boston Celtics of the late 1950s and 1960s, ran maybe a half-dozen set plays. Everybody in the league knew what they were—most teams copied the plays and ran 'em themselves. Yet nobody could stop them because the Celtics ran them so well and because they had such great players. Look at the way today's Utah Jazz use the pick-and-roll. It's the simplest play in the game—every high school coach teaches his team how to run it and how to stop it. Everybody in the building knows it's coming, yet game after game the Jazz frustrate teams with it.

In this part, I'll discuss some basics of basketball strategy and why teams win. I'll look at both the offensive and defensive aspects of the game and some of my favorite players at each end of the court. Then I'll take a stab at answering 10 questions I often hear from fans.

Plan "A"

Chapter 15

Winning Isn't Everything, or the Only Thing, But It Sure Beats Losing

---

In This Chapter

➤ The keys to winning

➤ John Wooden's concept of threes

➤ Rebounding: you can't win if you don't have the ball

Winning isn't everything, or the only thing, but it sure beats losing.

Let's be honest: Nobody plays a game to lose. We compete—put ourselves on the line—because we love the feeling that comes with winning. Athletes are competitive by nature, and it's no coincidence that the best athletes are often the most intensely competitive. Exhibit A is Michael Jordan. He hates to lose, and it doesn't matter what the game is.

There is absolutely nothing like the feeling you get after your team has won the championship. I was fortunate enough to experience it twice with the Knicks, in 1970 and again in 1973. There is just no way to describe it. I'll never forget it.

What Makes a Winning Team?

The two keys to winning basketball are teamwork and defense.

If you have those two elements, all other things tend to work themselves out.

Defense Wins Championships

Although the object of the game is to score more points than the other team, it's not the act of scoring, but rather the act of preventing your opponent from scoring, that is the key to success. I firmly believe that winning teams are built upon defense rather than offense, and I think a look through the record book illuminates this point.

Quote...Unquote

"Bill Russell didn't give you anything on defense. He didn't want to give you a shot if you were underneath the basket or 15 feet away or 20 feet away. He has this great desire and pride to stop you and instincts that were amazing."—*Johnny "Red" Kerr, a rival NBA center.*

What was the most important element of the Boston Celtics dynasty? Not any dominant scorer; though Boston had many prolific point producers such as Tommy Heinsohn, Bill Sharman, Sam Jones, and John Havlicek, it has never featured an NBA scoring champion. The presence of Bill Russell as a shot-blocking anchor to the team's defense as well as a dominant rebounder propelled the Celtics' success. The year after Russell retired, the Celtics' record dropped by 14 wins, and they failed to make the playoffs. The team's poorer performance was a direct result of not having Russell around anymore to patrol the lane.

The Showtime Lakers of the 1980s, for all their offensive flash and dash, were a team built upon solid defense. Michael Cooper was a stopper who could guard anyone from a point guard to a power forward, whereas Kareem Abdul-Jabbar gave them a big man to protect the basket.

Defense has been key to the success of the Chicago Bulls in the 1990s. In Michael Jordan, Scottie Pippen, and Horace Grant, the Bulls had three of the best defensive players in the game. When Grant left, they eventually replaced him with Dennis Rodman, another outstanding defender and an extraordinary rebounder.

Good defense can be psychologically devastating to an opponent. Consider:

➤ You put on your best move only to find your defender right up in your face.

➤ You put up a series of fakes only to have your shot slapped away from the basket.

➤ You try to push the ball up the floor only to find your path blocked by your man.

➤ You attempt to pass to a seemingly open teammate only to have an opponent step into the passing lane and pick it off.

What could be more vexing? Great defense frustrates and devastates.

There's No "I" in Team

You can't build a winner without teamwork—five guys who play together as a team.

Teamwork is the key to effective offense. You don't win with one or two prolific scorers; you win consistently with a team that can score in many ways. Just about any individual can be shut down, but you can't contain a team that has many weapons and can beat you in several different ways. Diversity leads to prosperity.

Teamwork also is the key to effective defense. Players have to be ready, willing, and able to help their teammates on defense by switching over and picking up their men, stepping out and blocking their path to the basket, or sliding over and swatting away a shot in the lane. Effective traps and double-teams can disrupt a team's half-court offense, whereas well-executed presses can prevent a team from even getting into its offensive scheme.

Whatever the players do reflects what the coach is like. When you see unbridled players on the court throwing the ball all over the place and taking wild shots, that's the way the coach is. When you see players who are well-disciplined, altruistic, and team-oriented, it's a reflection of their coach.

A person's character is revealed in many ways. I can watch a team warming up and tell whether the players are team-oriented.

Character was big with my former coaches. You had to be a person of good character. It helped to be a good player, but character overruled that. Many guys didn't play because they lacked the kind of good character that makes a person a good team-mate and a good leader.

I grew up in Atlanta under segregation. The older people were very cognizant of who you represented—not just you, but the entire black race. It was instilled in us as youngsters. So you had to carry yourself in a positive way that made you a good example.

A strong work ethic also evolved from the older people's direction. They kept telling us you had to be twice as good as the other guy and never to rest on your laurels. I'd score 20 or 25 points in a high school game, and the coach would tell me about some white guy across town doing the same thing and how I had to do better. It was the carrot coaches and other mentors dangled in front of you to keep you motivated and keep you from becoming complacent.

Clyde's Tip

I always had coaches who were team-oriented. They only had one set of rules: If you didn't play defense, you didn't play; and if you didn't play team ball, you weren't on the team. We had guys in high school who could score 20 or 25 points a game on the playground, but they were not on our school team because they were individuals who could not play team ball. And for our coaches that wasn't good enough. So don't be a gunner or a ball-hog when you're trying out for your team—coaches look for players who know the value of teamwork.

Quote...Unquote

"I wanted players to play hard, play together and to play the team game. I also wanted to help them by constructing an approach that would utilize their talents best. Coaching is like conducting an orchestra, getting all the parts to play in harmony so that what comes out of all those instruments is a pleasing sound, a positive, beautiful sound."—*Dr. Jack Ramsay, a Hall of Fame coach who won an NBA championship with the 1977 Portland Trail Blazers.*

It was the same thing with grades. I always heard how I needed to improve, "You can't go to a big school if you don't make the grades." I heard that at home—from my parents and grandparents. You know how they say it takes an entire village to raise a child? It was that way with me. I was lucky because nobody would let me drink or smoke or do anything like that. They said, "Hey, you're going to be a ballplayer. You can't do that." Teachers, my mom, neighbors—there was a whole community to keep me in line and make sure I never let down my guard. They made sure I developed a positive, strong character that would serve me in basketball and in life.

John Wooden's Concept of Threes

John Wooden, the Wizard of Westwood who coached UCLA to 10 national championships and 20 Pac 10 titles, had an interesting way of looking at basketball.

He saw it as a game of threes:

➤ Forward, guard, center

➤ Shoot, drive, pass

➤ Ball, you, man

➤ Conditioning, skill, teamwork

The meaning of the first group of threes is obvious: the three basic positions in the game. The second group covers the three fundamental skills you need on offense—shooting, driving (which includes dribbling), and passing.

John Wooden, a member of the Basketball Hall of Fame as both a player and a coach, guided the UCLA Bruins to 10 NCAA championships.
Associated Press

That third group reminds me of what my coach on the Knicks, Red Holzman, always emphasized: "See the ball!" He meant that any time you are playing defense, you must see the ball and your man simultaneously, creating the "ball, you, man" triangle that Wooden was talking about. Usually guys see their man; by constantly telling us to "See the ball!", Red was emphasizing that you must be aware of the ball as well, or you're vulnerable to backdoor plays and just being a step slow on defense.

The last group of threes represents the foundation of what Wooden called his Pyramid of Success, and I couldn't agree more. Conditioning and teamwork are every bit as important as skill when it comes to winning basketball.

The Value of Rebounding

You can't score and win if you don't have the ball, and you get the ball by rebounding.

Rebounding requires perseverance and resiliency—a willingness to mix it up under the basket and take your lumps to get your hands on the ball. It helps to be tall and able to leap through the roof, but that won't make you a resourceful rebounder. You need a willingness to pound the glass, quickness in getting to missed shots, and also an attitude of invincibility, that nothing will keep you away from the ball.

You need tenacity and audacity to bound and astound.

Why is rebounding important? Because over the long haul, team shooting percentages tend to be similar. Most NBA teams shoot between 43 and 47 percent from the field, with a few exceptions at both ends. So if teams are going to make roughly the same percentage of shots, it stands to reason that the team that attempts more shots will have an advantage. And outrebounding your opponent will lead to more shot opportunities, as long as you don't give the ball back on turnovers.

Quote...Unquote

"Every time a shot goes up, I believe the rebound is mine. I really believe it. I go after every ball because I believe it belongs to me."—*Moses Malone, three-time NBA MVP and six-time rebounding champion.*

Clyde's Tip

Check out the boxscores in your newspaper. Look at the figures under total rebounds for both teams. Chances are the team with more rebounds won the game.

Clyde's Tip

When a shot is taken, instead of watching the flight of the ball, try watching what's going on near the basket. The battle for rebounding position among the game's big men is fascinating and will make you appreciate the physical nature of the game.

Moses Malone, who won an NBA Championship with Philadelphia in 1983, was among the most effective offensive rebounders of all time because of his tenacity. Associated Press

Positioning is vital to success in rebounding. You must be smart enough to get good rebounding position, which generally means being between your man and the basket so that you'll have first crack at a shot as it bounces off the rim. You also must be strong enough to hold that position after you get it because you can be sure your opponent is going to try to push you out of the way.

This positioning is known as boxing out, and it's a lost art today. It used to be one of the basics, but today's players are all caught up in athleticism and jumping ability and don't pay enough attention to fundamentals such as boxing out. They think all they have to do to get rebounds is be able to jump, and they're wrong.

It's easy to overlook the importance of strength in rebounding. A player who is not strong enough to maintain his position and hold off his man under the basket will not be a good rebounder. And after he grabs the ball, he must be strong enough to hold onto it amidst the crashing bodies and flailing arms.

After positioning, which includes the strength needed to maintain position, the most important quality for a rebounder is quickness to the ball. Knowing when to jump is more important than how high you can jump. A player should grab a rebound at the top of his jump, using his elbows, shoulders, and body to shield the ball from his man.

Although most rebounds are grabbed by a team's center or power forward, it helps if every player can rebound because it takes the pressure off the big men, especially at the defensive end of the court.

Rebounding is divided into two categories— offensive rebounding, or going after your own missed shots while you are on offense, and defensive rebounding, or going after an opponent's missed shots while you are on defense.

Quickness is more important than strength in offensive rebounding because generally you start out in poor rebounding position—with your man between you and the basket. It's not a matter of using your strength to stay in good position, you have to use your quickness to get out of bad

Clyde's Chalk Talk

Offensive rebounding means trying to get your own team's missed shots for another chance at scoring. *Defensive rebounding* means going after the opposing team's missed shots, so that they have just one opportunity to score. Both are important to a team's success.

Clyde's Record Book

Today's rebounding statistics aren't as impressive as in the past. Wilt Chamberlain and Bill Russell averaged more than 22 rebounds a game for their careers, whereas today you won't find more than a handful of players at 10 rebounds a game in any given season. There are two reasons for the difference: Today's teams take far fewer shots per game, and they make a higher percentage of their shots. The result is fewer rebounding opportunities and lower rebounding stats.

position. When a shot is launched, a good offensive rebounder will try to anticipate which direction it will go if it misses and try to beat his man to that spot on the court, which is where quickness comes into play.

One player on the court has an advantage over all the others when it comes to offensive rebounding and can be most effective. That's the shooter. He often knows as soon as he releases the ball whether it is going to be off target and in what direction the rebound likely will bounce. For example, in the key play of Game 2 of the 1998 NBA Finals, Steve Kerr attempted a three-point shot that missed. But he knew where the rebound likely would go, and even though he was the smallest player on the floor, he followed up his shot, got the rebound and passed it to Michael Jordan for a vital basket. Kerr's play emphasizes why coaches are always telling their players to follow their own shots and go to the basket, even if they're not otherwise strong rebounders.

The Least You Need to Know

➤ Defense wins championships, in basketball as well as other sports such as baseball and football.

➤ Teamwork and character, which are fostered by discipline, are key elements for success in basketball as well as in life.

➤ Rebounding is the blue-collar job of basketball and lays the foundation for a winning team.

Chapter 16

Offensive Basketball

In This Chapter

➤ Teamwork: five egos must share one ball

➤ Taking care of the rock

➤ Good shots, bad shots

➤ To run or not to run, that is the question

➤ When five-on-five becomes one-on-one

➤ End-game strategy

➤ My favorite offensive players

The basics of offensive basketball are simple, but the real fun comes when you begin to understand the subtleties of why one player or team succeeds when another does not.

The goal in basketball is to score more points than the opposing team. Because it's much easier to score when you are not closely guarded than when you are covered like a blanket, the goal in offensive basketball is to create open shots for yourself or your teammates.

Some players are so talented offensively that they can create open shots on their own. Michael Jordan or Grant Hill can take the ball facing an opponent, use a variety of dribbles and fakes, and all of a sudden shake himself free for an open shot at the basket. This is known as creating your own shot, and only a select few players in the NBA can do this consistently.

More often you need a little help from your friends. Two, three, or even five players, moving precisely and passing the ball crisply between them, will eventually shake somebody free for an open shot. That's because the offensive player always has the basic advantage of knowing where he's going and where the ball is going, whereas the defender does not and must rely on his ability to react. That always puts the offensive player at least a half-step ahead, and often that's all he needs.

In this chapter, I'll talk about the importance of teamwork, of taking care of the ball, and of getting good shots at the basket, and how this is done. Without getting too technical, I'll look at the two basic types of offense, the running game and the set-up offense, and tell you what to look for in both. I'll also tip my cap to the offensive players I most enjoy watching and describe why I feel they are special.

Five Egos Must Share One Ball and One Goal

Basketball is a team sport, and the best offense operates smoothly as a team.

This sounds simple, but you'd be amazed how many players are baffled by it.

That's because basketball is also an individual sport—one-on-one, me against you, take it to the hoop and show me what you got. Anybody who has ever picked up a basketball has been in that position. Let's face it: It's energizing and revitalizing to beat your man to the basket.

Problems arise when players start to let that ego boost get in the way of the team goal. A player can get so caught up in his individual duel, in trying to prove what he can do on his own, that he loses sight—literally and figuratively—of his teammates.

A hallmark of the Knicks teams I played on was our teamwork. With player movement and ball movement, we got the most out of each other's skills. It really became a case where the whole was greater than the sum of the individual parts.

This was true even after Earl Monroe, one of the unique one-on-one players in basketball history, joined our team from Baltimore. He understood what we were all about, which was winning as a team, and was willing to subjugate his own game for the good of the team. It helped that he'd already proven his prowess as an individual talent when he was in Baltimore because now he put winning above all else. That's why he fit in so well with us.

Clyde's Tip

Look for signs of ego overload when you're watching a game. A player may get scored on and take it personally, so he'll try to come back on offense and beat that man one-on-one. But in doing so, he neglects what has been working for his team, he stops functioning as part of a unit, and, invariably, his team suffers. Even if he does beat his man once or twice, the rest of the team gets so out of rhythm that the overall impact is negative.

Treat the Rock Like a Diamond

On the playground, you'll often hear the ball referred to as "the rock"—as in "I'm open, gimme the rock!"

I like to think of that rock as a diamond, and I know many coaches wish their players thought the same way.

Because you can't score if you don't have the ball, it stands to reason that you should try to take care of the ball after you get it. A *turnover* is when you give up the ball without getting off a shot attempt—something you want to avoid.

Coaches constantly preach against turnovers. Bringing the ball downcourt and then turning it over before you can attempt a shot is a wasted opportunity. Too many squandered opportunities will cost you the ball game.

A certain number of turnovers is acceptable because a player has to be creative and take chances to be effective. If all a guy does is make the safe pass, he's not turning the ball over, but he's also not helping his team much. Sometimes a player has to force the issue and put pressure on the defense with a riskier pass. This might result in a few more turnovers, but if the player knows what he's doing, those will be outweighed by the baskets they'll produce.

Think of those passes as calculated risks, which are essential to success in any field. That's why Pat Riley didn't mind most of Magic Johnson's turnovers; he knew the creativity that lay behind them was essential to the Lakers' success.

Here's another example of where calculated risks paid off. In 1989–90, Isiah Thomas led the NBA in turnovers with 322. He also led the Detroit Pistons to their second consecutive NBA Championship.

Clyde's Record Book

Sometimes, I'll admit, one-on-one shootouts can be spectacular. I remember one in the playoffs several years ago between Larry Bird of Boston and Dominique Wilkins of Atlanta, when it seemed that neither one could miss in the fourth quarter. They went back and forth, bang, bang, like two gunfighters in the Old West. Dominique outscored Larry, but Boston won the game. So I guess you could say, Dominique won the battle but lost the war.

Clyde's Chalk Talk

A *turnover* is when the offensive team loses the ball to the defensive team without taking a shot. This happens when a player makes a bad pass that is intercepted or goes out of bounds, or is sloppy with his dribbling so the other team can take the ball away. An offensive foul also results in a turnover because the offending team must give control of the ball to the team that was fouled.

Clyde's Record Book

In what seems a paradox, some of the best ballhandlers in NBA history have committed the most turnovers. Isiah Thomas, Magic Johnson, and John Stockton all rank among the top five in career turnovers. But it makes sense, when you think about it, because they had the ball in their hands so much of the time. These three guards handled the ball so much, they were bound to commit some turnovers. (By the way, the NBA didn't start keeping track of turnovers until the 1977–78 season, so most of mine went unrecorded!)

Quote...Unquote

"Any time you're focusing on unorthodox maneuvers, a lot of them are not going to work. The thing to remember if you're an athlete is not to be insecure just because a couple backfire. Don't be inhibited or frightened by throwing a few away, because eventually your talent will come to the fore."—*Bob Cousy, Hall of Fame guard of the Boston Celtics.*

And he was voted the MVP of the NBA Finals even though he committed 25 turnovers in the series, more than any other player.

So what coaches really look for, and what you should look for as a fan, is not the total number of turnovers but the types of turnovers. If a player is trying to beat a defense with a tough pass, and it's a good gamble within the context of the game situation, it's one thing if the pass goes awry. If a player throws a lazy pass that's intercepted or a sloppy one that goes out of bounds without really trying to accomplish anything, that's an entirely different matter.

One statistic more meaningful than total turnovers in judging effective ballhandling is the assist-to-turnover ratio—the number of assists a player accumulates compared with the number of turnovers he commits. This measures productivity and gives a player credit for making good plays instead of just penalizing him for poor plays.

The most efficient point guards in the NBA will compile assist-to-turnover ratios of 3-1 or better. Long-time Charlotte Hornets guard Tyrone "Muggsy" Bogues, at 5'3" the shortest player in NBA history, is the league's career leader in assist-to-turnover ratio with a mark of nearly 5-1. Utah's John Stockton is next at nearly 4-1.

Give Me Your Best Shot

Invariably, the team that takes more good shots wins the game.

Obvious, right? It seems basic, but again this fact tends to get lost amidst all the details.

What's a good shot? The easy answer is any shot that goes in. It's like the coach who jumps off the bench and screams "No! No! No!" when a guy puts up a 30-foot off-balance shot in traffic and then changes it to "Yeah! Great shot!" when the ball goes in. As long as it finds the bottom of the net, it's a good shot—no matter how bad it looked when it left the shooter's hands.

Seriously, I think a good shot should measure up to three criteria:

➤ It should be within a player's comfort zone, a shot he regularly takes and makes.

➤ It should come within the framework of the team's offense (except for a bail-out when the shot clock is running down).

➤ It should make sense within the context of the game.

Let's look at each of these yardsticks.

A good shot is one a player is comfortable taking. It's one he practices regularly and makes most of the time, whether or not he's being guarded. The type of shot varies from player to player. Some players can hit hook shots; some can't. Some can turn around and shoot; others must start by facing up to the basket. Some can shoot from long distances; others must be near the basket. The bottom line is if a player shoots a shot he's comfortable with, he has a much better chance of making it than if it's outside his comfort zone.

A good shot springs from within the team offense. If a team plays a running game, it might be a layup or a spot-up jumper off the fast break. If a team likes to run specific patterns, the shot that comes at the end of that pattern figures to be a good one. Shots don't occur in vacuums. They all take place within the context of team play, and good shots are ones that come naturally from that context.

Finally, a good shot makes sense according to the score and time of game. If your team is ahead late in the game, you might be better off passing up a seemingly easy shot and instead running some time off the clock, so that your opponent won't have a chance to catch up. If the other team has just scored two or three quick baskets, you might want to take your time before you attempt a shot to slow down their momentum.

Getting the shooter the ball when he wants it, where he wants it, and how he wants it are all important to setting up a good shot.

Some players like to catch and shoot without taking a dribble, whereas others prefer to catch the

Clyde's Tip

Turnovers have a parallel in tennis, where you have forced errors—a player hits the ball out while trying to make a tough shot—and unforced errors—a player hits the ball out without really trying to make much of a shot. The forced errors are the calculated risks—you're trying to hit a winner, you figure out what the margin of error is, and decide whether to take a chance. If your calculations are good, you'll succeed. That's the way any aspiring star has to think.

Clyde's Tip

When a team gets possession of the ball with less than 24 seconds left in the quarter, the coach usually will hold up one finger and call out, "One shot!" He wants his team to hold onto the ball and not shoot it until the clock is approaching zero. That way, even if the shot misses, the other team won't have enough time to come back and score. A shot taken with 15 seconds left is often a bad shot because the other team has time to score before the quarter ends.

ball, dribble once or twice, and then shoot. Just about every player has his favorite spots on the floor, those places where his shot is virtually automatic to go in. Players prefer one side or the other. Some prefer to be along the baseline, whereas others like to shoot from around the top of the key. Some players prefer to shoot off a pass that comes straight to them; others prefer a bounce pass that comes up. Still others like a lead pass that makes them move to a spot on the floor before shooting.

All these things go into getting off a good shot. A good point guard understands this and knows the preferences of his teammates. He'll keep them happy by giving them the ball when they want it, where they want it, and how they want it. Then it's up to them to finish the play.

Band on the Run

To run or not to run, that is the question every team must answer in developing its offense. When is it best to push the ball up the floor quickly and try to play at a fast tempo, and when is it best to slow things down and fall back into a patterned (planned or set-up) offense?

It's really no question at all. Every coach loves to run and every fan loves to watch a team that runs. Unfortunately, not every team has players suited for a running game.

Clyde's Tip

To play a running game, a team must have a quick guard who loves to run and makes good decisions on the run. That's why it's so important that point guards show dexterity off the dribble and handle the ball smoothly with both hands. The mechanics must be second nature, so that a player can concentrate on making the right choices while the game is being played at a fast tempo.

The idea behind a running game is to move the ball toward the basket quickly, before the defense has time to adjust and get set up. This often leads to manpower advantages, such as two-on-one or three-on-two, and that can create open shots, the kind coaches strive for.

Every coach likes to have a team that can run at least once in awhile. You need some of those easy shots over the course of a game. Otherwise, you have to rely on a slower, patterned offense to create every shot opportunity, which is much more difficult.

But a team can be successful playing a set-up offense if it is disciplined. If players know and accept their roles and can be relied on to do what they're supposed to do, a half-court offense can be very effective. Teamwork, precise ball movement, and constant player movement without the ball all can wear down an opponent. Former Celtic, John Havlicek, and one of my old teammates, Bill Bradley, were known for wearing out their opponents by their perpetual motion on the court. Both were effective within the set-up offense.

Clyde's Rules

Remember that playing a running game is only a means to an end. You don't get any bonus style points just for running. The object is to get good shots at the basket, and if a running game helps a team accomplish this, then it should run. If playing a running game only leads to confusion, poor decisions, and sloppy play, it should not be played.

Pat Riley had players suited for a running game in Los Angeles. Kareem Abdul-Jabbar was the dominating center for rebounds, and Magic Johnson was the player to race the ball up the court and then pass it off to players such as Norm Nixon, Byron Scott, Jamaal Wilkes, and James Worthy for baskets. So Riley's Lakers played a running game.

When he came to New York, Riley found a team not suited to running. The team was built around Patrick Ewing and Charles Oakley, two slower players who are better suited to a half-court offense. There was no point guard like Magic and no players who could get out and fill the lanes on the break like those Laker teams had. So Riley's Knicks played at a slower tempo, using a set-up, ball-control offense.

Now, in Miami, Riley is trying to come up with a combination of the two styles. Some of his players, especially star center Alonzo Mourning, are better suited to a slower, patterned offense. But Riley also knows how much the easy shots that come out of a running game can mean to a team, so he has tried to get the Heat to push the ball up whenever they have the opportunity.

Clyde's Tip

Another thing to look for if a team is to succeed at a running game is a center who can rebound and fire an outlet pass to get the break going. The outlet pass is thrown quickly to a guard who should already be near midcourt, and it should hit him in stride so that he can keep running toward the basket. Wes Unseld, a Hall of Famer who played for the Bullets, was among the best ever at throwing strong, accurate outlet passes.

So the question of whether to run ultimately should be decided by the skills of the players on the team.

The best teams can be effective either way.

When Five-on-Five Becomes One-on-One

You know the line about how the best-laid plans often go awry? That happens in basketball, too—rather frequently, I might add.

A play might look impressive when it's drawn up on paper or a chalkboard, with Xs and Os and solid lines and dotted lines. But in real life, what are the chances of all 10 players on the court moving along the exact paths that correspond to the lines on the diagram? You got it: slim to none. All five offensive players would have to remember their assignments perfectly and run them in precise coordination with each other, and all five defenders would have to react exactly as expected by the offensive team. Not likely.

Also, there are no secrets when it comes to basketball plays. The movement of coaches and players from one team to another, plus the sophisticated scouting available thanks to video and computers, makes it impossible for a team to keep a play all to itself.

Virtually all plays involve picks, or screens, where an offensive player tries to shed his defender by running him into a pick set by a teammate. I've already described many of these plays, such as the pick-and-roll or the give-and-go, in Chapter 5.

Clyde's Tip

Watch how a team reacts when one of its plays doesn't work. Is there any sign of confusion or panic? Do the players regroup and run another play in the time remaining on the shot clock? Or do they run an isolation play, where they give the ball to one player and clear enough space so that he can work one-on-one against a defender? How well the players react when things don't go right says a lot about a team.

But what happens when things go awry? What does a team do when a play doesn't work?

Usually, there are several options to make any play pay off, and if a defense takes away the first option, a team should be able to swing over to a second option pretty easily. If there is enough time left on the shot clock, another option is to bring the ball back out and run a new play—what we call *resetting the offense*. But because there might not be much time left, often all a team can do is dump the ball in to its center and let him use his pivot moves. Shaquille O'Neal of the Lakers, Hakeem Olajuwon of the Rockets, and Patrick Ewing of the Knicks are especially effective in this manner.

Another option that doesn't take much time is to isolate one offensive player against one defender on the outside and let the offensive player try to drive to the basket or work his way free for an open jumper. This is when five-on-five basketball reduces to one-on-one, and it happens in every game. Each team has one or two players it likes to fall back on and use in just such an isolation situation.

Some teams, such as the Detroit Pistons with Grant Hill, run frequent isolation plays in their half-court offense to take advantage of an especially gifted player. They try to force an opponent into double-teaming Hill, which leaves someone else open for a quick pass and shot.

Clyde's Rules

For an isolation play to work, an offensive team needs proper spacing on the court. Teammates must be far enough away from the player with the ball so that he has enough room to operate one-on-one. Should the defense then elect to double-team, if the offensive players are properly spaced somebody should be open for a quick pass and shot.

A team must simply pick its poison when considering whether to run isolation plays, and sometimes there is no correct choice, as Michael Jordan showed the Utah Jazz in the 1997 NBA Finals. He beat them in Game 1 with a shot when they chose not to double-team him, and he beat them in Game 6 with a pass when they elected to double-team. As Utah coach Jerry Sloan found out, there are times when you're damned if you do and damned if you don't.

End-Game Strategy: How to Make Time Stand Still

The last two minutes of an NBA game can take 10 or 15 minutes of real time to complete. That's because smart coaches conserve their timeouts in case the game is close down the stretch.

Not only do they get to stop the clock and discuss strategy with their players, they can gain a territorial advantage as well. Under NBA rules a team that calls an immediate timeout upon gaining possession of the ball in the final two minutes of a game may inbound the ball from midcourt rather than from under its own basket, thus saving the precious seconds it takes to advance the ball into the offensive zone.

Let's say you get possession with two seconds on the clock. If you have to go the length of the court, it's unlikely you'll be able to get off a good shot unless you happen to complete a very long inbounds pass (which is unlikely but does occasionally happen—Duke fans remember Christian Laettner taking just such a pass from Grant Hill and beating Kentucky in an NCAA playoff game not long ago. But if you can throw your inbounds pass from midcourt directly into the offensive zone, you're much more likely to get it to a player in good shooting position. With two seconds on the clock he has time to catch the ball and perhaps dribble once or fake his defender out of position before taking his shot—keep in mind that as long as the shot has left a player's hand, it still counts even if time expires before it goes through the basket.

Remember that in order to call a timeout, a team must have possession of the ball or the clock already must be stopped, as when a player commits a foul or the ball goes out of bounds. The defensive team cannot randomly call a timeout just to stop the clock. Therefore, if a team has a lead late in the game, it is wise to run as much time as possible off the 24-second shot clock before attempting a shot at the basket. That gives the opposing team less time in which to try to score and catch up.

A team trailing late in the game often goes to a pressure defense to try to force turnovers that will give it a chance to cut into the lead. That's why the team with the lead will usually have its best ballhandlers on the court late in the game, even if that means going with a lineup of three, four, or even five guards. The most important thing at that stage of the game is to protect the ball and not give the other team chances to catch up.

Often the trailing team, unable to create turnovers, finds itself with no recourse but to commit fouls. Although this puts the opponent at the foul line with a chance to increase its lead, it stops the clock and the trailing team gets the ball back after the successful free throws. Even if the team in the lead makes both free throw attempts, the trailing team can cut into the margin by coming back and making a three-point field goal.

Naturally, the trailing team will try to foul the opponent's worst free throw shooter in these late-game situations, hoping he'll miss one or both of his attempts. That's why it's vital for a coach whose team is ahead to make sure he has his best free throw shooters on the floor, even if it creates an unorthodox lineup.

My Favorite Offensive Players

Obviously, I'm partial to guards, and I played against two of the best: Jerry West and Oscar Robertson, consummate players who had no weaknesses. They could beat you from inside or outside, by driving or shooting jumpers, in a running game or a half-court game. And they could adjust to anything the defense tried to do to stop them—they always seemed to have another way to beat you.

Another omnipotent offensive player, whom I played both against and with, was Earl Monroe. When he was with Baltimore, the Pearl was known for his shaking and baking, driving and jiving. He had more moves than anybody and loved to put on a show. When he came to New York, he had to tone that down to fit into our offensive scheme, and to his credit, he made the adjustment and helped us win a championship.

Some players are just so good with one move that they cannot be stopped. Kareem Abdul-Jabbar was that way with his sky-hook, which was the single most potent weapon in basketball history. When he got the ball in the low post, he could not be stopped because he could wheel in either direction or go away from the basket to get off his sky-hook, and he shot it from so high up that it could not be blocked.

Hakeem Olajuwon of the Houston Rockets is very effective with his spin moves out of the low post, what have become known as the Dream Shake. He's so quick and agile, he's tough to defend.

Speaking of centers, I'd be remiss if I didn't mention Wilt Chamberlain. He was the unstoppable force going to the basket, the only Superman to play the game.

Lenny Wilkens is now the coach of the Atlanta Hawks, but many young fans don't know what a great guard he was in his playing days, especially with the St. Louis Hawks in the 1960s. He was the best at going to his left. In fact, he could only go left—he knew it, opponents knew it, everyone in the arena knew it—but nobody could stop him. It was uncanny the way he was able to slice and dice you going to his left, even though you knew it was coming.

Michael Jordan, of course, belongs among the elite. Early in his career he was unstoppable driving to the basket, and as the years went by he developed a jump shot out to three-point range. That perimeter shooting made him much more effective and probably added several years to his career, if only because he can avoid the pounding he takes every time he takes it to the hoop.

Larry Bird of the Celtics and Magic Johnson of the Lakers were outstanding offensive players because of their versatility. They could beat you so many ways.

Finally, another guy I'd like to mention is the Mailman of the Utah Jazz, Karl Malone. I really respect his game. He and John Stockton, because of their longevity together, have developed a unique kind of offensive ESP. They instinctively know what's going to happen and what the other is going to do, and that's the essence of an effective offense.

The Least You Need to Know

➤ Teamwork is essential for a cohesive offense.

➤ Taking care of "the rock" (the ball) is very important, but a playmaker must not be too conservative, either.

➤ A good shot for one player is a bad shot for another; game situations also help determine whether a shot is wise or ill-advised.

➤ Some players are better-suited for a running game than a slower, half-court set offense. A shrewd, sagacious coach will design his offense around the skills of his players.

Chapter 17

Defensive Basketball

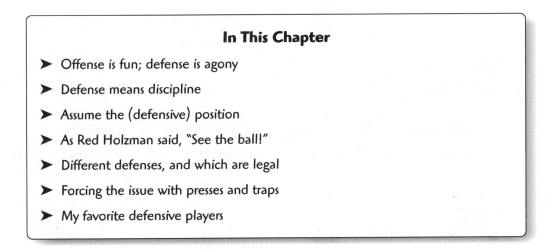

In This Chapter

➤ Offense is fun; defense is agony

➤ Defense means discipline

➤ Assume the (defensive) position

➤ As Red Holzman said, "See the ball!"

➤ Different defenses, and which are legal

➤ Forcing the issue with presses and traps

➤ My favorite defensive players

If the object of the game is to score more points than the other team, one way to do that is by preventing the other team from scoring. And that's where defense comes in.

The best shooters in basketball miss about half their shots overall. If left unguarded, however, their percentage goes way up. A good shooter at the NBA level should be able to make 70 or 80 percent—or more—of his open shots. I say "should" because some of today's young players don't measure up to that standard. While growing up, they were too mesmerized by video clips showing fancy dunks and razzle-dazzle moves to practice something mundane like shooting, and as a result they don't measure up to players of a generation ago—at least in this one area.

But I digress into one of my pet peeves. My original point is that it's infinitely easier to sink a shot when you are open than when you are closely guarded. A good defender will make sure that a shooter has no open space in which to get off his shot and will have to contend with a hand or two in his face (and perhaps a little nudge in his hip as well). Though occasionally a hot shooter will sink his shot no matter how tightly he's guarded, aggressive, persistent defense invariably sends shooting percentages plummeting.

Good defense, however, involves more than just harassing a shooter. Good defense makes life difficult for the offensive team every step of the way by contesting everything, from putting the ball in play to bringing it upcourt to passing it from one player to the next. Defense can be a devastating weapon, both physically and psychologically. Think how frustrated an offense is going to feel going into the fourth quarter if its every move has been hounded over the first three quarters.

In this chapter, I'll discuss what makes for good defensive play, both by individuals and as a team. I'll also discuss the two basic types of defense played in basketball, which are man-to-man and zone. Even though zones are illegal in the NBA, they are common in college, high school, and women's ball, and the principles behind an effective zone are often incorporated into defenses used in the NBA. I'll also look at some of the defensive trickery you might want to watch for and pay homage to some of my favorite defensive players.

Don't Expect Headlines for Playing Defense

Playing offense is fun. Name a player who doesn't like to pick up a ball and shoot it. Even Dennis Rodman has been known to launch a three-pointer every now and then.

Defense, on the other hand, is hard work. And don't expect kudos for it, either.

When you pick up the paper, the articles hardly ever mention defense. When the average aficionado looks to see what happened in a game, he invariably looks at who scored. The scorers get the adulation. It's rare when the defensive standout even gets a mention, although Scottie Pippen changed that a bit in recent NBA Finals.

In baseball they used to say that home run hitters drive Cadillacs. In basketball, the high scorers drive the fancy cars (probably Porsches rather than Cadillacs) and get all the attention.

Defense gets less attention because it's intangible. It's mundane. Look at Charles Oakley, formerly of the Knicks. His stats every night are about 10 points, 10 rebounds—nothing special, but he does it on D. He plays the kind of pounding, physical defense that really takes its toll and frustrates opponents. The stat sheet won't reflect that.

Quote...Unquote

"The art of defense is really an art based on hard work."—*Bill Russell, the Hall of Fame center of the Boston Celtics who revolutionized defense in the NBA with his shot-blocking skills.*

Charles Oakley (34) uses his strength to keep Dennis Rodman away from the basket and maintain position for a defensive rebound, one of the many little ways he helps his team. Associated Press

When Red Holzman took over as coach of the Knicks back in the 1960s, he said he was going to focus on defense and teamwork. We had some talented players, but some weren't prepared for the tenacity that goes into playing defense. I was about the only guy who was happy. Defense was my forte. I loved defense. I saw the situation as my opportunity to get more playing time, and I relished the thought.

My attitude toward defense stems from my college days. After my sophomore season, I was ineligible to play because of poor grades. So every day in practice I was placed on the "scout" team and had to play defense against the regulars. It was sort of a punishment by the coaches, never letting me play offense.

Now, I didn't blame the coach for my grades or get angry at him for putting me on defense. I just said I'm going to be the best damn defensive player I can be. The way I got back was by playing tenacious defense. I'd have the guys on the scout team all revved up, and we'd create havoc with our defense. Finally the coach would say, "Frazier, sit down so we can get something done on offense." Now guys who were on the team tell me they dreaded playing against us because of the way we attacked them on defense. I take that as quite a tribute.

Defense = Discipline

I'll keep this short and sweet.

You must be disciplined to play good defense. Discipline to me is everything. If you don't have discipline, you don't have anything.

No one particular skill is needed to play good defense. It helps to be quick, that's for sure, and it also helps to have a good sense of anticipation for what is about to happen on the court.

But what you really need most is an old fashioned blue-collar work ethic. Defense consists of hard work and a lot of hustle. And that stems from discipline.

You Play Defense with Your Feet and Head, Not Your Hands

It's a common misconception that you must have quick hands to play good defense. What you really need are quick feet rather than quick hands, and a strong court sense to know how to use them.

Defense is about positioning rather than reaching and grabbing. If you can maintain good defensive position, which generally places you between your man and the basket, that's half the battle. You also want to maneuver your opponent to a place on the court where he is less comfortable—if he likes to go to his right, you overplay him in that direction and force him to go left, where he's less comfortable and less dangerous. That's all part of defensive positioning.

Anticipation and footwork help you establish and maintain good position on defense. If you can anticipate what a team is going to try to do on offense, you can get into position to stop it. And if you have good footwork, you can maintain that position.

As far as footwork goes, you start by mastering the stagger stance. Your feet are shoulder-width apart, the same as if I'm going to punch you, to get some momentum. You never want to cross your feet and you never want to have a parallel stance. You want to slide, slide, slide along with your man. Once you cross your feet, you're beaten.

You should have your butt down and your head up. Most guys try to play defense standing straight up, which is wrong. You should feel it in your back. You should be balanced on the balls of your feet—not the toes, not the heels. You can have your left foot forward or your right foot forward, whichever is most comfortable. That's the key, being comfortable.

Seattle's Gary Payton has a good defensive stance against Chicago's Michael Jordan, with his knees bent, his feet staggered, and his head up. Associated Press

In guarding a man with the ball, a defender must train himself *not* to watch the ball. This sounds antiproductive, but not when you stop and think about it. A player with the ball in his hands can deceive a defender with a series of ball fakes before he even starts his move. What the defender must do is train himself to watch from the top of a guy's chest to his waist. Wherever that part of the player's body goes, he must go.

"See the Ball!"

Our coach on the Knicks, Red Holzman, was constantly imploring us to "See the ball!" It became one of the catch phrases associated with our team, but it was often misunderstood. What he was really telling us was that in guarding a player without the ball, it was vital to see not only the man we were trying to guard, but also where the ball was on the court.

Any time you play defense away from the ball, you must see the ball and see your man simultaneously. Usually guys see their man because that's the natural thing to do on defense. You're assigned to guard a man, so you watch him closely.

Red was emphasizing the importance of seeing the ball as well, and of understanding the relationship between where your man is and where the ball is. If you know that, you can position yourself effectively; if you don't, you're vulnerable.

If you're guarding a man away from the ball, you're really not playing the man, but rather a lane. You should overplay the passing lane between your man and the guy with the ball. That way, you'll be in position to step in and pick off an errant pass.

Man-to-Man Versus Zone: Which Is Better?

The two basic types of defense in basketball are man-to-man and zone. Each has advantages and disadvantages.

Man-to-Man Defenses

In man-to-man defenses, each player is assigned to guard a specific player on the opposing team. In zone defenses, each player is assigned to an area of the floor and guards any offensive player who comes into that area.

In man-to-man coverage, a defender knows what player he's responsible for and should be on that player wherever he goes on the court. If that player is particularly explosive, then guarding him one-on-one could be a problem. Man-to-man coverage also leaves a player more vulnerable to screens and picks because his first priority is following his man, and he might not see a screen or pick in time. A teammate must then help out by switching, or changing defensive assignments, and picking up his teammate's man if that teammate runs into a screen.

The diagram at the bottom of this page illustrates how two defensive players, playing man-to-man defense, might execute a switch.

See how much easier it is for the second defender to pick up the man with the ball and block his path to the basket.

Clyde's Chalk Talk

Switching is a defensive tactic where two players trade defensive assignments, switching the men they are guarding. It most often occurs after an offensive player runs his defender into a screen set by another player on the offensive team. Rather than try to run around or through the screen, the initial defender might find it simpler to switch defensive assignments with the defender guarding the man who set the screen and is in better position to pick up the man with the ball.

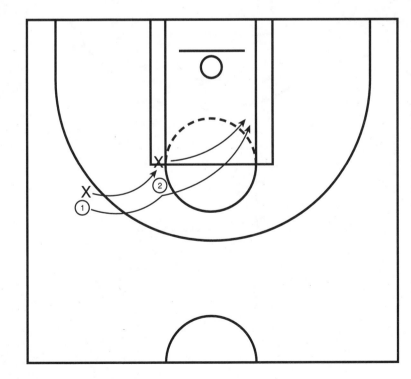

When the player with the ball (1) tries to lose his man in a screen set by a teammate (2) and then drive toward the basket, it's often easier for the two defenders (X) to switch assignments. The man originally guarding the player with the ball stays with the man who set the screen, while his teammate picks up the man with the ball.

Zone Defenses

Playing a zone defense might be easier for some players because they only have to guard a designated area of the floor and don't have to chase a man all over the court. But a defender must be able to guard anyone who comes into his area of the zone, whether it's a big guy or small, fast or slow. Also, if an offensive team tries to overload the zone by putting two men in an area guarded by one defender, that defender must be able to contain them both until help arrives, as it should quickly.

One advantage to a zone is that each area of the floor always is covered, so the defense should not be vulnerable to lobs or crosscourt passes. Another is that it becomes relatively easy for players in adjoining areas of the zone to converge and double-team the man with the ball when he goes into the seam between their two areas. This extra defensive pressure can force the man with the ball into a turnover.

The following three diagrams illustrate the most basic zone defenses:

The 2-1-2 zone puts two men outside, one in the middle near the foul line, and two along the baseline, on either side of the basket.

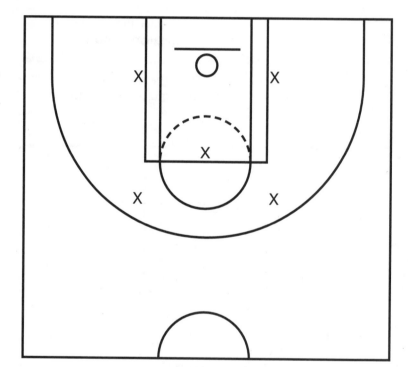

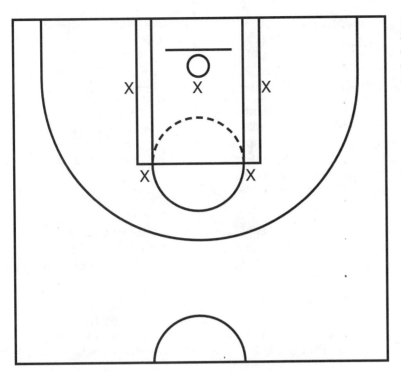

The 2-3 zone puts two men outside and three along the baseline, one on each side of the basket and one in the lane.

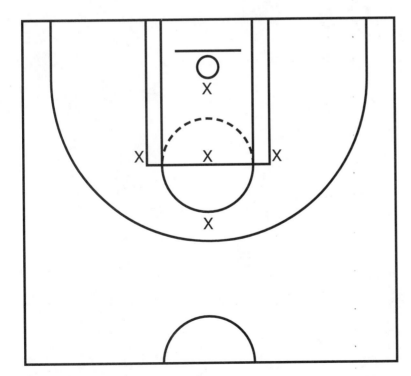

The 1-3-1 zone puts one man outside, three across the foul line extended, and one under the basket.

In each case, the defenders in the zone hope to be able to double-team the offensive player with the ball and force him into a mistake. In the 1-3-1, for example, the player on the outside will try to force the offensive player with the ball to one side or the other and follow him there, where he can be joined by a defensive teammate playing the wing in a double-team while the other three defenders cover the rest of the court.

Zones are useful when a team has a size advantage and wants to pack the middle, or keep as many players as possible near the basket and the key area. This forces the other team to shoot from outside, which generally are lower percentage shots. This became such a prevalent strategy that rules-makers introduced the three-point basket, awarding three points for a shot made from beyond a certain distance. The idea was to force defenders away from the basket and make them guard players farther away, thus opening up the lane for drives.

A zone is often used when a team wants to apply full-court defensive pressure—guarding a team closely all over the court in an attempt to force turnovers. That's because when you have to cover the 94-foot length of the court, it's much easier for players to guard specific areas rather than chase opponents all over the floor.

The 2-2-1 zone press shown on the next page is an example of where defensive players would be stationed in such a full-court pressure defense. Two players try to steal the inbounds pass or go for a quick double-team; then two more players are stationed near midcourt for additional double-teaming possibilities. One player hangs back to guard against the long pass.

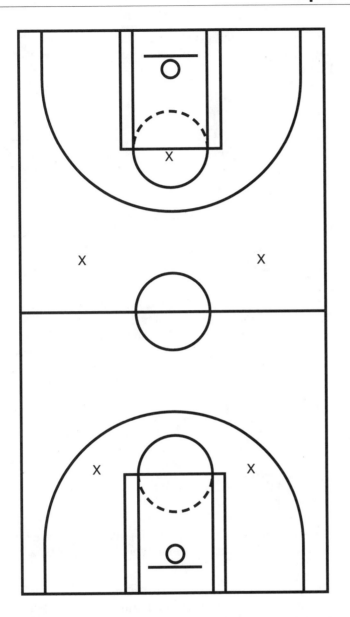

In the 2-2-1 zone press, defenders try to create double-teams and force turnovers all over the court.

So Which Defense Is Better?

Both man-to-man and zone defenses can be effective, depending on the skills of the defensive players.

Slower players are better off in a zone, where they are only responsible for a limited area of the floor and don't have to chase an opponent all over the court. The same is often true for bigger players, who can be stationed near the basket where their height can have greatest impact. A zone also is useful if a high-scoring player gets into foul trouble because he won't have to guard a man too closely, and there will always be a teammate nearby to help him out.

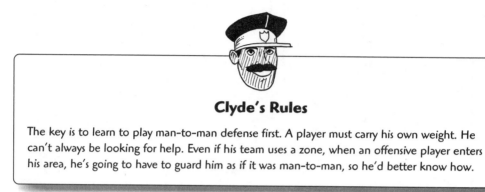

Clyde's Rules

The key is to learn to play man-to-man defense first. A player must carry his own weight. He can't always be looking for help. Even if his team uses a zone, when an offensive player enters his area, he's going to have to guard him as if it was man-to-man, so he'd better know how.

Players who are quick and fundamentally sound defensively might be better off in a man-to-man situation, where they can really apply their skills to frustrate an opponent. If a talented defensive player is used in a zone, the opponent can avoid him by running its plays to the other side of the court. In man-to-man, there's no avoiding him.

NBA = NZA: No Zones Allowed

Although zone defenses are common in high school, college, and women's ball, zone defenses are not allowed in the NBA and haven't been since early in the league's first season.

League officials always have wanted the NBA and its athletes to be known for quickness and athleticism rather than size and strength. To encourage swoops to the hoop, which are arguably the most spectacular plays in the game, they knew they couldn't allow a defensive team to clog the middle with big, lumbering players. So they prohibited zone defenses, forcing every defender to chase a man wherever he goes on the court.

NBA coaches have spent much time over the past 50 years trying to figure out ways around the no-zone rule. As soon as a coach discovers a loophole, the rules committee meets and plugs it. As a result, the NBA doesn't simply say zone defenses are not allowed, but instead has developed a complicated system of illegal defense rules based on players' positions on the court and how far they are from an opponent. If a team violates these rules, it is issued first a warning and then a technical foul for each subsequent violation.

Unfortunately, these rules are so complex that players, coaches, media members, and fans are often baffled when a referee blows his whistle for an illegal defense violation.

This is one area where everybody agrees that simpler rules would be helpful, but the rules get more complicated each season.

Presses, Traps, and Other Defensive Chicanery

The object of a defense is to harass and ultimately stymie an offense. So it stands to reason that the trickier and more complicated you can make a defense, the more effective it will be in achieving that result.

Man-to-man defenses, the only kind allowed in the NBA, tends to be the most straight-up, with each defender responsible for guarding one man. Any double-teaming must be done with lightning quickness, or the other three defenders will be left at the mercy of the offense. The man with the ball must be trapped and harassed immediately.

Zones make it easier to *press* and *trap* because the three players not involved in the double-team can just lay back and cover areas near the basket. In the NBA, they must cover specific men, or their team will be called for an illegal defense violation.

Whether playing man-to-man or zone, defenders like to use the sidelines, the baseline, and the midcourt line to help them trap a man with the ball. The corners, where the sideline meets either the midcourt line or the baseline, are especially deadly for a ballhandler because they cut off his avenue of escape in two directions. That's one reason coaches constantly are imploring their players to keep the ball in the middle of the floor when they bring it up.

Clyde's Chalk Talk

To *press* is to guard closely or otherwise apply increased defensive pressure. For example, guarding opponents over the full length of the court rather than just in the offensive zone is called a *full-court press*. To *trap* is to force an offensive player with the ball into a situation where he is guarded by two defenders, or where one defender has him pinned against the sideline, baseline, or midcourt line. These situations decrease his options and increase chances for a turnover.

The center has a special role on defense, whether playing man-to-man or zone. The center is the last line of defense, like the goalie in soccer or hockey. His job is to keep players from driving the lane to the basket. He has to intimidate not only with his skills but also with his persona, the way Bill Russell did with the old Celtics. Russell was the best at scaring people out of the lane, and many times when you did go in, you would rush your shot because you'd be afraid he would block it.

A key element in playing good defense is savvy. A lot of the defense I played was an illusion. I would try to beguile my opponents. I gave them plenty of room to hang themselves. My reasoning was that if I was all over my opponents on defense, they would be more alert. I would play off them, so it looked like they could do a lot of things. They'd start to feel comfortable that they could do anything, and they'd become careless or lazy. That's when I'd make them pay.

You have to know your opponents. Some players like contact; I didn't give it. Others don't like it, so I'd give them contact. You have to know who likes to go right, who likes to go left. You have to know what each player wants to do with the ball. Nine times out of 10, if a player was right-handed, I'd force him to the left because he would not be as adept that way. I knew that going left, when the player stopped to shoot, he had to bring the ball right back into my face. The ball was exposed to me, and that made it easier for me to block or to distract him.

So much of defense is savvy.

My Favorite Defensive Players

Start with Jerry Sloan and Norm Van Lier, who teamed in the backcourt for Chicago in the early 1970s. Those Bulls teams were predicated on defense. Most players hated to play them, and I had to do it a lot. They would push and scratch and claw every inch of the way. They were indomitable.

Joe Caldwell, who played for a number of teams including the Hawks in St. Louis and Atlanta, was another guy who was tough for me. He was so quick, he could get all over you on defense. They called him "Pogo Joe" because of his leaping ability.

Gus Johnson, who played forward for the Bullets, was another tough defender. In those days, players were allowed to hand-check more than they are today, and he was so strong he could manipulate you around the court just by sticking one hand in your back. I'd get hot, and they'd switch him over on me, and it would be all over.

Among centers, I've already mentioned Bill Russell, who changed the way defense is thought of in the NBA with his shot blocking and his intimidation in the lane. Another intimidating defensive center was Nate Thurmond of the Warriors. He wasn't as spectacular as Russell, but he was tough and relentless. Everybody hated to play against him.

Dennis Rodman ranks among the best all-around defensive players I've ever seen. He's talented and relentless and can guard players of any size, from guards to forwards to centers.

I'd put Michael Jordan in there too, definitely. He's so good offensively that people overlook his defense, but he can shut you down. Scottie Pippen is much the same way. Gary Payton of Seattle is another defensive standout, pesky and persistent around the ball. And the best guy I've seen at fighting his way over screens is Mookie Blaylock of the Atlanta Hawks.

The Least You Need to Know

➤ Defense is hard work, but without it you don't win.

➤ Positioning is vital to good defensive play.

➤ You need quick feet and a quick mind to play defense, more so than quick hands.

➤ When guarding a man with the ball, a defender who watches the player's waist will never get faked out.

➤ When guarding a man without the ball, a defender who sees both his man and the ball can often pick off a pass.

➤ Both man-to-man and zone defenses can be effective, depending on players' talents.

➤ Zone defenses are prohibited in the NBA to keep the lane open for driving and jiving to the hoop.

Chapter 18

Clyde Handles the Tough Ones

In This Chapter

➤ Clyde answers 10 really tough questions about basketball

➤ What more could you ask?

I've been involved with basketball for most of my life, and I hear the same questions over and over. Some are questions about the nature of the game, whereas other questions seek my opinion on the kinds of subjects that every fan loves to discuss like who's the greatest player of all time or who was the best team ever assembled.

Let's switch gears and see whether we can answer some of those questions once and for all, or maybe start a few arguments.

Why Does It Take So Long to Play the Last Two Minutes?

Those last two minutes on the game clock can last 15 or 20 minutes on the real clock because of the finality of it all. You know that if you don't do this or that, you're going to lose the game. Everybody is more focused in the last two minutes.

Each timeout becomes more important, not only to break a run by the other team, but because more strategy is involved. Players know that the crucial time is upon them, so they want to talk it over and devise the best opportunity.

People say that you don't have to watch an NBA game until the last two minutes, but those people don't appreciate the beauty of the NBA game. A great play can happen anytime, in the first quarter as easily as the fourth, and you'll miss it if you only watch the last two minutes.

I will say the game is more intense, more excruciating, in the last two minutes or the last five minutes. That's because it becomes a half-court game. Early on, there's more transition; but at the end, it's more physical, and the defenses become aroused. The cream rises to the top—your superstars, the players who can handle the pressure, come to the forefront. Many players don't want the ball in the last two minutes, but not the real stars of the game.

How Can an NBA Player Possibly Miss a Dunk?

It all boils down to lack of concentration. A guy goes to the basket thinking, "Should I do a tomahawk? A Statue of Liberty?" He's worried about what kind of dunk he's going to do so that he can make it to the highlight reels. He's not focusing on the job at hand, so he drifts too far toward the basket and bounces it off the back of the rim.

I remember once in the playoffs, Michael Jordan wanted to put a little mustard on it. He wanted to make a statement, and he missed the dunk. There's probably nothing more humiliating than that, to miss an open dunk shot in the pros.

How Can a Team Be So Good in One Half and So Bad the Next?

That's part of the grandeur of the pro game. It's a game of momentum. Obviously, when momentum comes, it's contagious. Guys get involved; they start to strive and thrive. It's a game of spurts, and for four or five minutes, you can get on a roll.

Primarily, a team's momentum is predicated on defense. Your defense becomes your best offense by forcing turnovers, capitalizing on transition, and contesting every shot. When the other team misfires, it does not get a second opportunity.

But momentum can go as quickly as it comes. A team gets overconfident and starts going away from its game plan, and things can change in a hurry. A couple of shots from the baseline bounce out to the top of the key and set up fast breaks the other way, and all of a sudden that 20-point lead is gone.

No first quarter or first half lead is safe in the NBA, no matter how big. The level of talent is so high that any team can come back in a hurry.

Who Was the Greatest Player in Basketball History?

I'd have to say Kareem Abdul-Jabbar. He encompassed everything, no matter what standard you want to measure greatness by. Winning? He won championships in grade school, high school, college, and the pros. Scoring? He scored more points in the NBA than anyone else in history. Longevity? He played 20 seasons in the NBA. He also was respected as a team player. He could have scored many more points if he had been a selfish player.

It's tough for me to pick him over Bill Russell, Wilt Chamberlain, and Michael Jordan; but because of teamwork and everything else, I would have to pick Kareem. His sky-hook is the most lethal weapon the game has ever seen. For 20 years, he shot over 50 percent from the field. That's a phenomenal statistic.

If You Could Pick One Player, in His Prime, to Start a Team, Who Would It Be?

Again I'd have to say Abdul-Jabbar, for all the reasons given previously. But I might need an asterisk today, because the big man ain't what he used to be. The big man isn't as dominant as in the past because of swarming defenses, which can dictate what a big man does. You can take him out of the game by double- and triple-teaming him in the last four or five minutes.

That's why Michael Jordan has been the premier player of the past decade. He can create. If you take away his inside game, he comes out on the perimeter and beats you. In today's NBA, you need guys who can create opportunities. If a center such as Patrick Ewing has to come outside and become a power forward, he's not as effective.

So in today's game, I might go for Michael more than Abdul-Jabbar, or I might take Magic Johnson rather than the big guy. I know I'm going to need his creativity down the stretch. Today, you can build a team with a swarming defense that can take a big guy out of the game, so I might think differently.

In the 1970s, I would have gone with Abdul-Jabbar, Bill Russell, and Wilt Chamberlain unequivocally. But the game was different then.

Why Can't NBA Players Make Their Free Throws?

That's a pet peeve of mine. Look at the women. The WNBA had a higher league-wide free throw percentage in its first year than the men did that season. That's because the players in the WNBA are hungrier. They're seeking recognition; they're not complacent. Their egos haven't come into play. NBA players make a lot of money, and they just forget about the basics.

It's despicable for NBA players to shoot 50 or 60 percent from the line. They do not practice. Or if they practice, they're practicing the wrong technique. I read about Chris Dudley, the way he shoots 200 free throws a day in practice but still has trouble hitting 50 percent. Yeah he shoots a lot in practice, but he's just standing on the line. It doesn't compare to what it's like in a game.

I used to shoot until I missed. And when I missed, I ran a suicide drill or two, a sprint from one end of the court to the other. I would punish myself for missing. In a game, you're going to be winded, huffing and puffing, so that's how I practiced. Shooting's easy if you stand on the line and somebody shags the ball for you. For more realism, you have to punish yourself. That's the pressure. I knew that if I missed, I had to run one or two suicides, so I was going to focus more. I'd remember all I learned.

What Was the Greatest Basketball Team of All Time?

In my opinion, the 1967 Philadelphia 76ers were the greatest basketball team of all time. They had Wilt Chamberlain, Hal Greer, Chet Walker, Lucious Jackson, Wali Jones, and Billy Cunningham. They were phenomenal.

Playing against that team was like playing a football game. You were so battered running around chasing after Greer or Jones when they were using screens by Chamberlain or Luke Jackson. My body aches just thinking of it. They were so physical; they would hound and pound you.

By that year, Wilt had won seven scoring titles, so he was no longer enthralled with scoring. By then, he wanted to win more than anything else, so whatever had to be done, he did. Rebound, dish the ball, whatever the team needed at the time, that's what he provided. That change in Chamberlain really brought this team together.

With the Game on the Line, Who Would You Want to Take the Last Shot?

I can think of a number of guys. Start with Abdul-Jabbar and that sky-hook. That was unstoppable.

Then you have guys like Michael Jordan, Oscar Robertson, Jerry West, and Earl Monroe, who could create their own shots, and if you fouled them, you might as well give them the basket. Plus, they all wanted the ball in that scenario.

Rick Barry is another guy who comes to mind. He was a lethal shooter who could create his own shot and had range on his jumper. And he relished the pressure.

If the Players on a Team Like Each Other, Is That Team More Likely to Win?

It helps if there's cohesion on a team, but it's not essential. Look at the Bronx Zoo. The Yankees dispelled that notion, winning championships with total chaos.

It's human nature to be envious. Do you think everyone liked Abdul-Jabbar or Magic on those Lakers teams? Believe me—they didn't all like each other.

I liked Willis Reed because I respected him. He taught me a lot about how to be a professional. Even though he traded me later in my career, the positives outweigh the negatives, and I'll always have respect for him. He's a man's man. But early in my career, my agent tried to separate us because he felt we were competing for the same endorsements, to be the star of the team. When you're young, it's easy for people to separate you and pit one player against another. When you cross the lines to step on the court, those things should not enter into it. You have to be focused on the game. If you're thinking about off-court stuff, the team is not going to be successful.

I saw that in some of the Knicks teams after I retired. Some players had to see who was in the jersey before they would give a teammate the ball. Hey, if you see a white jersey and he's open, give him the ball. Don't stop and think about who it is and whether you get along.

Our Knicks teams epitomized teamwork on the court, but we were not close off the court. It's almost impossible to live in New York and have the closeness teams have in smaller cities because there are so many more places to live and hang out. We lived all over the place, and I rarely saw my teammates until game time. Los Angeles is like that, too. We didn't have that closeness I noticed when we went to other places.

Who's Your All-Time Starting Five?

I would choose Elgin Baylor, Oscar Robertson, Michael Jordan, and Kareem Abdul-Jabbar… Can I put Bill Russell on there? I know that gives me two centers, but I'm having trouble with the second forward. I'll take Russell if you'll let me. If not, if I have to take a forward, maybe Karl Malone.

The Least You Need to Know

➤ Two minutes on the game clock can mean 20 minutes on a real clock because so much is at stake.

➤ Kareem Abdul-Jabbar was the greatest player of all time. But because centers no longer dominate, Michael Jordan might be the player to pick if you were starting a team from scratch.

➤ NBA players should be embarrassed when they miss free throws or dunks.

➤ The greatest team of all time? The 1967 Philadelphia 76ers.

Part 5

From the Playgrounds to the Pros

Basketball is often called the city game, as inner-city playgrounds resonate with the hypnotic rhythm of a basketball bouncing on blacktop. But basketball is played with just as much passion on the beaches of California, the bluegrass of Kentucky, and the dirt driveways of Indiana. Wherever you look, you'll find a hoop, whether it's hanging from a wooden garage door or a chain-link school yard fence or a fancy adjustable metal pole.

Basketball is a decidedly American game, though it was invented by a Canadian and is now played by billions around the world. It ranks right up there with McDonald's and Coca-Cola among this country's most popular exports.

In this part, I'll look at basketball on many different levels, from the NBA to pro leagues abroad to the college and high school games to playground ball. I'll also take a look at women's basketball, which is virtually as old as the game itself and over the past decade has enjoyed a phenomenal growth in popularity.

Chapter 19

The NBA

> ### In This Chapter
>
> ➤ Humble beginnings as a league struggles for acceptance
>
> ➤ Red Auerbach, Bill Russell, and the Celtics dynasty
>
> ➤ The age of expansion is not without growing pains
>
> ➤ Magic, Larry, and Michael usher in a golden era
>
> ➤ The future: can the NBA survive without Michael?
>
> ➤ Clyde's tips for making the NBA even better

Nowhere is basketball played on a higher level than in the National Basketball Association. Of the players who are good enough to make their high school varsity teams, only a tiny percentage go on to play college ball, and only a tiny percentage of them go on to play in the NBA. And with the influx of talented foreign-born players, a trend that is only going to grow with the booming popularity of the sport overseas, the competition for jobs in the NBA is that much more intense.

This chapter takes a look at the NBA today, its history, and its future.

A Stage for the Stars: the NBA's Structure Today

As I said in Part 2, the NBA is a players' league. Everything is focused on the talents of its players. The rules are designed to showcase their skills and encourage them to stretch the limits of their abilities until they are bound only by their imagination. Players today are treated like traveling dignitaries, jetting from city to city on luxury charters, staying in the finest hotels, and playing in arenas that are more like multi-media malls than basketball gyms. And they are paid on a scale with leading entertainers from film, music, or theater.

The NBA provides the framework, the stage on which they perform. Comprised of 29 teams in four divisions and two conferences, the league stretches from coast to coast and into Canada, with recent expansion franchises placed in Toronto and Vancouver. Teams play 82-game regular-season schedules, beginning around November 1 and lasting nearly six full months, with the four division winners and the next six teams in each conference qualifying for the playoffs, which can go on for another two months.

Here is the current NBA Divisional alignment:

Eastern Conference

Atlantic Division	Central Division
Boston Celtics	Atlanta Hawks
Miami Heat	Charlotte Hornets
New Jersey Nets	Chicago Bulls
New York Knicks	Cleveland Cavaliers
Orlando Magic	Detroit Pistons
Philadelphia 76ers	Indiana Pacers
Toronto Raptors	Milwaukee Bucks
Washington Wizards	

Western Conference

Midwest Division	Pacific Division
Dallas Mavericks	Golden State Warriors
Denver Nuggets	Los Angeles Clippers
Houston Rockets	Los Angeles Lakers
Minnesota Timberwolves	Phoenix Suns
San Antonio Spurs	Portland Trail Blazers
Utah Jazz	Sacramento Kings
Vancouver Grizzlies	Seattle SuperSonics

After a regular season that begins around November 1 and stretches nearly six months, the playoffs take on a life of their own for the next two months, beginning in late April and ending in mid-June. Unlike the regular season, where teams might not play each other for several months, in the playoffs, two teams hook up for best-of-5 or best-of-7 series. The familiarity of playing the same opponent repeatedly over two weeks leads to intense rivalries and fascinating strategic moves.

The playoffs culminate in the NBA Finals, a best-of-7 series between the champions of the Eastern and Western Conferences, with the winner being crowned NBA champion. It's amazing how much attention is focused on the playoffs. Last spring, I went to my cleaner because I needed a button sewn onto a jacket. Now, this is a guy who has never talked to me about basketball, but all of a sudden he says, "Mr. Frazier, do you think the Knicks will win against Miami?" I couldn't believe it!

Two other major events are on the annual NBA calendar.

The All-Star Weekend is held in early February, is rotated between various league cities, and includes the All-Star Game, skills events such as the long distance shootout, and a gala interactive fan festival. This weekend has become the league's showpiece, with thousands of corporate executives in attendance to see where their sponsorship and licensing dollars go. It is also a media mecca, drawing more than 1,000 writers and broadcasters from around the globe.

The NBA Draft is conducted following the playoffs and enables teams to select the rights to the top players from college, high school, and foreign ranks. To give weaker teams a chance to improve, teams make their selections in inverse order of their regular-season record from the previous year, so the weakest teams get to pick first.

Humble Beginnings

While the NBA reaches millions of fans today, it took a long time for it to become such an important part of our culture.

The first professional basketball game that can be documented took place in 1896 in Trenton, New Jersey, just five years after the sport was invented. There are sketchy reports of a play-for-pay game in Herkimer, New York, as early as 1893 but no solid verification.

By 1896, a group of men regularly played basketball at a YMCA in Trenton. One day they found that building unavailable, but when you gotta play, you gotta play. So they rented out a local Masonic Hall and then decided to charge admission to recoup their costs. So many spectators showed up that they not only covered expenses but had money left over, which they decided to divide among themselves. Each player earned $15, and there was an extra $1 left over that went to Fred Cooper, who had organized the game. Cooper thus became the first "highest paid player in basketball history."

The first known professional basketball league was formed two years later, in 1898, and called itself the

Clyde's Record Book

Not only was Fred Cooper the organizer of the first recorded pro basketball game, but he also designed the uniforms worn during that game in 1896. Cooper's uniforms included velvet shorts and tights, a far cry from the baggy shorts en vogue today.

National Basketball League. But because all its teams were from the area in and around Philadelphia, it was hardly national in scope.

Many leagues would come and go over the next 50 years. It was not uncommon for top players in the 1910s and 1920s to play in two or three leagues at the same time, sometimes under assumed names. The best teams of the era either supplemented league play, or bypassed it entirely, by barnstorming—traveling from town to town, taking on any local team that would put up enough money to play them.

One of the strongest of the early leagues was the American Basketball League that existed from 1925 to 1931 before falling victim to the Depression. A few years later, the backing of several large companies, including Firestone, Goodyear, and General Electric, gave rise to the National Basketball League in 1937. That league, based in the Midwest, attracted the top players of the time and achieved a high level of play in its dozen years of existence. But its growth was limited, and its fate eventually sealed, by the relatively small cities and arenas in which it played.

Birth of the NBA

The end of World War II in 1945 ushered in a new era in American professional sports. With so many soldiers coming home with peacetime dollars to spend, existing leagues flourished, and new leagues were born. Among them was the Basketball Association of America, created on June 6, 1946, by the owners of major arenas and hockey teams in Boston, Chicago, Cleveland, Detroit, New York, Philadelphia, Pittsburgh, Providence, St. Louis, Toronto, and Washington, D.C.

The men who gathered that day at the old Commodore Hotel next door to New York's Grand Central Terminal had no huge passion for basketball. They simply were looking for something that might draw people into their buildings on days and nights they otherwise would be dark. They already had hockey, the circus, ice shows, and other such events, so they turned to hoops, which was already hugely popular on the high school and college level but had never really caught on professionally.

On November 1, 1946, at Maple Leaf Gardens in Toronto, the New York Knicks defeated the Toronto Huskies 68-66 in the league's first game. The leading scorer of that initial contest was Toronto player-coach Ed Sadowski, who tallied 18 points, and tickets for that game were priced from $2.50 down to 75 cents—a far cry from today's going rate.

Although the BAA struggled for its first two years, its birth signaled the end for the better-established NBL, which could not hope to compete for players against a league playing in larger arenas in major cities. In 1948,

Clyde's Record Book

The first basket in the history of the BAA, forerunner of the NBA, was scored by New York's Ossie Schectman. Even then the league was promotion-minded: Any fan taller than Toronto's 6'8" center, George Nostrand, was admitted free.

the BAA added four of the strongest teams from the NBL, including the league champion Minneapolis Lakers (the same team that would move to Los Angeles in 1960), who featured the top player of that time, George Mikan. One year later, the NBL folded, and six teams were admitted into the BAA, which was renamed the National Basketball Association.

The First Lakers Dynasty

With the 6'10" Mikan as its hub, the Minneapolis Lakers became the NBA's first dynasty. They won championships in 1949, 1950, 1952, 1953, and 1954—five of their first six years in the league. Add NBL titles with Chicago in 1947 and Minneapolis in 1948, and Mikan personally played on seven title-winning teams in eight years.

The Lakers' success was both good news and bad news for the young NBA, which was struggling to gain a toehold on the sports scene. Fans flocked to see Mikan and star teammates like Jim Pollard, Vern Mikkelsen, and Slater Martin, but at the expense of other teams. And Minneapolis's success kept other teams from building a winning tradition. The NBA, which had 17 teams in 1949–50, was down to eight teams by 1954–55.

Quote...Unquote

"The game was stagnant. Teams literally started sitting on the ball in the third quarter. That was the way the game was played: Get a lead and put the ball in the icebox while the paying customers started reading the program. The whole game slowed up."—*Bob Cousy, Hall of Fame guard of the Boston Celtics who played in the 1950s and early 1960s.*

The Shot Clock Saves the NBA

Minneapolis's success wasn't the only thing hurting the NBA. The game itself had become slow-paced and marred by rough play. Fouls were plentiful because when a team got the lead, it would go into a stall. Its players would just stand around and hold the ball, not even trying to score, content to wait until they were fouled and then take their free throws. Games became free throw shooting contests, while the fans snored on.

Enter Danny Biasone, owner of the NBA's Syracuse Nationals. He and his general manager, Leo Ferris, developed a device to speed up play: the 24-second shot clock. The idea was simple. A team would have to attempt a shot within 24 seconds or lose possession of the ball. No more stalling.

Quote...Unquote

"Things were going from bad to worse. The games were interminable. Attendance was suffering. We were in a desperate situation."—*Maurice Podoloff, president of the NBA from 1946 to 1963.*

Quote...Unquote

"Basketball needed a time limit. In baseball you get three outs. In football you have to gain 10 yards in four plays or you give up the ball. But in basketball, if you had the lead and a good ballhandler, you could play around all night. The number of seconds really wasn't that important. No matter what, the game needed a time element."
—Danny Biasone, inventor of the 24-second shot clock.

Clyde's Tip

Not long after the shot clock was introduced, the NBA became truly a national league. In 1959–60 there was no team west of St. Louis, but in the summer of 1960, the Minneapolis Lakers moved to Los Angeles, stretching the NBA out to the West Coast. Two years later, they were joined by the former Philadelphia Warriors, who moved to San Francisco and became the team now known as the Golden State Warriors.

How did Biasone arrive at a 24-second shot clock? He took the average number of shots two teams would take in a game during the previous few seasons, which was about 120, and divided that into the number of seconds in a game, which was 2,880. The result was 24, which Biasone reasoned would be enough time for a team to run several plays and get off a good shot. Biasone's 24 seconds remains the NBA's standard to this day.

Biasone's clock was tested in the summer of 1954 and adopted for use in the 1954–55 season, along with a rule that limited the number of fouls a team could commit in one quarter to six (later reduced to five and then to four) before penalty free throws would be assessed. The rules worked hand-in-hand, and the results were no stalling and less frequent fouling, bringing scoring and excitement back to the pro game.

The results were dramatic. In one season, average scores rose 14 points per team, an 18 percent increase. The number of teams scoring 100 or more points in an NBA playoff game rose from 3 in 1954 to 18 in 1955. Fittingly, Biasone's Syracuse Nationals won their only NBA championship in 1955, the first year of the shot clock, rallying from a 17-point deficit to beat Fort Wayne 92–91 in Game 7 of the NBA Finals—a comeback that would not have been possible without the shot clock because Fort Wayne surely would have gone into a stall.

The shot clock paved the way for a new breed of stars to enter the NBA. High scorers like Wilt Chamberlain, Oscar Robertson, Elgin Baylor, and Jerry West would bring new excitement to the pro game in the 1960s. But the big story of that decade was no one individual, but rather a team—the Boston Celtics.

The Boston Celtics: The NBA's Greatest Dynasty

No team has ever dominated a major American pro sport like the Boston Celtics. From 1956–57 through 1968–69, the Celtics won 11 NBA championships in 13 seasons, including eight in a row in one remarkable stretch. Red Auerbach served as coach for the first nine of those championship teams, as general manager for the final two.

Red Auerbach, with his trademark cigar, celebrates another Boston Celtics victory.
Associated Press

It is no coincidence that Boston's dynasty overlapped, precisely, the playing career of William Felton Russell. The agile, shot-blocking center changed the way the NBA thought about defense, serving as an anchor for the Celtics. He allowed their other players to overplay their men and apply extra pressure, knowing there was a safety behind them in case they got beat. Willis Reed played that same role on my Knicks teams, and I know I appreciated it!

Auerbach and Russell were the constants during the Celtics dynasty. The others players came and went, like interchangeable parts in a well-oiled machine with Auerbach at the controls, but Russell was always there as the hub that held it all together. K.C. Jones succeeded Bob Cousy at point

Clyde's Tip

Bill Russell not only guarded the opposing team's center, he played a role similar to that of a goalie in hockey or soccer. If another player got past his Boston defender, Russell always seemed to be back around the basket to prevent him from driving in for an easy layup.

253

guard; Bill Sharman gave way to Sam Jones at shooting guard; and the forwards went from Tom Heinsohn, Jim Loscutoff, and Satch Sanders to John Havlicek, Don Nelson, and Bailey Howell. Through it all, Russell was there in the middle, blocking shots, rebounding, and intimidating opposing players.

The Celtics won their first championship in 1957 and then bowed to the St. Louis Hawks the following season. In 1959, they began a string of eight consecutive NBA titles, by far the longest streak in league history—no other team has won more than three in a row. Auerbach retired as coach following the 1966 championship, and Boston's reign came to an end in 1967 when the Philadelphia 76ers won the crown. But with Russell serving as player-coach, the Celtics bounced back to win titles again in 1968 and 1969.

Growing Pains

After the glory years of the Celtics, the NBA enjoyed another surge in popularity when my Knicks teams won titles in 1970 and 1973. Kareem Abdul-Jabbar, Oscar Robertson, and the Milwaukee Bucks, and Wilt Chamberlain, Jerry West, and the Los Angeles Lakers took the two championships in between. Having championship teams in New York at that time seemed to really give the league a boost.

It was a time of expansion for the NBA, which had only nine teams—the eight from the 1950s and a Baltimore franchise that had begun in Chicago in 1961 and moved two years later—as late as 1965–66. The Chicago Bulls joined the league in 1966–67, followed by San Diego and Seattle the following year and Milwaukee and Phoenix the year after that. Buffalo, Cleveland, and Portland swelled the ranks to 17 in 1970–71, and New Orleans made it 18 in 1974–75.

One reason for that expansion was the birth of the rival American Basketball Association in 1967. The NBA didn't want to lose any lucrative markets to the upstart league, and although the ABA attracted and developed many outstanding players and fine teams, it never attained the broad popularity of the NBA, largely because of the lack of a strong national television package to provide exposure. By the mid-1970s, the ABA was on its last legs, and in 1976, the NBA absorbed its four surviving franchises. Pro basketball was back to one major league, a 22-team NBA.

The late 1970s were a tough time for the NBA, whose resources had been sapped during its war for survival against the ABA. Interest in the league was lagging, and most teams were losing money. The league's championship series, the NBA Finals, wasn't even shown live on network television, but instead was replayed on tape after the late-night news.

The NBA was badly in need of a jump-start, and it got it from two young stars who had battled it out for the 1979 collegiate championship—Earvin "Magic" Johnson of Michigan State University and Larry Bird of Indiana State University.

Star Power Leads to a Golden Era

Johnson and Bird were exceptional in that they were more than just great scorers. Both were complete players, the kind who truly made their teammates better. Both were naturals, possessing an innate sense that allowed them to see not only what was happening on the court but what was about to happen. Both were brilliant passers who delighted in setting up their teammates. They delighted basketball purists and won over a new generation of fans.

It helped the NBA that they joined two of the league's premier franchises on opposite coasts, teams that had been used to winning but had hit hard times—Johnson going to the Lakers and Bird to the Celtics. A transcontinental rivalry was born, and it didn't take long for the young stars' impact to be felt. Johnson led the Lakers to the title as a rookie in 1980, and Bird guided the Celtics to the crown the following year.

Johnson led the Lakers to five championships in the 1980s; Bird took the Celtics to three. They met head-to-head in three NBA Finals: Bird and the Celtics winning in 1984; Johnson and the Lakers coming out on top in 1985 and 1987. Together they led an NBA revival, taking a flickering torch that had been kept alive by Julius Erving and passing along a shining flame to Michael Jordan.

Quote...Unquote

"We're both the same—we'll do anything to win. You can list all the great players you want, but there are only a couple of winners."—*Magic Johnson, on his rivalry with Larry Bird.*

Meanwhile, with David Stern taking over as NBA commissioner in 1984, the NBA worked to clean up its tarnished image by instituting a salary cap and an antidrug program and going all-out to market its stars. Jordan's arrival, with an NCAA championship, an Olympic gold medal, and a heavy promotional boost from Nike, enhanced this strategy and took it to a new level.

Jordan began winning scoring championships, and suddenly everyone wanted to "be like Mike," a phrase driven by another company with which Jordan had a promotional deal, Gatorade. When the 1990s came and the stars of Johnson and Bird faded, Jordan shone brightly—a proven individual superstar who now showed he could lead his team to the top. Jordan guided the Chicago Bulls to NBA titles in 1991, 1992, and 1993; retired and spent one season pursuing a baseball dream in the minor leagues; and then returned to lead the Bulls back to the top.

By the mid-1990s, Jordan was the most acclaimed athlete in the world, and the NBA's appeal had reached global proportions. Telecasts of NBA games were seen in nearly 200 countries around the world, and hundreds of foreign journalists came to the United States every year to cover the NBA All-Star Game and NBA Finals.

The NBA, which now lists 29 franchises including Toronto and Vancouver in Canada, has never been more popular than it is today, especially with younger sports fans both in the United States and around the world.

Can the NBA Survive Without Michael?

The multi-billion dollar question is how will the NBA do after Michael Jordan retires. Can a league built on star power survive the loss of its greatest star and continue to thrive?

The TV networks say yes. NBC and Turner will pay the NBA a combined $2.64 billion for the rights to broadcast games over four years beginning with the 1998–99 season, even though Jordan might not be around for most or all of that period.

The league has always managed to find new stars, and players such as Shaquille O'Neal, Kobe Bryant, Grant Hill, Kevin Garnett, Stephon Marbury, Allen Iverson, Tim Duncan, and Keith Van Horn, all of whom were high draft choices in the 1990s, appear to be capable of capturing fans' attention.

Clyde's Tip

In the summer of 1997, Kevin Garnett, 21 years old and a veteran of two NBA seasons after turning pro out of high school, signed a six-year contract extension with the Minnesota Timberwolves worth a reported $123 million. That's more than $20 million a year for a player who had averaged 13.7 points and 7.1 rebounds in two pro seasons. Is this a great country or what?

The league, however, is not without problems that need to be addressed. Skyrocketing salaries have blown budgets out of whack as teams try to outdo each other finding loopholes in the salary cap rules. Fiscal responsibility is out the window, with some players demanding and getting upwards of $10 million a year and the league-wide average ticket price reaching a reported $36.32 in 1997–98.

Even with all the money coming in from television rights, corporate sponsorships, and global licensing deals, most teams in the NBA were operating at a loss as of the summer of 1998. That prompted the league to take dramatic action: It scrapped the Collective Bargaining Agreement it had reached with the Players Association in 1995 and opened talks on a new deal, even though that raised the prospect of a work stoppage prior to the 1998–99 season.

The NBA Draft, which lately includes players from foreign countries and high schools as well as colleges, replenishes the talent pool each year. Associated Press

Clyde's Tips for Improving the NBA

The league has done a stupendous job when it comes to rules, which have evolved over the years to a point where they really let the players showcase their talent, and that's what the fans want to see.

Each year or two the league seems to do a little tinkering to make things even better. Last year, for example, the NBA got rid of one of my pet peeves when it ruled that a player could no longer call a timeout while he was flying out of bounds. That always used to annoy me. If he can't keep the ball inbounds, why bail him out by giving him a timeout? I'm glad the league got rid of that one.

The league also introduced a semi-circle under the basket to give the officials some guidance on when to call charging or blocking or when to let it go. I think this change helped, too. I think it shows that the rules committee has been creative and innovative in helping the officials as well as the players.

Here's an example of something the league's done to make the game better, and I bet most fans aren't even aware of it. When I was a player, the 24-second clocks were sitting on the floor in two of the four corners of the court, while the game clock was up above your head. When you were dribbling the ball upcourt, you couldn't see them both at the same time. You had to look up for the game clock and then find the corner where the shot clock was. Now both clocks are up above the basket, so you can see both in one glance as you go upcourt. It's a little thing, but as an ex-player, I can tell you it's a big help.

I really don't have many problems with the rules the way they are today. I'll tell you one rule I wouldn't change, and that's the ban on zone defense. If the league allowed zones, scores would be even lower than they are today. Imagine how clogged the court would be with all of today's big players hanging around under the basket. There would be no room to shoot. Allowing zones would be a disaster for the NBA. It would take away the players' creativity that fans want to see.

One thing that has changed over the years is the way players can play defense. Early NBA players tell me how they used to put two hands on their man and push him out of position, with no foul being called. When I played, it was one hand. Now it's no hands, although the rules allow a forearm in the back.

Even though this seems to favor the offensive player, it really doesn't vex me. That's because you don't play defense with your hands, but with your feet and your head. You have to keep your feet moving and stay in good position, and all good defensive players know that. So those changes really don't bother me.

Clyde's Tip

When people say that the NBA should allow zone defenses, I have an easy comeback for them. Did anybody know that Michael Jordan could be as spectacular as he is when he was in college? No. And one reason was because with zone defenses, not even Michael could slice and dice to the basket the way fans want. Do you really want to take that out of the NBA? I don't think so.

Is an 82-game season too long? Sure, but I'm a pragmatist. I know the owners have to make money. It's easy to say cut it to 62 games, but you know the players are going to want the same salaries. They're not going to take a cut in pay. So that just wouldn't work.

I really don't mind 82 games that much. After the first half of the season, you start to feel some fatigue and get a little jaded, but the All-Star break comes at a good time and seems to get players and teams refocused. Then you get into the races for playoff berths and positioning over the second half. Finally, you reach the playoffs and then it's all adrenaline. Everybody is revved up and moving quicker and faster. So I think the schedule works well enough as it is.

Expansion is another matter. Unequivocally, it has watered down the league. You had teams last year that just couldn't compete—Denver, Dallas, Toronto at times, some of the other teams in the West. There's a dearth of talent throughout the league, especially at center but now also at the point guard position.

I don't know why there are not enough players—that mystifies me. Now that it's an international game, you would think there would be more good players than ever. Players have the benefit of modern training techniques, strength coaches, nutrition experts—you'd think there would be an abundance of talent. Yet the bottom line is that they're going to continue to expand because of the popularity of the game, so you've got to be practical about it.

Clyde's Rules

You want to know one of my pet peeves? It's when guys try to come off the bench and enter the game, and the refs don't allow it. I know the rule book says a player must come off the bench, check in with the official scorer and be sitting or kneeling in the area in front of the scorer's table before the stoppage of play in order to be permitted to enter the game, but I think sometimes this gets a little too petty. Maybe they weren't kneeling in the box long enough, but to me that's no real reason to keep them out. Let them in. That's why they're there. Let them play.

The Least You Need to Know

➤ Pro basketball began in Trenton, New Jersey, in 1896—50 years before the NBA's forerunner, the Basketball Association of America, was created.

➤ Red Auerbach's savvy and Bill Russell's defensive skills helped the Boston Celtics win 8 championships in a row and 11 in 13 years—the NBA's greatest dynasty.

➤ Magic Johnson and Larry Bird led an NBA revival in the 1980s and then Michael Jordan carried it to greater heights.

➤ Today's NBA consists of 29 teams divided into 4 divisions, with the 4 division winners and 12 additional teams qualifying for the playoffs.

➤ The regular season begins around November 1 and lasts until mid-April. The playoffs begin shortly thereafter and run approximately two months, into mid-to late June.

➤ The midseason All-Star Weekend is a gala affair consisting of skills contests, a fan festival, and the All-Star Game itself.

➤ Can the NBA survive and thrive without Michael? That's the multi-billion dollar question. I think the answer is yes.

Chapter 20

Pro Ball Beyond the NBA

In This Chapter

➤ Hooping it up around the world

➤ Basketball may be played a little differently around the world, but it's still the same game

➤ Dream Teams and their impact on basketball's global growth

➤ The Harlem Globetrotters: basketball's goodwill ambassadors for nearly 75 years

➤ The CBA and other minor leagues are courts of dreams

Basketball is the fastest growing sport in the world. In most countries, it ranks either first or second in popularity—as measured by participation and spectator interest—along with soccer, or what is known outside the United States as football. And that order may be changing in the not-too-distant future. As one Spanish youngster told NBA officials on the occasion of the Boston Celtics' participation in the McDonald's Championship in Madrid in 1988: "Football is our fathers' sport. Basketball is our sport."

It's easy to see why. All you need is a ball and a hoop, and you can be playing basketball, even if you're all by yourself. For soccer you need a large field, and if not two full teams, at least several other players for teammates and opponents.

The sport's global growth was accelerated by the participation in the 1992 Olympics in Barcelona by the original Dream Team. With the prohibition on NBA players in global events such as the Olympics having been lifted, USA Basketball was able to put together the finest assemblage of talent any sport has ever seen, from Michael Jordan, Magic Johnson, Larry Bird, and on through the roster. The Dream Team captivated the public's fancy and was by far the premier attraction of the Barcelona Olympics, giving the growth of basketball a major boost throughout Europe and the world.

Clyde's Tip

Why is the international basketball federation known as FIBA? The acronym comes from the original French name, Federation Internationale de Basketball Amateur. The word *Amateur* was dropped in 1989 when the distinction between amateurs and professionals was eliminated, but the acronym was kept for traditional reasons—and let's face it, FIBA sounds better than FIB.

Clyde's Record Book

Hall of Famer Bill Bradley, the former Princeton All-American and one of my teammates on the New York Knicks, played for a team in Milan, Italy, in the mid-1960s, while he was on his two-year Rhodes Scholarship at Oxford. Because European teams generally play no more than two games a week, he found he could fly over from England and make most of the Milan team's games. That gave him a chance to stay in competitive basketball shape before beginning his NBA career.

In this chapter, I'll look at the pro basketball world beyond the NBA, from minor leagues in the United States to thriving pro leagues overseas. I'll examine the impact of the original Dream Team and its successors, as well as the role the Harlem Globetrotters have played in furthering the growth of the sport for nearly three-quarters of a century.

The World Learns to Hoop It Up

Basketball has long been a global game. Although it was invented in the United States, its inventor was a Canadian, Dr. James Naismith. And because 5 of the 18 students who participated in the first basketball game were from Canada and one was from Japan, they quickly brought news of this innovative activity to their homelands.

In 1932, the International Basketball Federation (FIBA) was founded in Geneva, Switzerland, with eight member national federations: Argentina, Czechoslovakia, Greece, Italy, Latvia, Portugal, Romania, and Switzerland.

The world governing body for basketball, FIBA includes 206 member national federations and governs all international competitions including the World Championships for men and women and the basketball competitions at the Olympics. Basketball made its first appearance as a demonstration sport at the 1904 Olympics in St. Louis and became a medal sport in 1936 in Berlin. FIBA staged the first World Championship for men in 1950 in Buenos Aires, Argentina, and for women in 1953 in Santiago, Chile.

Sports in Europe and much of the world feature long-standing athletic clubs steeped in tradition, which often have thousands of members who participate in various sports on a recreational basis. These clubs also field competitive teams at both junior and senior levels in sports such as soccer and basketball, and these senior teams are the equivalent of professional franchises in the United States.

Recently, these senior club teams have attracted corporate sponsors willing to spend big money to finance or support these teams, much the way sponsors attach themselves to NBA teams in the United States. These club teams compete in leagues in their own individual countries, in special tournaments and Cup events that cross national borders, and most recently in a European super-league that includes the best teams from several countries.

The influx of sponsorship money to these athletic clubs led to a competition for talent because they are allowed to have two and sometimes three players on their roster who are not citizens of that country. For a long time, those imports were NBA players seeking to extend their pro careers, fringe NBA players, or college players who couldn't make it in the NBA. But recently they have included some top collegians seeking an alternative to the NBA and European-born players who either chose to bypass or were not ready for the demanding competition in the NBA. Rosters of top Spanish, Italian, French, and Greek League teams are dotted with players from Eastern Europe, for example, in addition to Americans.

A Different Game, the Same Game

For many years, it was easy to tell the difference between an American-born and -raised player and a foreign-born and -raised player. That's because for many years players in Europe, Asia, and Africa learned and played the game without being overly influenced by the American game because game telecasts or clinics by visitors were rare.

American players were more fluid and seemed smoother in their actions. They drove to the basket more and jumped better. Foreign players were more mechanical, skilled in fundamentals but not as comfortable at improvising, making up moves and plays on-the-fly.

These tendencies have changed in recent years, as more of the world is exposed to the NBA style of play. More foreign-born players are attending college in the United States and going on to play in the NBA, whereas former NBA players are plentiful in foreign pro leagues. So there has been a merging of styles. Croatian Drazen Petrovic, who played for the New Jersey Nets before he was killed in a car crash in 1994, was as fluid and daring as any American-born player.

But some differences in the style of play remain.

Perhaps because of the larger, trapezoidal foul lane and the shorter three-point line used in international play, big men overseas tend to roam outside and shoot more three-pointers than their American counterparts, who tend to stay closer to the basket.

Three-point shots abound in international ball, where the pure shooting skills of the players often compare well with those of NBA players. International players also tend not to be as aggressive inside, as adept at going one-on-one offensively, or as tenacious defensively as American players, although these gaps too are rapidly closing.

As was seen in Olympic competitions prior to the Dream Teams' dominance in 1992 and 1996, the rest of the world is rapidly catching up to the United States in terms of skill level. Many national teams could compete successfully with top college teams or perhaps even struggling NBA teams.

Clyde's Rules

There are several key differences between international play and what we're used to in the NBA. They include:

➤ The foul lane is shaped like a trapezoid (with the wide side at the baseline) instead of a rectangle.

➤ The three-point line is at 20'6", compared with 19'9" in American college ball and 22' to 23'9" in the NBA.

➤ The shot clock is 30 seconds, compared with 35 in college and 24 in the NBA.

➤ Games consist of two 20-minute halves, the same as college but shorter than the NBA's four 12-minute quarters.

Dream Teams Make Their Impact

On April 8, 1989, the FIBA World Congress voted to eliminate the distinction between amateurs and professionals—a fuzzy distinction at best. Players who were paid to compete for European club teams or received government stipends to compete in the former Soviet Union were somehow considered amateurs by FIBA, whereas NBA players were considered professionals.

In any case, the vote opened the way for NBA players to participate in FIBA-sponsored international events such as the Olympics. There was immediate skepticism about whether highly paid NBA stars would want to spend the 1992 off-season competing in the Olympics, but this failed to take into account the huge marketing opportunity that the Olympics represented for these players and their corporate backers, to say nothing of the national pride and competitive instincts of these players.

Every player who was asked to compete agreed, and USA Basketball went out of its way to make it a pleasant experience by staging training camp in Monte Carlo, housing the players at a private hotel in Barcelona, and paying for the players' families to accompany them.

The roster of that original Dream Team reads like a nominating list for the Hall of Fame. Start with Michael Jordan, Magic Johnson, and Larry Bird, three of the greatest players ever to lace on sneakers. At center were David Robinson and Patrick Ewing, at power forward Karl Malone and Charles Barkley. For versatility, there were Scottie

Pippen, Clyde Drexler, and Chris Mullin, while all-time assists and steals leader John Stockton provided another playmaker. The 12th man was Christian Laettner, a future NBA All-Star who had been the top college player of 1991–92 at Duke yet was something of a babe in the woods in this company.

The Dream Team dominated its opponents, winning its eight Olympic games by an average of nearly 44 points. Yet nobody complained about the lopsided nature of the competition, for the other teams knew that only by playing against the very best could they measure their own progress. They were honored to be on the same floor as these living legends, and it became a ritual for the Dream Team to pose for pictures with their opponents before each game.

It's difficult to describe the reaction to the Dream Team to anyone who wasn't in Barcelona. The players were mobbed wherever they went by people young and old, male and female, basketball fans and non-fans alike. Coach Chuck Daly said it was "like Elvis and the Beatles put together," and he wasn't far off.

The impact the Dream Team had on the global popularity of the sport is indisputable. Competing on the world's greatest athletic stage, the Dream Team won millions, perhaps billions, of new fans for the game of basketball simply by showing how beautiful it can be when played at its highest level. Demand for NBA merchandise and telecasts of NBA games exploded in countries around the world, and the NBA office was deluged with requests from promoters for teams and players to make global trips overseas.

People quickly began asking whether the NBA would consider expanding to Europe, perhaps forming a European division. Commissioner Stern responded by saying that the league had no plans to expand beyond North America and that it chose to work with FIBA to strengthen existing leagues in European nations and build the sport at the grass roots level. I think that's a wise policy because the

Clyde's Record Book

Coach Chuck Daly had only one problem with the original Dream Team: how to come up with enough playing time to keep everyone happy. It was resolved when Stockton got hurt and could see only limited action, and Daly decided to keep Laettner for the most part on the bench as insurance in case his big men got in foul trouble. Then he divided the time pretty much equally among the remaining 10 players, even mixing and matching his opening lineup each game to give everyone a chance to start.

Quote...Unquote

"They knew they were playing the best in the world. They'll go home and for the rest of their lives be able to tell their kids, 'I played against Michael Jordan and Magic Johnson and Larry Bird.' And the more they play against our best players, the more confident they're going to get."—*Chuck Daly, coach of the Original Dream Team, on the way other teams approached his squad.*

NBA has more than enough to concern itself with here at home without trying to expand overseas.

Nonetheless, the NBA worked hard to capitalize on global opportunities. With basketball becoming hugely popular in the Far East, the league has had two teams open the regular season with a pair of games in Japan every other year since 1990. Teams have played exhibitions regularly in Europe and Mexico, and more are anticipated for other parts of the world. Meanwhile, Dream Teams of NBA stars participated in the 1994 World Championship in Toronto and the 1996 Olympics in Atlanta, appearances that bolster the growth of interest in basketball globally.

In addition, the NBA has opened offices, largely for marketing and public relations purposes, in Paris, London, Barcelona, Mexico City, Hong Kong, Taiwan, Tokyo, Melbourne, and Singapore, with more to come. Its mandate is to focus both on growing interest in the NBA in particular and basketball in general because what's good for the sport could only be good for the league.

Basketball's Ambassadors of Goodwill

The Harlem Globetrotters made their first competitive appearance in Hinckley, Illinois, on January 7, 1927, and for nearly three-quarters of a century they have been delighting fans around the world with their mixture of basketball skill and high-jinx.

The Globetrotters were born not in Harlem, New York's famous uptown neighborhood, but in Chicago, where Abe Saperstein, a London-born son of Polish immigrants was coaching a team named the Savoy Big Five. When the Savoy Ballroom on Chicago's South Side decided it no longer wanted to sponsor a team, Saperstein renamed his club the Harlem Globetrotters—Harlem to indicate that the team was comprised of African-American players, Globetrotters to project a glamorous image.

Clyde's Record Book

The Harlem Globetrotters' first trip didn't exactly live up to the team's nickname. It covered only 50 miles, the distance from Chicago to Hinckley, Illinois—hardly what you'd call trotting the globe.

As I mentioned earlier, pro leagues regularly came and went in the 1920s and 1930s, and the top teams made most of their money by barnstorming—traveling from town to town, usually by car or bus, and playing any local team that would pay to host them. The Globetrotters became one of the best teams of that barnstorming era, winning 101 of 117 games in their first year of existence.

But Saperstein quickly realized that storming into town and whipping the local team probably wouldn't get his team invited back for a return engagement, and eventually they'd run out of places to play. So the Globetrotters began to focus on entertainment in addition to competition, weaving fancy shots and tricky ballhandling routines into their games to delight the fans. That formula was an immediate success and enabled the Globetrotters to survive and thrive long after other barnstorming teams had died.

Throughout the 1930s, despite their focus on razzle-dazzle entertainment, the Globetrotters remained a highly competitive basketball team that ranked among the best in the nation. In 1939, they reached the semifinals of the prestigious World Professional Tournament in Chicago that included all the top teams of that era, and the following year they won the tournament.

After World War II, the Globetrotters began to live up to their name, traveling the world and winning new fans for the sport of basketball. In 1951, they embarked on a tour of Europe that included, at the request of U.S. government officials, a stop in Berlin. More than 75,000 fans filled the Olympic Stadium on August 22, 1951, to watch the Globetrotters in the same venue where Adolf Hitler had snubbed another African-American, Jesse Owens, at the 1936 Olympics.

Fred "Preacher" Smith of the Harlem Globetrotters enters the Guiness Book of World Records in 1997 by dunking on a basket set at 11 feet, 11 inches in Birmingham, England, during the Globetrotters' tour of Europe.
Associated Press

From then on, the U.S. State Department began referring to the Globetrotters as "Basketball's Ambassadors of Goodwill." They have appeared in numerous television shows and films and continue to tour the world, delighting a new generation of fans with their antics.

Courts of Dreams

The NBA is the professional basketball league to which all players aspire, but it is not the only pro league in the United States. I've already mentioned the ABA, which lasted for nine seasons and produced great players like Julius Erving and David Thompson among many others. Another circuit, the American Basketball League, had visions of competing against the NBA in the early 1960s but lasted little more than a season before disappearing.

Quote...Unquote

"The CBA has been a proving ground for players, coaches and referees. The CBA has been instrumental in the development of many of the people you see in prominent positions all over the NBA today." —Rod Thorn, *NBA senior vice president, basketball operations.*

Many regional leagues, which sought to fill the gap between the NBA and college ball, have come and gone over the past half-century. But one minor league that has survived is the Continental Basketball Association (CBA), which began life as the Eastern Basketball Association and actually predates the NBA by one month.

The CBA now has a working agreement as the NBA's official developmental league. The NBA uses the league to test out possible rules and equipment changes and as a place for referees to gain experience. The CBA also has fed more than 100 players and several coaches to the NBA, including players such as Anthony Mason, Isaac Austin, John Starks, Matt Maloney, and Mario Elie and head coaches Phil Jackson, George Karl, Flip Saunders, and Dave Cowens.

Clyde's Record Book

Phil Jackson is the only man to coach teams to championships in both the NBA and the CBA. Before leading the Bulls to their first NBA crown in 1991, Jackson guided the Albany Patroons to the CBA crown in 1984. He's also the only man to win Coach of the Year honors in the NBA (1996) and CBA (1985).

Founded in 1946–47 as the Eastern Basketball Association with six franchises, all in Pennsylvania, the league changed its name to the Continental Basketball Association in 1978–79. The name change made sense because the league had placed a team in Anchorage, Alaska, the year before!

The Anchorage franchise lasted five seasons, which was four more than the Hawaii Volcanos, whose only CBA season was 1979–80. Other exotic CBA franchises that have come and gone include the Atlantic City Hi Rollers, the Puerto Rico Coquis, the Alberta Dusters, the Toronto Tornados, and the Mexico Aztecas. As you might guess, franchises coming and going is a fact of

CBA life, although several franchises have achieved stability in recent years, and expansion teams cost more than ever before.

The CBA, which plays a 56-game winter schedule, had nine teams in 1997–98, with three more scheduled to join in 1999–2000. The league is working hard to dispel its long-held image as a circuit of long bus rides, fast food joints, and second-rate hotels, preferring to stress its position as a launching pad for careers in the NBA.

Numerous pro and semipro leagues in existence today play summer schedules. Perhaps the best-known is in Los Angeles, where several NBA teams annually send young players to gain experience in the LA Pro Summer League. Another, along the East Coast, is the United States Basketball League.

The Least You Need to Know

➤ Basketball is the fastest growing sport in the world, second in popularity only to soccer.

➤ The Dream Team was the sensation of the 1992 Olympics in Barcelona and gave a major boost to the sport's global popularity.

➤ The Harlem Globetrotters have brought smiles to fans' faces for nearly three-quarters of a century.

➤ The Continental Basketball Association is the official developmental league of the NBA, sending players, coaches, and referees to the big time.

Chapter 21

The College Game

At its best, college basketball combines the intimacy and spirit of high school ball with the high skill level of the pros. It gives fans the best of both worlds, which is why college hoops loyalists are so passionate about their obsession.

Each year, college basketball reaches a climax with March Madness, more formally known as the NCAA Division I Men's Basketball Championship. The single-elimination format gives the tournament a sense of urgency rarely found in other sports (except pro football), where championships are decided in multi-game series.

Women's college basketball has enjoyed a tremendous growth spurt in recent years, with women's teams emerging from the shadows of their male counterparts and becoming nationally televised attractions on their own. Gone, or at least rapidly fading, are the days when the women's team was relegated to playing in the preliminary game before the men's team took the court. Women's programs such as those at Tennessee, Connecticut, and Stanford have rapidly developed a tradition to match the best of the nation's men's programs.

Clyde's Record Book

A crowd of 17,623 turned out at New York's Madison Square Garden on December 29, 1936, to watch Stanford beat LIU 45-31. The attraction was Stanford's Hank Luisetti, the first player to popularize the one-handed shot, who drew a standing ovation from the Garden crowd.

Clyde's Chalk Talk

Point-shaving refers to a player intentionally holding down his team's score—shaving points off it. This is done so that his team either loses or else wins by fewer points than expected. Remember that sports gambling works with a point spread, the number of points that a favorite must win by before somebody betting on that team is a winner. This is called *covering the spread*. Thus, in paying a player to shave points, a gambler doesn't have to convince the player to make his team lose—only to make sure his team wins by fewer points than the spread.

I should emphasize that the college years are a special time of maturing for a young athlete. Players who are raw in high school come into their own and refine their games, developing the skills and personalities that will mark their careers. It is at the college level that players who had little competition in high school get to test themselves against players every bit as good as they are, and learn to do what they need to do to take their games to the next level. Beyond all that, the college years are a vital time for the mental and emotional maturing process that takes place off the court. That's why I feel strongly that young players should spend at least a few years in college rather than try to rush into the pros, as tempting as that may be.

This chapter takes a look at college basketball and the special allure it has on players, students, alumni, and fans.

Beyond the Campuses

Once college basketball was an intercollegiate activity among neighboring schools played in campus gyms before students, family, friends, and faculty. But that was a long, long time ago.

By the 1930s, college basketball had hit the big time. Teams traveled around the country and played in big-city arenas such as Chicago Stadium or New York's Madison Square Garden. In fact, college hoops was a staple at the Garden, with local teams such as Long Island University, New York University, City College of New York, and St. John's hosting national powers before sellout crowds.

While this brought revenue to the universities and pleased alumni who loved to cheer on their alma mater, it also exposed the college game to gambling. College basketball has been hit by a number of *point-shaving* scandals, which continue to make news as recently as this past season.

Despite these setbacks, the growth of interest in college basketball has been tremendous and continues unabated. More schools are investing in building their basketball programs, confident that the positive publicity and enthusiasm that a successful program generates outweighs the costs. Leading programs are as likely to play games in big-city arenas as in campus gyms, and they have become the modern barnstormers, traveling the country to play any school that will come up with enough money to make the trip worth their while.

March Madness: Everyone Into the Office Pool!

Division I college teams (generally comprised of the bigger or more prestigious schools that have more resources to attract top players) play about 30 games a year. The object is to win at least 20 of them, which should qualify your team for a place in March Madness, the 64-team field of the NCAA tournament. (See the later section called "There's Life Beyond Division I" to learn more about other college divisions.)

The college season begins in November and runs until March. Most teams belong to *conferences*, so they'll play games against both conference rivals and non-conference foes. They'll also usually play in at least one tournament, at the start of the season or during the holiday break.

In the 1950s and 1960s, you had to win your conference schedule to qualify for the tournament, but that's not the case anymore. With so many teams in the field, some of the major conferences, like the Big Ten or the Big East, often send five or six teams to the tourney.

Conference tournaments usually take place in early March, with the NCAA tournament and the 32-team National Invitation Tournament beginning in mid-March. The NIT is actually older than the NCAA tourney and used to be more prestigious, but now it only gets teams that don't qualify for bids to the more lucrative NCAA event.

Clyde's Chalk Talk

The *National Collegiate Athletic Association (NCAA)* is this country's governing body for all college sports, including basketball. In addition to administering the championship tournament, the NCAA oversees the playing rules and ensures that schools abide by regulations on recruiting and other matters.

Clyde's Chalk Talk

Conferences are alliances of schools, usually from within one geographical region and sharing a similar academic/athletic philosophy, that are the collegiate counterpart to a professional league. Rivalries develop between schools that are members of the same conference, enhancing the competitive appeal of their games. One such rivalry is that between Harvard and Yale, members of the prestigious Ivy League.

What makes the NCAA tournament so special? The urgency of the single-elimination format, combined with the unpredictability of college players (as compared with pros) gives each game extra tension. You never know what's going to happen. Every year

Clyde's Tip

You can even get into the NCAA tournament with a losing record. That's because the automatic berths reserved for conference champions (which make up nearly half the field) go to the teams that win the conferences' postseason tournaments, not the regular season leaders. The motto is if you're not going to win many games, don't waste your wins early; get hot at the right time, and you're in.

upsets abound and a Cinderella story emerges—in 1998 it was Valparaiso that surprised the experts and captured fans' imagination around the country, because everybody loves an underdog.

The fact is, people who don't regularly follow sports sit up and take notice during March Madness. So much emotion comes through on those national telecasts that it's hard not to get caught up in rooting for one school or another.

Oh yes, there's one more reason to get into March Madness: the office pool. Is there an office in this country where a tearsheet of the tournament brackets from the local paper isn't circulated so that everyone from the boss to the mail clerk can make their picks? People who wouldn't consider gambling don't think twice about diving right into the office pool. Just remember to keep a copy so that when you're watching on TV, you can check off all your winners.

Cheerleaders, like these from Syracuse University, add to the fun and spirit of college basketball. Associated Press

Coaches Call the Shots

The NBA is a players' league. College basketball is a coach's game.

The reason is simple: The players on a college team change every four years, if not sooner. The coach, on the other hand, may be there for much longer. The coach builds the program and provides the stability to see it through. More than any other single person, the coach gives the school's basketball program its identity. He implements his system and lets it develop over the years, to the point where it often becomes associated with the school.

The college coach has to do much more than just prepare his team for an opponent and then make the right substitutions. He must first recruit the players who will make up his team. Then he must monitor their academic performance, providing guidance and arranging for tutoring as needed, to make sure they are eligible to suit up. Then he must spend time speaking to alumni groups to help raise money for the school and the athletic program, and to rally campus and civic groups to help build support for the team.

With all the preliminary work, the easiest part of the coach's job may well come once the game starts.

As you might expect, players at the college level tend to be more coachable than after they turn pro. They're younger, of course, and more open to guidance and correction. They also have had less time to develop bad habits or negative attitudes, and are more likely to follow a positive role model, such as a coach.

The nature of the college game itself also makes for more of a coach's game. The pace is significantly slower than in the NBA, which lends itself to more play-calling from the bench. The players, overall, are not as athletically gifted or refined, which increases the importance of strategy and coaching. Zone defenses are permitted, giving the coach more defensive strategies to work with. Finally, players come and go quickly, so the college coach can't depend on having quality players every season. He must put in a firm structure so all players will have something they can cling to for stability. That becomes the signature of his program and his school.

Clyde's Tip

Don't pick all favorites in filling our your office pool bracket sheet, because those are the teams most people will pick. Try to find an underdog that finished the season strong and might be capable of an upset or two. Consider a team that played in an especially strong conference or beat some tough teams down the stretch. And if that team is led by an experienced coach who has proven himself in previous tournaments, so much the better.

Clyde's Tip

When you think of North Carolina, who do you think of first? Long-time coach Dean Smith, of course. Not Michael Jordan, James Worthy, nor any of the other Tar Heel stars. That proves that college basketball is a coach's game.

John Wooden and the UCLA Dynasty

As a player, John Wooden was known as the Indiana Rubber Man. Later, as a coach, he became better-known as the Wizard of Westwood, so he can lay claim to two of basketball's more interesting nicknames. Wooden is one of only two men to be inducted into the Basketball Hall of Fame as both a player and coach; Lenny Wilkens joined him as a dual honoree when he was named as a coach in 1998.

Wooden was an outstanding high school player in Indiana—the high school he played at is now located on John R. Wooden Drive—and a college star at Purdue, but it was as the coach of the UCLA Bruins that he made his most lasting impression. In 27 seasons at UCLA, Wooden's Bruins won 20 championships in what is now the Pacific-10 Conference.

But the Bruins were far from just a regional power. During that time, UCLA won 10 national championships in a 12-year span, including seven in a row from 1967 through 1973. Four times, Wooden's Bruins went undefeated, including consecutive 30-0 seasons in 1972 and 1973 as part of a record 88-game winning streak that covered parts of four seasons.

Quote...Unquote

"I played my heart out for Coach Wooden. It meant that much to me. He deserves to go out a winner." —*Dave Meyers of UCLA, after leading the Bruins to a 92–85 victory over Kentucky in the 1975 NCAA championship game, John Wooden's final game as coach.*

Wooden was named the national coach of the year six times by UPI, five times by AP and the U.S. Basketball Writers Association. Among the stars he coached are Kareem Abdul-Jabbar, Lucius Allen, Henry Bibby, Gail Goodrich, Walt Hazzard, Marques Johnson, Dave Meyers, Curtis Rowe, Bill Walton, Mike Warren, Richard Washington, Sidney Wicks, and Jamaal Wilkes—each of these players was an All-American.

It was the greatest dynasty in college basketball history, one that ranks right up there with the Boston Celtics' 11 championships in 13 seasons when it comes to total domination.

Campus Kings: College Hoops' Perennial Powers

Some teams can always be found in the NCAA tournament and somewhere in the Top 20 or Top 25 polls conducted by AP and *USA Today*. They are the campus kings, the perennial powers of college basketball.

What they have in common is a winning tradition, usually generated by at least one highly successful coach who stayed with the school for many years. Schools at lower levels tend to be stepping stones for coaches on the rise, so even if they achieve prominence for a few years, the program may have trouble maintaining its winning ways when the coach moves on. But the elite schools stay on top because their coaches are fixtures.

These schools also stay on top because of the exposure they receive on national television. High school kids see these teams on TV all the time, and it's natural for them to want to go there. Recruiting becomes a breeze; these schools get the cream of the crop.

I already mentioned UCLA and Wooden. While it's true that Gary Cunningham and Gene Bartow, the coaches who succeeded Wooden, could not duplicate his success, the bottom line is that no one in history has been able to, either. Although it would be two decades until UCLA won another national title in 1995, the Bruins remained at or near the top of the Pac-10—and even reached the NCAA Finals in 1980 under Larry Brown.

The college basketball program with the most wins is the University of Kentucky, where Adolph Rupp reigned as the Baron of the Bluegrass. In 41 years as the head coach at Kentucky (from 1931 through 1972), Rupp compiled a record of 875-190 for a winning percentage of .822 and led the Wildcats to four NCAA titles. Not even a recruiting scandal could keep the Kentucky program down very long, as Rick Pitino brought the Wildcats back to championship level in 1996.

The only man with more major college victories than Rupp is Dean Smith, who compiled a record of 879-256 in 36 years as the head coach at North Carolina from 1962 through 1997. Smith led the Tar Heels to two national titles and eight other NCAA Final Four appearances. He succeeded another great coach at North Carolina: Frank McGuire, who guided the Tar Heels to the NCAA title in 1957.

Other major colleges that seem to win 20 games or more each season and that often rank near the top of the polls include Duke under Mike Krzyzewski, Kansas under Roy Williams, Indiana under Bob Knight, Arizona under Lute Olsen, Louisville under Denny Crum, Syracuse under Jim Boeheim, and Georgetown under John Thompson.

Clyde's Record Book

This table lists the five winningest coaches in NCAA Division I, with the schools they are most commonly associated with and their career victory totals:

Dean Smith (North Carolina)	879
Adolph Rupp (Kentucky)	876
Henry Iba (Oklahoma State)	767
Ed Diddle (Western Kentucky)	759
Phog Allen (Kansas)	746

Dean Smith, who retired in 1997 as the coach with the most wins in college basketball history, makes a point to one of his North Carolina players. Associated Press

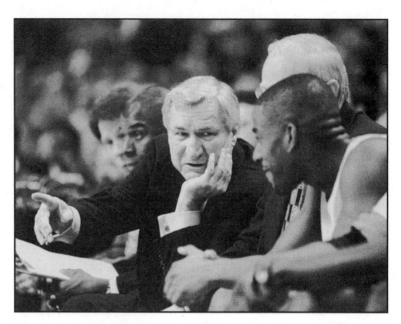

There's Life Beyond Division I

Clyde's Record Book

Some great players have come from the so-called small-college ranks, including Earl Monroe (Winston-Salem State), Willis Reed (Grambling), George Gervin (Eastern Michigan), Jerry Sloan (Evansville), Joe Fulks (Murray State), Vern Mikkelsen (Hamline), Jack Sikma (Illinois Wesleyan), and Dennis Rodman (Southeastern Oklahoma). And, oh yes, Walt "Clyde" Frazier (Southern Illinois).

When you think of college basketball and March Madness, you're thinking of the NCAA's Division I—the big guys. But there are many other levels of competition in the college ranks, and the games they play are just as spirited and hard-fought as those you see on national TV.

The NCAA also includes Division II and Division III, while the National Association of Intercollegiate Athletics represents nearly 500 schools. These are all four-year colleges, but many have smaller enrollments than their Division I brethren, so they prefer to compete on a more limited scale—at least in terms of expenses, though certainly not in spirit.

Then there are the more than 500 two-year junior or community colleges that field basketball teams. Many fine players who could not qualify academically for a four-year college when they came out of high school have gone to junior colleges, where they worked on their grades as well as their game.

How the Game Has Changed

The tremendous media exposure that college basketball receives has brought the game more in line with the NBA as far as entertainment value and excitement. Gone are the days of stall-ball, thanks to the introduction of a shot clock. And the geniuses who outlawed dunking in college ball—an absurdity that somehow lasted nine seasons from 1967–68 through 1975–76—wouldn't have a prayer of pushing that rule through today.

Besides the shot clock, the rule that has produced the biggest change in the college game has been the three-point shot. With the line set at just 19 feet, 9 inches from the basket, this is a very makeable shot—I'd say too makeable. Every big-time school has at least a couple of players for whom 20-foot jumpers are a piece of cake. Some teams—such as Kentucky when Rick Pitino was coaching—seemed to design their entire offense around the three-point shot.

Clyde's Record Book

Among the current and former NBA stars who once played junior college ball are Mitch Richmond, Larry Johnson, Sam Cassell, Mookie Blaylock, Tiny Archibald, Artis Gilmore, Spencer Haywood, Dennis Johnson, Gus Johnson, Vinnie Johnson, and Bob McAdoo.

I really think the three-pointer has hurt the game. How many times have you seen a player come down on a fast break and, instead of heading to the basket, spot up behind the three-point line? Players are so conscious of the line that they have forgotten how to shoot medium-range jumpers. Those have become virtually extinct, and it's hard to argue with the logic: Why shoot a 17-footer for two points when you can back up a step and try for three points?

One good thing that the three-point rule has done is bring the small player back into the game. Guards who can create and make their shots are more valuable than ever. Many teams will use three-guard lineups on offense to get more three-pointers and will employ scrambling, pressure tactics on defense to prevent teams from setting up for threes at the other end.

Why Great College Players Don't Always Make Great Pros

Despite the evolution of the game, not every great college basketball player makes it big in the NBA.

I see three main reasons: size, quickness, and maturity.

The average NBA player stands 6'7" and weighs 223 pounds. That's big. Many college players find they have to learn a new position if they want to make it in the pros. The 6'8" college center has to learn to play facing the basket as a forward, while the 6'5" college forward has to learn to handle the ball and play the perimeter as a guard. Often this transition becomes a major roadblock to success, and good college players fall by the wayside because they can't adjust.

Quickness among NBA players is a trait that is underestimated by the average fan, who sometimes fails to see beyond the size of these athletes. The NBA is a game based on quickness. Whether making moves to the basket on offense or reacting to an opponent's efforts on defense, the single most important attribute an NBA player needs to succeed is quickness. College players often can get by on size and shooting ability to become stars, but in the NBA you've got to have quickness.

Clyde's Rules

The importance of quickness to an NBA player is true even among centers, where you'd think size was the most important trait. Look at Hakeem Olajuwon, David Robinson, Patrick Ewing, even Shaquille O'Neal—they're all remarkably quick.

Maturity may be the single greatest reason why not every college star succeeds in the NBA—and that means both physical and emotional maturity.

The NBA game is much more physical and grueling than college ball, and some players can't handle the pounding of NBA play or the demanding nature of the 82-game schedule. Remember, college players usually play just 30–35 games a year, their games are only 40 minutes long (as opposed to 48), and playing in zone defenses often saves wear and tear on their bodies.

Clyde's Record Book

Steve Alford was a high school Mr. Basketball in the state of Indiana who led Indiana University to the 1987 NCAA title, earning All-American honors. Though a great shooter and sound fundamental player, at 6'2" Alford was undersized for a pro shooting guard; he also lacked the quickness to succeed in the NBA. He played sparingly in four pro seasons before moving into the college coaching ranks.

Besides, different players reach their physical peak at different stages of their careers. Some players are as good as they'll ever get early in their college careers, or even while they're still in high school. Others don't really come into their own until several years into their pro careers.

As for the emotional factor, some college players simply can't deal with life in the pros. For many, joining a pro team is the first time they are on their own, out of their cocoons. And more players are turning pro at a younger age, before they complete (or in some cases even attend) college, which only means they are less emotionally prepared for the move. Even though the NBA runs special programs to help rookies make the transition to pro life on—and especially off—the court, not all college stars can handle it.

Can College Basketball Survive Early Entry?

Colleges used to be able to count on three (before freshman eligibility) or four years of play from a player they recruited. Not anymore. When Bobby Cremins recruited Stephon Marbury to Georgia Tech, he knew he'd be lucky to get two years out of him before he left for the NBA. He turned out to be half-lucky—Marbury stayed for only one year.

The NBA used to have a rule saying a player was not eligible to be drafted until his college class graduated. But in 1970, Spencer Haywood sued the league, claiming this rule unfairly prohibited him from making a living. The courts agreed.

The NBA tried a hardship system, whereby players had to prove financial hardship to enter the league early, but this proved unrealistic. Finally, the league agreed to open its doors to any player, and that's the way things stand today.

Now, players regularly turn pro after one or two years of college ball. They feel their games are ready for the NBA, and in many cases they're right. Remember that Magic Johnson was a sophomore when he turned pro, and he did fairly well.

Some players are even bypassing college entirely. And with the success of Kevin Garnett, who made the move to the NBA from high school in 1995, more likely will follow.

What does this do to the college game? For one thing, it has brought about tremendous instability, because a coach can't count on keeping his star players for very long. And one star can make a tremendous impact in college basketball, turning a mediocre team into a champion—or, by leaving, turning a champion into an also-ran.

Recruiting is more important than ever. A coach used to recruit a star point guard and know that position would be filled for four years, but now he feels the need to constantly replenish the talent on his roster.

The lack of player stability hasn't seemed to have affected the popularity of the college game, though. Fans tend to root for their favorite programs regardless of the players. And, at least so far, the stream of talent from the high school ranks has been more than enough to replace players lost early to the pros. But whether this will continue bears watching.

The Least You Need to Know

➤ March Madness, culminating in the NCAA Final Four, is one of the great events of the sports calendar.

➤ The NBA is a players' league; college basketball is a coach's game, because the coach is the constant who shapes a school's basketball program.

➤ John Wooden made UCLA the Boston Celtics of college basketball.

➤ Most of the big-time schools you see on national TV each week compete in the NCAA's Division I, but games played by smaller schools in other divisions can be just as spirited and competitive.

➤ Not all great college players make great pros; a lack of size, quickness, or maturity can be major impediments to success.

➤ Early entry into the pro ranks has created quicker turnover than ever before among college basketball's stars, but so far it hasn't hurt the game's popularity which continues to grow each year.

Chapter 22

High School Happenings

In This Chapter

➤ A game everybody plays, or at least watches

➤ High school hoops hysteria

➤ Milan High School: the real-life *Hoosiers*

➤ The dream is to go from high school to the pros

➤ The reality is that BMOC rarely lasts very long

It's easy to like high school basketball.

The energy in a high school gym on game nights is something special. The players are swooping and hooping, the cheerleaders are dancing and prancing, all to the delight of classmates and relatives cheering from the stands.

No, the level of play isn't what you see in the NBA or in big-time college basketball. Yet that is part of the charm. High school players make up in enthusiasm and effort what they may lack in excellence. They work harder at the fundamentals of the game, such as making a crisp bounce pass to get the ball past a defender or boxing out an opponent to grab a rebound—or shooting free throws, which is a lost art in the NBA.

And (gasp!) they listen to what their coaches have to say.

On the high school basketball courts, so many teenagers—girls as well as boys—learn values such as teamwork, cooperation, and sportsmanship—and one, in particular, that was instilled in me: discipline. They experience the joy of victory and the agony of defeat, and they learn how to handle both powerful emotions—valuable lessons indeed.

Everybody's Involved

High school basketball is part of Americana, bridging the distance from the inner cities to the Great Plains. The sport is played by about one million student-athletes annually and watched by millions of family and friends, fellow students, alumni, and other school supporters.

About 17,000 member schools make up the National Federation of State High School Associations. Of those, 16,594 had boys' basketball teams and 16,198 had girls' basketball teams in 1995–96, the most recent season for which data is available. According to the Federation, more students play high school basketball than any other sport—a total of 545,596 boys and 445,869 girls in 1995–96. And that doesn't include all the others who play *intramural* basketball or just play the game for fun in gym class.

Clyde's Chalk Talk

Many youngsters like to play basketball and compete, but lack the *skill* to play on a varsity team. For them, an *intramural* team, often composed of similarly enthusiastic classmates, is a perfect answer. Many high schools and colleges offer elaborate intramural leagues to satisfy these eager players.

The reasons for this popularity are obvious. Basketball is a game that promotes teamwork and other positive values, making it appealing to educators. It stresses skill over strength, opening it up to all students, not just the biggest and strongest. Basketball can be played indoors, throughout the long winter months that make up the heart of the school year. And because you don't need a whole lot of kids to get a team together or expensive equipment or facilities to make it happen, it's accessible to even the smallest schools that might not be able to field a football team or baseball squad.

Clyde's Rules

Rules for high school basketball are similar to college, although some states don't use shot clocks. The three-point line is the same: 19 feet, 9 inches. One major difference is that the game is divided into four eight-minute quarters (for a total of 32 minutes) instead of the 40-minute college game that is divided into 20-minute halves.

Some High School Hoop History

High school basketball has a rich tradition, dating back nearly to the day the sport was invented. And that makes sense, because it was created by an instructor as an indoor exercise for a class of students.

The first interscholastic basketball game supposedly took place between Holyoke (Massachusetts) High School and Philadelphia (Pennsylvania) Central High School in 1897, just six years after the sport was invented. Holyoke played several games that year against various schools and in 1890 won an 11-team tournament held in Boston.

The first statewide invitational tournament is believed to have been held in 1905 at Lawrence College in Appleton, Wisconsin. Such tournaments quickly became popular and were sponsored throughout the country by individuals, companies, civic groups, or colleges until state athletic associations took them over. The first state association-sanctioned events were held in 1908 in Illinois, Kansas, and Utah; by 1920, when the National Federation of State High School Associations was founded, half the states in the country were running tournaments.

To this day, "going to the States" is the goal of high school players throughout the land.

High School Hoops Hysteria

You've probably heard about Hoosier Hysteria, which grips the state of Indiana every February and March. During this time a statewide high school basketball tournament is played, the climax of which takes place in the state capital. But hysteria of this type doesn't just affect Hoosiers—it's a nationwide epidemic.

Clyde's Chalk Talk

The *National Federation of State High School Associations* provides leadership for high school sports, including basketball, much the same way the NCAA does for colleges. The Federation publishes record books, casebooks, game administration handbooks, and manuals for players and officials. It also coordinates and updates the rules used in high school play.

Clyde's Record Book

Some of the most successful high school basketball teams played for Passaic High School in New Jersey more than 70 years ago. Beginning on December 17, 1919, Passaic won 159 consecutive games before losing to Hackensack High 39-35 on February 6, 1925. But believe it or not, the girls' winning streak is even longer: The Baskin (Louisiana) High School girls' team won 218 games in a row from 1947 through 1953.

Warsaw's Kevin Ault drives against New Albany's Lamont Roland in the Final Four of the 1996 Indiana state championship, also known as Hoosier Hysteria. Associated Press

Clyde's Record Book

St. Anthony's High School in Jersey City, New Jersey, holds the record for most consecutive boys' state titles won: nine, from 1983 through 1991. But once again, the girls' record is even longer: Pius XI in Milwaukee, Wisconsin, won 12 straight girls' titles from 1982 through 1993.

Tournament time is an exciting time in states all around the country, as the best teams from the big cities and the small towns meet to play opponents they don't normally play, with statewide bragging rights at stake.

High school basketball is big in California, where the weather enables hoopsters to play outdoors as well as in for most of the year. It's big in the Eastern Seaboard cities such as Boston, New York, Philadelphia, and Washington, where school yard heroes take games they've honed on the blacktop playgrounds and test them in a more structured environment. It's big in states such as Kentucky and North Carolina, where countless youngsters go to bed dreaming of playing for their storied state colleges and universities and knowing they must first prove themselves at the high school level.

*Basketball is taken seriously in Hoosier country, where Indiana University coach Bob Knight slams a cup of water to the floor during a 1997 game against Minnesota.
Associated Press*

Some states hold open tournaments, inviting all the best schools in the state regardless of size. Other states divide schools into divisions according to enrollment and run separate tournaments for each division or class. The idea is that it's not fair to expect a small-town school with perhaps 100 students to compete against a big-city school that might have an enrollment of 5,000 or more. While this might level the playing field for smaller schools, it also takes away their chance to play David and slay a Goliath, much like Milan High School of Indiana did in 1954.

The Real-Life *Hoosiers*

You may recall the movie *Hoosiers*, in which Gene Hackman played an aging coach who led a team from a rural town in Indiana to the state championship, beating a big-city rival in a dramatic state finals game. Hackman's character was an old-line coach who believed in discipline—much like my coaches did when I was growing up in Atlanta—and taught a team-oriented game in which passing and fundamentals were stressed over individual play.

Well, *Hoosiers* really did exist. In 1954, Milan High School, with just 161 students, won the Indiana State Championship at Butler Fieldhouse on the Butler University campus in Indianapolis, defeating big-city Muncie Central 32-30 in the championship game.

When the real-life David took on its Goliath, the team was at a disadvantage not only because of the size of the schools but also because of the size of the players. Milan's starting center stood just 5'11", and its tallest player was only 6'2"; the Muncie front line went 6'5", 6'4", and 6'2".

But Milan's disciplined style of play managed to keep the game close throughout, and a basket by Ray Craft on a driving layup tied the score at 28-28 late in the game. Two free throws by 5'10" guard Bobby Plump put Milan in front, but a long shot by Gene Flowers of Muncie tied the score in the final minute. With 18 seconds left, Milan coach Marvin Wood called a timeout to set up one last play.

Wood declared that the ball go to Plump, a two-time Indiana All-Star. With five seconds left, Plump started to drive to the basket, and as his defender backed off, he lofted a jumper that went in at the buzzer, giving Milan a 32-30 victory.

Clyde's Rules

While the movie makes much of how the coach stressed teamwork and that the ball had to be passed a number of times before a shot should be attempted, the big play for the real-life *Hoosiers* was just the opposite. On the winning play for Milan High School, the team's star, Bobby Plump, was given the ball in an isolation situation. His teammates were told to stay on the other side of the court, out of his way, and Plump scored the winning basket by going one-on-one against his defender.

The Dream: From High School to the Pros

The recent success of Kevin Garnett and Kobe Bryant may be the worst thing to happen to the sport in years.

Garnett went from high school to the pros in 1995—and in three years he's twice been an NBA All-Star and has signed a contract for more than $20 million a year. Bryant followed him a year later and made the All-Star Game in his second season, when the national media dubbed him the "Air Apparent" to Michael Jordan—a lot to ask of a teenager!

So many young kids have seen their success as NBA All-Stars—Garnett with the big contract and Bryant with all the endorsements and publicity—and then fantasize about following in their footsteps from high school to the NBA.

The truth is, 99.9 percent of them will never make it.

An orderly progression used to exist from high school basketball through the college ranks and then on to the NBA. By the time players reached the pros, they had ample opportunity to receive coaching in the fundamentals of the game and to learn the discipline and dedication needed to succeed.

Clyde's Rules

There's no denying that some players are ready to turn pro before they complete four years of college. But these players are the exception, not the rule. Each year, most of the players who leave school early will never play a game in the NBA. Only a select few will follow in the footsteps of Magic Johnson, Isiah Thomas, and, yes, Michael Jordan. The NBA would prefer that players go to college and play four years there, so they are as prepared as possible both physically and emotionally when they turn pro. But the courts have ruled that to keep underclassmen out of the draft would be denying them their opportunity to make a living, so any player can turn pro simply by informing the NBA of their desire to be declared eligible for the draft.

After the courts ordered the NBA to remove restrictions from underclassmen in its draft process, however, the floodgates opened. First you saw college juniors passing up their final year, and maybe an occasional sophomore hoping to follow in the footsteps of a Magic Johnson. Now, players such as Stephon Marbury make a one-year pit stop at Georgia Tech before turning pro, or they go straight to the NBA out of high school.

Moses Malone, Darryl Dawkins, and Bill Willoughby did it back in the mid-1970s, with mixed results. Malone went on to a great pro career and is a future Hall of Famer. Dawkins, a tremendous physical specimen and an engaging personality, had a long and productive NBA career but never became the superstar he might have become had he gotten some solid schooling and discipline at the college level. And Willoughby was inept, averaging just 6.0 points per game and bouncing between six teams in eight NBA seasons.

Shawn Kemp was among the top high school players in the nation at Concord High School in Elkhart, Indiana, in 1988. Kemp chose to enroll at the University of Kentucky but dropped out, then attended a community college in Texas but did not play basketball. When he was drafted on the first round by the Seattle SuperSonics in 1989, Kemp became the first player to go from high school ball to the NBA in more than a decade. After a year on the bench, Kemp developed into one of the NBA's better forwards and a perennial All-Star, yet even he is probably not the polished player he might have been with some good early coaching and playing experience at the college level.

In the last three or four years, players are coming into the NBA earlier and earlier. Several have come in directly from high school, and while the jury is still out on such as Jermaine O'Neal and Tracy McGrady, Garnett and Bryant already have made their mark.

The Reality: BMOC Doesn't Last Long

I'm happy for Garnett and Bryant's success, but it gives too many youngsters the wrong idea.

Just look at the numbers. More than 500,000 boys play competitive high school basketball every year. Only 58 players get drafted into the NBA every year. A few more might make it without getting drafted, but not enough to change the impact of those numbers.

Clyde's Record Book

Have you ever heard of Danny Heater or Greg Procell? Heater set a high school record by scoring 135 points for Burnsville, West Virginia, on January 26, 1960. Procell scored 3,173 points for Noble Ebarb, Louisiana, in 1969–70 and 6,702 points in his high school career, both records. Neither ever played a minute in the NBA.

The inescapable fact is that the odds against a high school player making it to NBA success are staggering. Only the very best beat those odds, if they have luck and good health on their side. Most high school players find they can't even compete on the college level, where just about every player on the team was a Big Man On Campus in high school.

Instead of focusing on the NBA, high school players should concentrate on parlaying their talents into a college scholarship that will afford them a chance at an education and something they can fall back on if they don't realize their hoop dreams.

And if their hoop dreams do come true, they can still put their college educations to good use. Business courses and public speaking classes are of particular benefit to an athlete who makes it to the pros.

The Least You Need to Know

➤ About one million high school players—both boys and girls—play interscholastic basketball, more than any other sport.

➤ Indiana is renowned for Hoosier Hysteria, but state tournaments create hoops excitement all around the country.

➤ The movie *Hoosiers* was based on the David vs. Goliath saga of tiny Milan High School, which in 1954 defeated Muncie Central for the Indiana state title.

➤ Despite the recent success of Kevin Garnett and Kobe Bryant, who went directly from high school to the pros, only a tiny fraction of high school players ever make it to big-time college ball, much less the NBA.

Chapter 23

Women Hoop It Up, Too

In This Chapter

➤ Senda Berenson Abbott: the mother of basketball

➤ 6-on-6 and other oddities

➤ From humble beginnings to the big-time

➤ A Dream Team of their own

➤ The pros: Is there room for two?

Women's basketball is growing faster in the United States than the men's game, in both participation and popularity. The days when women's college teams were relegated to playing before empty gyms in the preliminary games of doubleheaders before the men's teams took the floor are dead or dying. Today, women's teams from schools such as Tennessee, Connecticut, and Stanford regularly play before crowds of 15,000, 20,000, or even more.

Nearly half a million girls play interscholastic high school basketball, and thousands more compete in intramural hoops. Women's college basketball has hit the big-time, too, with the NCAA Women's Final Four an annual sellout that is televised nationally to ever-rising ratings. More than 5.2 million fans attended women's college games in 1995–96 (not counting doubleheaders with men's teams), the last year for which statistics are available. And not one, but two, pro leagues are vying for public attention—and getting it.

Fans have discovered the beauty and excitement of women's basketball. Everybody can relate to this game, which is played below the rim. Dunks are extremely rare at even the highest levels of women's basketball. Women's basketball is a game of skill, finesse, coaching, and discipline, all aspects that are the essence of the sport. It's a game that features precise passing, controlled dribbling, boxing out for rebounds, and teamwork at both ends of the court—the way the men's game used to be.

Women may not be as strong or as fast, but when it comes to the fundamentals of basketball, they are every bit the equal of men—if not better—as you'll learn in this chapter.

The Mother of Basketball

Senda Berenson Abbott, the director of physical education at Smith College in Northampton, Massachusetts, in the 1890s, read about a new indoor game called basketball that had been invented by Dr. James Naismith in nearby Springfield. She attended a seminar about the game, got to know Naismith, and decided to integrate basketball into her women's exercise classes.

Abbott set about adapting Naismith's game into something that would be appropriate for women of that period. Using his rules as a guide, she created the first basketball guidebook for women and developed a more orderly and refined game that tried to stress socialization and cooperation rather than competition.

Clyde's Rules

Keep in mind that a century ago, vigorous exercise for women was frowned upon. And it was not considered appropriate for young women—or women of any age, for that matter—to be too competitive. So pioneers such as Senda Berenson Abbott had to think not only about trying to popularize basketball, but also making it acceptable within the social framework of that era.

Because it was not considered proper for women of the 1890s to be running up and down a gymnasium floor, Abbott divided the court into three equal sections. She then assigned players to each section and required them to remain within its boundaries, using passes to advance the ball from section to section toward the team's goal.

The first women's collegiate game was played between the freshman and sophomore classes at Abbott's Smith College in 1893. No men were allowed in the gym, to prevent them from seeing the players wearing bloomers.

Such rules of modesty were the norm, not the exception. No men were permitted to attend the first intercollegiate women's game, between teams from Stanford and the

University of California on April 4, 1896. When two men were called into the gym to prop up a basket, it was reported that "the Berkeley team screamed and hid in a corner." After the basket was fixed and the men left the building, the game resumed and Stanford posted a 2-1 victory.

Even before Abbott brought basketball to the Smith women, the first women's game on record was played early in 1892, just weeks after Naismith invented basketball. Some teachers at Buckingham Grade School in Springfield tried out the new game with their students. Among them was Maude Sherman, who later met and married Naismith.

But because of her early adaptation of basketball, her service for a dozen years as Chairperson of the Women's Basketball Committee, and her editorship of the women's rules book, Abbott is regarded as the Mother of Basketball.

Early Oddities of the Women's Game

In 1895, Clara Baer, a teacher at Newcomb College in New Orleans, heard about basketball and wrote to Naismith for the rules of the game. Along with his reply, Naismith sent her a diagram of the court, on which he indicated where players usually were stationed. Baer, more than 1,000 miles away, took this to mean that the players were not allowed to leave the immediate areas that Naismith had indicated.

Due to this misinterpretation—combined with Abbott's concept of dividing the court into thirds—women were not allowed to run the entire court for more than a half-century. In the 1920s, the three-sectioned court was the standard for women's basketball, with the number of players per team varying between 5 and 10. In the 1930s, the court was divided into two sections, and six players per team—three guards and three forwards—became the norm. The players on each team were assigned to opposite halves of the court and were not permitted to cross the midcourt line.

That's the way women's basketball remained until the 1960s, when a movement to switch to men's rules began to pick up steam. At first, two of the six players were designated as "rovers" and were permitted to cross midcourt, but this proved to be just a stop-gap measure. In 1969, women began experimental use of five-player teams playing a full-court game, just like men, in intercollegiate competition.

Clyde's Record Book

Six-girl basketball meant specialization, because three players on a team tried to score and the other three could only play defense. This led to some high-scoring performances, topped by the 156 points scored by Marie Boyd of Central High School in Lonaconing, Maryland, in a single game on February 25, 1924; the 1,986 points scored by Denise Long of Whitten High School of Union (Iowa) in the 1968–69 season; and the 6,736 career points scored by Lynne Lorenzen of Ventura (Iowa) High School in 1984–87. All far exceed the records for five-girl basketball.

The cat was out of the bag. Within two years, this became the official standard for women's play, although what became known as "six-girl basketball" continued into the early 1990s, especially at the high school level in states such as Iowa and Oklahoma.

When the court opened up, excitement came to the women's game. The new game showed that women can actually play basketball, that they can compete like men, that they can do some of the shaking and baking—and I mean on the court!

From AAU to AIAW to NCAA and the Big-Time

The evolution in rules is reflected in the administration of women's basketball in the United States. Several different organizations have played prominent roles in the sport's leadership over the years.

The AAU

The Amateur Athletic Union (AAU) organized the first National Women's Basketball Championship in 1926, and by 1929 this became an annual event. The famed Babe Didrikson, playing for a team called the Golden Cyclones, averaged more than 20 points per game in leading her team to the 1931 AAU title.

Two schools you've probably never heard of—Wayland College of Plainview, Texas, and the Nashville Business College in Tennessee—played key roles in the development of women's basketball in the 1950s and 1960s.

Clyde's Tip

The Wayland College women's team was flying on a private plane in the 1950s, when NBA teams considered themselves lucky to be on any kind of airplane at all. Even commercial flights were rare for the NBA in those days and were reserved for trips to the league's westernmost cities such as St. Louis or Minneapolis. Trains and buses were the standard means of transportation in the NBA.

Wayland, coached by Harley Redin, was one of the first schools to offer full scholarships to women basketball players. In addition, thanks to the generosity of local businessman Claude Hutcherson, the team flew on a private plane to all its road games. The Hutcherson Flying Queens, as they became known, won 131 consecutive games in one stretch and compiled a 431-66 record, winning the National AAU Tournament 10 times and finishing second 9 times.

Wayland's 131-game winning streak came to an end at the 1958 AAU Championships, when the team was beaten 46-42 by an amateur team sponsored by the Nashville Business College. Nashville, coached by John Head, won 96 games in a row and took 11 National AAU titles, including eight in a row from 1962 through 1969.

Nashville's superstar was Nera White, a brilliant shooter with great range who could run and jump like the best men of her day. White, who attended George Peabody College in Nashville before playing on the amateur team sponsored by the Nashville Business College, was voted the Most Valuable Player of the AAU Tournament 10 times. She was named an All-American—a designation open to all amateur players at that time, not just collegians—15 years in a row.

The AIAW

In 1969, the first National Intercollegiate Women's Basketball Tournament was held at West Chester State College in Pennsylvania and was won by a nearby school called Immaculata. This was the dawning of a new era in women's college basketball.

Two years later, the Association of Intercollegiate Athletics for Women (AIAW) was formed, and from 1971 to 1982 the AIAW served as the governing body for women's intercollegiate sports. While the NCAA was administering the more profitable men's sports, the understaffed, underfunded AIAW organized and promoted championships in basketball and other sports for women and played a key role in the development of women's athletics in the United States.

A major boost came with Congress' passage of Title IX of the Educational Amendments of 1972, which sought to promote gender equity. Title IX stated, in part, "No person in the U.S. shall, on the basis of sex, be excluded from participation in, or denied the benefits of, or be subjected to discrimination under any educational program or activity receiving federal aid." Because virtually every college and university receives some sort of federal aid, this forced schools to devote greater resources, including scholarships and better facilities, to women's athletic programs.

In keeping with the early tradition of women's athletics, the AIAW was a relatively low-key group that stressed the "student" part in "student-athletes" and disdained a "win at all costs" mentality. As a result, schools that did not offer athletic scholarships and that ran programs on tight budgets enjoyed great success in the AIAW, including Delta State, Immaculata, Montclair State, Queens, and Wayland Baptist.

But women's basketball was growing, and even in the understated world of the AIAW, major schools began to rise to the top. UCLA won the AIAW title game in 1978, beating the University of Maryland. The University of Tennessee reached the finals twice, and in the AIAW's final year, Rutgers defeated Texas for the 1982 crown.

Clyde's Record Book

Some of the greatest players in women's basketball history played college ball when the game was run by the AIAW, not the NCAA, so they go unrecognized in the NCAA record book. These include Carol Blazejowski of Montclair State, Nancy Lieberman-Cline and Anne Donovan of Old Dominion, Ann Meyers of UCLA, and Lusia Harris-Stewart of Delta State. All are members of the Basketball Hall of Fame.

The NCAA

The NCAA took over administration of the women's game in 1982 and set up its first Division I National Basketball Championship.

Clyde's Tip

The physical fitness craze has helped the growth of women's hoops. In the '60s, you didn't see women pumping iron or doing any of the exercise things they do now. Back then, girls who played ball were called tomboys and often were ostracized by other girls. Now they are encouraged—by peers, teachers, coaches, and parents—to play and compete. Women are much more into their health and fitness now.

The AIAW had laid the foundation, but the NCAA had the resources to build the building. The NCAA Women's Final Four, supported by national television, has grown into a major event on the sports calendar, adding to March Madness.

Any question as to whether women's college basketball was ready for the big-time was answered on December 9, 1987, when a crowd of 24,563 (including 23,912 paid fans) saw Texas defeat Tennessee 97-78 at Thompson-Boling Arena in Knoxville, Tennessee.

Tennessee's Lady Vols, coached by Pat Head Summitt, have been a national power for the past decade, winning NCAA titles in 1989, 1991, 1996, 1997, and 1998—the last three with the brilliant Chamique Holdsclaw leading the way. Two spectacular NCAA Finals preceded the Lady Vols' three-peat: In 1994, the North Carolina Tar Heels beat the Louisiana Tech Lady Techsters 60-59 on a last-second shot by Charlotte Smith; in 1995, a popular Connecticut Huskies team led by Rebecca Lobo, Jennifer Rizzotti, and Kara Wolters capped an undefeated season by beating the Tennessee Lady Vols 70-64 in the title game.

USA Basketball Steps Up

While women's basketball was thriving on the college level, the same was not true on the international front. The United States women could do no better than a bronze medal at the 1992 Olympics (while the Dream Team was romping to a gold) and were beaten by Brazil in the 1994 World Championships.

In 1995, USA Basketball—the sport's governing body and Olympic member—decided to do something about the situation. The old method of putting together an Olympic team in tryouts a few months before the event clearly wasn't working. A longer-range commitment was needed, so USA Basketball—with the marketing support of the NBA—decided to bring the best American players together for a year of practice and competition prior to the 1996 Olympics.

Chosen as coach of the USA Basketball Women's National Team was Tara VanDerveer, who took a sabbatical from her job at Stanford, which she had coached to two NCAA titles. The team's 12 players were the best of their era, a women's Dream Team:

Jennifer Azzi, Ruthie Bolton, Teresa Edwards, Venus Lacy, Lisa Leslie, Rebecca Lobo, Katrina McClain, Nikki McCray, Carla McGhee, Dawn Staley, Katy Steding, and Sheryl Swoopes. The players were given a salary to live, train, practice, and compete together, a concept that seemed perfectly logical but had never been done before.

Backed by corporate sponsors the likes of which women's basketball had never seen (thanks to the NBA's marketing clout), the team was a year-long barnstorming sensation. It toured the United States playing the best college teams and traveled to Russia, the Ukraine, China, Australia, and Canada to gain international experience. It was a popular hit everywhere it went—and, oh yes, it also won all 52 games it played.

The team hit Atlanta on a roll and stormed through the 1996 Olympics, easily winning all eight games en route to the gold medal. Six of those games were played in the Georgia Dome and drew crowds of more than 30,000, further testament that women's basketball was ready for prime time.

The Pros: Is There Room for Two?

Women's professional basketball had long been played in Europe, Asia, and South America, but not the United States. Leagues would start up, often hoping to capitalize on some college or Olympic success, then quickly sink in a sea of red ink. So to make a living at the game they loved, the top college women stars in the United State had to travel overseas to play professionally—or else give up playing for a career in coaching, broadcasting, or marketing.

The success of the USA Basketball Women's National Team on and off the court changed all that. It directly led to the formation of not one, but two professional women's leagues.

The eight-team American Basketball League (ABL) was the first to try to capitalize on the Olympic hoopla, playing its inaugural season in the winter of 1996–97. Then came the eight-team Women's National Basketball Association (WNBA), backed by the NBA, which played its first season in the summer of 1997.

The two leagues took very different approaches. The ABL played a conventional winter schedule and placed teams in mid-sized, non-NBA cities where the college game was popular, such as Hartford, Connecticut, and Columbus, Ohio. The league spent what little money it had on signing as many top players as it could, luring them with the idea of not having to travel overseas to play professionally.

Clyde's Tip

When you go to a women's pro game, whether it's ABL or WNBA, you'll see many women in the crowd, more so than at an NBA game. The crowd also tends to be younger, at least partly because tickets are much more affordable than for NBA games. This is good for the growth of the women's game and should build more new fans.

Rebecca Lobo, who won an NCAA title with Connecticut and a 1996 Olympic gold medal, is now one of the WNBA's marquee players, playing with the New York Liberty.
Associated Press

Unlike the ABL, the WNBA was driven by marketing, with its teams owned by NBA franchises and playing in NBA arenas. WNBA teams played a summer schedule because that was when network television time was available, so it benefited from coverage by three national networks in its very first season. The league spent far more money on promotion than players and, as a result, drew the type of corporate sponsorship no start-up league ever has had. It did sign a few marquee players for big bucks (using them as centerpieces in its marketing campaign), then filled its rosters with ex-collegians and foreign pros, available during their offseasons overseas.

The results were what you might expect, given these approaches. The ABL has been a modest success, earning positive reviews for the caliber of play and mixed reviews at the gate; ABL teams averaged 3,536 fans per game in the league's first season and 4,333 in its second.

The WNBA was a marketing smash, earning raves for its ability to attract fans to the tune of 9,669 per game in its first season. (The second season was being played as this book was being printed.) This league got somewhat lesser reviews for the caliber of play, but that didn't seem to bother fans who watched either in person or on TV. The WNBA entered with more professionalism—thanks to the NBA's money, everything about the league (such as arenas, television, and publicity) was first-rate.

Both leagues have expanded, but the question I have is whether we really have a need for both. The prudent thing for them to do would be to stop competing and merge, combining the assets of each. I think it's inevitable, and it behooves both leagues to address their differences sooner rather than later. The talent in a merged league would be overwhelming. As for the playing schedule, they probably would have to compete in the winter; I'm not sure that the novelty of a summer schedule won't wear off after awhile.

The Least You Need to Know

➤ Senda Berenson Abbott, who adapted the original rules of basketball for use by women in the 1890s, is regarded as the Mother of Basketball.

➤ For more than a half-century, women played on six-player teams comprised of shooters and defenders who were not permitted to cross the midcourt line.

➤ After the AIAW laid the foundation of the women's college game, the NCAA took over its administration in 1982 and ushered it into the arena of big-time athletics.

➤ The USA Basketball team that won the gold medal at the 1996 Olympics paved the way for two pro leagues, the ABL and the WNBA, whose merger seems prudent, if not inevitable.

Pickup Ball

Pickup basketball is the sport in its rawest form.

It's basketball without all the structure and restrictions that come with organized ball (although it most definitely has its own rules and culture). It's the game stripped down to its basics—some players, a ball, and a hoop or two. What more do you need?

Pickup basketball gets its name from the fact that teams are picked from whoever is at the playground or the gym. Say two teams are playing a game of five-against-five, full-court basketball, and you show up and want to play. You call out, "I got next," and when the game ends, you pick some of the players from the losing team or some others who are waiting to play, form a team, and take on the winners.

That's one of the rules of the playground: Winners stay. Other rules and customs may vary from playground to playground, but that one is universal. The winning team gets to keep on playing until it loses, so it's good to put together a strong team before you take the court. Otherwise, you might have to wait awhile until you get to play again. I'll go into more detail on the rules of the playground later in this chapter.

Clyde's Chalk Talk

So far in this book, just about everything I've talked about has been *full-court basketball*—the game played on a full court, with each team shooting at a basket at opposite ends. But many pickup games, whether played on playgrounds or in school yards, are often *half-court games*. The entire game takes place on half a court, with both teams shooting at the same goal.

Any Number Can Play

As I've mentioned, one of the best things about basketball is that any number of players can play the game. You don't need a whole bunch of players as in football or baseball, and nowhere is this flexibility more evident than at the playground.

If you get there early in the morning, you might see guys playing two-on-two, or even one-on-one. After awhile, though, play evolves into *half-court games* (usually three-on-three) and *full-court games* (four-on-four or five-on-five).

The reason for this is simple. Up to six people on half a court—even a playground court, which is often shorter and narrower than the official NBA and college court that measures 50 feet by 94 feet—leaves plenty of room for movement without bodies constantly crashing into each other. You can still get a good game going. But when you have at least four players on a team, you're better off stretching the game out to the full length of the court, or else things will get too crowded.

Two youngsters hoop it up at Anacostia Park in Washington, D.C., on a sultry summer afternoon. Associated Press

Half-Court vs. Full-Court

Which is more fun, a half-court game or a full-court game?

That may depend on what kind of shape you're in. If you like to run and you have plenty of stamina, you'll probably prefer the full-court game. Play is more wide open, and you can take advantage of your speed by outrunning the man who is guarding you down the court.

If you just don't like to run as much, then half-court basketball is for you. It's the same game, but you don't have to run all the way from one end of the court to the other. You still have to shoot, dribble, pass, rebound, and play defense, so you still must be able to move around. The only difference is that all the action takes place on a half-court—really, within 25 feet of the basket.

Smaller players who rely on speed and quickness often prefer the full-court game, which is more wide open. Bigger, slower players who are most effective around the basket tend to prefer the half-court game so they don't have to tire themselves out by running from end to end.

Clyde's Tip

Older players and players who have had knee or ankle injuries tend to prefer half-court basketball. They still get to compete and use the skills and savvy they have gained over the years, but they don't have to do all the running a full-court game demands, running that often can be taxing on an aging or infirm body.

Clyde's Rules

Don't think that because there is less running in half-court basketball, you don't have to be in shape to play. The quick starts and stops, the jumping and driving to the basket is the same—so if you're out of condition, you're going to find yourself at a big disadvantage, even in a half-court game.

Indoors, Outdoors

Pickup basketball games are played indoors as well as outdoors, wherever a court is available.

Indoor courts have some obvious advantages. You can play all year round, even in the dead of winter when it's freezing outside. Rain and snow are no problem. On a hot

305

summer afternoon, however, it can get pretty sweltering inside a gym that's not air-conditioned. You'll sometimes see portable fans set up around an indoor court in the summer, to circulate the air and also to try to keep the floor dry. Then again, if it's hot inside, it's probably pretty hot outside, too.

Indoor courts also tend to be in better condition than courts on outdoor playgrounds, which usually get less regular maintenance. In a school gym or a rec center, you usually can count on rims that are not bent, smooth backboards, and nets hanging from each basket; go to a playground, and you might not find any of these.

An air-conditioned gym can be a nice place to play some full-court basketball, especially on a summer day deep in the heart of Texas.
Associated Press

Another advantage to an indoor court is that you play on a wooden floor, or perhaps even one of those artificial surfaces that have a little extra bounce. These are a lot easier on the body than the cement courts of the playgrounds. And the basket poles in indoor gyms often are padded, a luxury you won't find outdoors.

Yet another advantage is that a school gym or rec center usually has a water fountain and a bathroom near the court. This can come in extremely handy, and you may or may not have access to such facilities on outdoor playgrounds.

For all that, outdoor courts still have their appeal. There's nothing like playing a game under the sun on a bright spring day or under the streetlights on a warm summer night. Besides, outdoor courts have character and reflect their locale. If you play indoors, you might be playing anywhere; if you play outdoors, you'll definitely know where you are, whether it's the streets of New York, the shores of California or Florida, or anywhere in between.

Playground Dreams and Dreamers

The thing to remember is that it's not the playground that makes a pickup game special—it's the players.

In any city, the good players seem to gravitate to certain gyms or playgrounds. Everybody seems to know where the best games can be found, and these are the places you want to seek out if you're a real aficionado.

The playground brings together the dreams and the dreamers. They watch the pros and then go out to the playground and try to emulate them. Imitation is the most sincere form of flattery, and in a good playground game you'll see a lot of imitation—and innovation, too.

You'll also hear an earful. There's a lot of hyperbolation and exaggeration; everybody on the playground brags about what they can do or what they have done.

That's part of the glamour of the playground—it's more loquacious and tenacious. There's more bravado. Everybody is always trying to show somebody else up.

Look at Mark Jackson of the Indiana Pacers and his helicopter swirls or his shimmy shakes, which come straight from the playgrounds of New York where he grew up. But that doesn't go over too well with some people—Larry Bird, now his coach with Indiana, had to tell him to cut it out in last year's playoffs.

Bird was one of the best trash-talkers in the league during his playing days, but he did it in a subtle manner. Instead of running over and getting in a guy's face or showing him up to the crowd, he'd get his point across while standing next to the guy at the foul line. Others might not have noticed, but his target sure would.

For Bird, trash-talking wasn't done to embarrass another player, but to rattle him and throw him off his game. But now the playground has invaded the NBA. Too many young players today resort to the kind of taunting and showboating we used to see only on the playgrounds. They try to humiliate other players—and that's not cool.

Clyde's Tip

The player I used to imitate was Hal Greer, the Hall of Fame guard who played for the Syracuse Nationals and the Philadelphia 76ers. I was always trying to use his moves and work them into my game.

Rules of the Playground

The basketball rules you may become familiar with from NBA or college games apply to playground ball, but with some modification.

No free throws are shot in playground games, because there are no referees present. Players call their own fouls: If you feel a foul has been committed against you, it's your job to call out "Foul!" immediately. Otherwise play will continue as if nothing had happened.

Clyde's Tip

Pickup basketball is not a game for the meek. You've got to call out "Foul!" when you get whacked, because nobody else is going to call it for you. I guess it's a good form of assertiveness training!

Because there are no free throws, a player fouled in the act of shooting is given the ball out of bounds and starts play again. That's why pickup games tend to get physical and there are few easy baskets. If a player drives in for a dunk or layup, the defender tries to block it even if he risks committing a foul. So what if a foul is called? The other team just gets the ball out of bounds, which is a lot better than giving up an easy basket.

Playground games are played to a certain number of points, with each basket counting as one point (remember, there are no free throws). Games usually go to 21 points unless the court is busy and many people are waiting, when they may be shortened to 15 or 11 points. Really, any number would work, but these seem to be the ones most often used in pickup games.

Generally, games must be decided by at least two points. That means if the score gets to 20-20, the next team that scores doesn't win even though it will have 21; the team must win by two. Thus, games can go on and on, which is great if you love playing but not so great if you have to be home in time for dinner! On a busy court or late in the day, this two-point rule may be waived and games may be played "straight up" so that the first team to reach 21 wins, even if only by one point.

The major rules difference in half-court basketball comes into play when the ball changes possession, such as after a missed shot. In a full-court game, the other team would then run toward the goal at the other end of the court. In a half-court game, it must move the ball out (by dribbling or passing) beyond a designated line on the court before attempting a shot. This line may be the free throw line, the top of the circle, or the three-point line, depending on court customs. Without this rule, a team could grab a rebound and immediately go up for a shot, which would take all the playmaking and strategy from the game. Yet growing up in the South, I often played in games where there was no bringing the ball out. These games were dominated by ferocious rebounders who kept pounding and bounding till the ball went in.

A Language of Its Own

If you're going to try your hand at pickup basketball, whether as a player or a spectator, you should learn to talk the talk.

You already know one key phrase: "I got next!" When the NBA was introducing its women's league, it adapted that phrase and used "We got next!" as its advertising slogan, letting everyone know that as soon as the NBA Finals were over the WNBA would be taking the court. It was a shrewd move, connecting the new women's league with both the established men's league and with playground ball.

"Take it back" is another phrase you'll hear on the playground, and I'm not talking about retracting a nasty remark in an argument. As I mentioned earlier, when a team gains possession in half-court basketball, it must take the ball back beyond a designated line before attempting a shot. Sometimes in the heat of a game, a player might be scrambling for the ball and forget that rule, so you'll hear a teammate remind him, "Take it back!"

"That's game" indicates when the game is over. Because playgrounds usually don't come with scoreboards, players have to keep score on their own. It's helpful if somebody calls out the score after each basket, but if one team is way ahead, this can be taken as rubbing it in, so it's up to each player to keep score in his head. When 21 (or whatever number has been agreed upon) is reached, somebody from the winning team should call out, "That's game."

"Game" also refers to a player's skill level. Guys standing by the side of the playground, watching the action, may point to a player and say, "He's got game" or "He's got no game." It's a comment not on any one specific skill but on the player's overall ability to play the game. The phrase is such a playground fixture that Spike Lee used it as the title for his recent basketball movie *He Got Game* starring Denzel Washington.

"Run" is another word you'll hear a lot in pickup games, and it usually means the same as "play." If somebody asks, "Want to run?" he's asking if you want to play ball, not go jogging. "Let's run again" means "Let's play again," which you should only try if nobody else is waiting to play.

Midnite Basketball and Drug-Free Leagues

It's midnight. Do you know where your hoopster is?

In a growing number of cities around the country, he or she may be playing in a program called "Midnite Basketball," designed to provide a safe alternative to the streets.

These games don't necessarily take place at midnight, but they do happen late at night, when gyms and recreation centers might otherwise not be used. The idea is to give boys and girls a place where they can go, after they've finished their dinner and homework, to compete in a structured, supervised environment.

Several of these Midnite Basketball leagues are sponsored by NBA teams and corporate partners, with local civic groups and youth associations providing organizational and management support. One such league is the Spurs/Pizza Hut Midnite Basketball League in San Antonio, which completed its seventh season in March 1998. Youngsters ages 17-25 played ball in three community centers under the coaching of off-duty police officers and other volunteers. The youths also were required to attend workshops in social subjects such as resume writing and conflict resolution. Another program in which the Spurs have been involved since 1991 is the Spurs/Nike Drug-Free Youth Basketball League, which involves more than 15,000 youngsters playing ball at some 68 locations throughout South Texas. Under this program—which received a "Point of Light" from George Bush when he was President—all players, coaches, and administrators sign a pledge to be drug-, alcohol-, and tobacco-free, and coaches talk to team members each week about the dangers of substance abuse. The program has expanded under the leadership of other NBA franchises including Denver, Indiana, Oakland, and Portland.

These are just two examples of the many types of programs in which pickup basketball can be used as a way to teach youngsters social responsibility.

Finally, a word of advice for all you weekend warriors: Go out and play! You can find a game just about anywhere—school gyms, playgrounds, community centers, YMCAs, churches, or other religious institutions. Often you'll be able to find a league of players whose skill level and competitive intensity matches yours; if not, get some like-minded souls together and start a regular game of your own.

The Least You Need to Know

➤ Pickup basketball may not have the organization and structure of the NBA or big-time college ball, but it definitely has its own rules and culture.

➤ Half-court basketball can be as intense and competitive as the full-court variety (if not more so), just without all the running of the full-court game.

➤ Indoor gyms may offer more in the way of creature comforts, but outdoor playgrounds often provide the best ambiance for pickup basketball.

➤ If a guys says, "Want to run?" don't expect to go off on a marathon; it's playground jargon for, "Do you want to play ball?"

➤ Many programs have been developed using pickup basketball as a lure to get youngsters off the streets and teach them social responsibility, teamwork, and sportsmanship.

Part 6
A Fan for Life

You can enjoy the game of basketball whether you're 8 or 80. It's a game of nuances, of subtle shadings, like the constantly changing colors of a sunset. Just when you think you've seen it all, you discover something new that changes the way you look at the game and enhances your appreciation for it.

The basics are simple: dribble, pass, shoot, as John Wooden said. The team that scores more points wins. And yet there is so much more, as I've tried to explain in this book. The game puts a premium on skill over strength, precision over power, agility over aggression. It's a thinking man's game—and a thinking woman's.

In this part, I'll give you some tips on how to get the most enjoyment, whether you are watching from the arena or from home. I'll discuss different ways to follow your favorite team and get an insider's look at what's going on, and I'll describe some of the many resources that are available to increase your game knowledge and appreciation. And for those of you with some Weekend Warrior in you, I'll give you one last push toward the court.

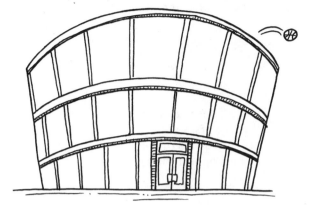

At the Arena

In This Chapter

➤ The best places to sit (besides the broadcast table)

➤ Learn to watch the ball

➤ Learn not to watch the ball

➤ Anticipate what's going to happen

➤ A few words about arena amenities

There's nothing quite like being at the game. It's true at any level—NBA, college, high school, even playground ball. There's an energy and an excitement at the game that makes it a riveting experience.

You can also see the big picture. You can see the interplay between the players, how player A telling player B to run in one direction opened the court so that player C could use screens set by players D and E to get free for his shot.

You develop an appreciation for the way athletes of such size and strength can move with such agility and amazing grace. You can feel the flow taking place on the court, and you can understand the constant movement that is so necessary for success. You can even feel the changes in momentum almost before they take place.

And then there's all that takes place off the court—the cheerleaders and dance teams, the provocative recorded music and the live bands, the celebrity fans at NBA games, and the vociferous student sections at college and high school games. A dazzling show goes on away from the court, a show that is only hinted at by TV and radio coverage of the game.

This chapter offers some tips on how to get the most out of the hoopla taking place on and off the court.

The Best Seats in the House

Where's the best place to sit at an NBA game?

Any place you can get a seat, is one answer. The NBA has played to more than 90 percent of seating capacity league-wide the past few years, so seats are scarce. And the best ones are sold on a season-long basis, often to executives or corporations who use them to entertain clients and enhance more business opportunities.

How to Get a Ticket

What's the average fan to do? Plan ahead. Let me repeat that: Plan ahead! NBA teams announce their schedules in July, so make sure you get one and pick out the games you want to see. Then find out when individual game tickets go on sale (teams are constantly selling season tickets but usually put tickets for individual games on sale on specific days), and be prepared to act fast. Also be prepared to replenish your bank account, since good seats to an NBA game regularly go for $30, $40, $50, or more.

Also consider mini-packages, groups of perhaps 6, 10, or 15 games that some teams will put together and offer as a package. There's usually a unifying element—all are week-end games or all are against rivals from within the conference—and, often, they are tied in with something else that makes the package attractive, such as free parking, dinner at a nearby restaurant, a promotional giveaway such as a jacket or basketball, or even a discount off the total ticket price.

If most of the dates are convenient and the games are against teams you want to see, this could be the way to go; usually these mini-plans go on sale before individual tickets or might include better seats than are sold individually.

As a last resort, on the day of a game you absolutely must see, you could try ticket agents, some of whom are listed in the phone book or in newspaper ads. Or you could show up early at the arena and see what is available on the street—although you should know that such unlicensed reselling of tickets (a.k.a. ticket-scalping) is illegal in many states.

What Ticket Should You Ask For?

Now, let's say your brother works for the team and tickets are no problem. Where do you want to sit?

Not courtside, where the celebrities sit. Most fans would love to sit courtside, but believe me, you really can't see the game evolve from there. Courtside seats are too close. It's like the head football coach who is standing on the sidelines—he needs to talk to his assistants up in the press box to find out what's going on. That's why a football team has to stop the game whenever those phone connections go down.

I think the best place to sit is up a bit, say 10 rows, above midcourt. While some people prefer to sit behind one basket so they can see players and plays coming right at them, I think it's best to be in the middle so you can see both sides equally and so you're not far from either basket. Being up a few rows from the court also lets you see plays evolve, which you really can't see from court level.

Of course, when you sit courtside you really can see the magnitude of the players and appreciate the agility and mobility of men of such size. You can also see and hear some of the shenanigans that happen on the court, whether it's the pushing and shoving for rebounding position, or the verbal play between players with long-standing rivalries.

So I guess if that brother of yours who works for the team offers you a pair courtside, don't turn him down. But after you've sat down there for a game or two, ask if he can get you anything a few rows up at midcourt.

Clyde's Tip

Skyboxes, luxury suites ringing the top of some NBA buildings, are terrible places for the hard-core fan. They are so far from the court that you really have no feel for the game as it is going on. However, the chance to sit in nice armchairs in a private box, with catered food and libations and a private bathroom, more than makes up for the distance. Private boxes a dozen rows or so from the court, which is the way they're being built in some of the newest arenas, are more ideal.

Keep Your Eye on the Ball

The easiest way to follow any sport—whether it's baseball, football, basketball, or soccer (I leave out hockey for an obvious reason, which I hope you can guess)—is to keep your eye on the ball. (That's right, there is no ball in hockey, so you can keep your eye on the puck instead.)

One of the really good things about basketball is that the ball is easy to see. First of all, it's big. How big? Nine inches in diameter, to be exact. That's big enough to be seen even from the cheap seats—or what passes for cheap seats today at NBA arenas.

Just in case size wasn't enough, the NBA got together with its official ball-maker, Spalding, about 20 years ago and had the company change the color of the ball. Out went the brown ball, replaced by a brighter, more orange-colored ball that was—you guessed it—easier to see.

So if you're at your first NBA game and you're struggling to follow the action, keep your eye on the ball. That's what the players are watching, so why not join them?

Take Your Eyes off the Ball

Watching the ball all the time is fine for beginners, but pretty soon you'll want more. The advantage to watching a game live, at the arena, is that you can watch whatever you want, not just what the TV camera is showing you. So learn to make the most of that advantage.

There are several ways to do this.

Watch Your Favorite Player

Pick a player, any player, and watch his every move. Pretty soon, you'll discover why he is (or isn't) a star.

Does he work diligently when his team has the ball, trying to get open for a shot or get one of his teammates open, or does he stand around and watch the action? If he's a big man, is he relentless in his effort to get to the boards (bounding and astounding, I like to call it), or does he give up if he's not immediately in good rebounding position? If he's a little man, does he have the strength and fortitude to fight his way through picks set by players 100 pounds heavier, or the quickness to run around them, or neither?

By picking a player and focusing on him for several minutes without being distracted by the ball, you can learn to appreciate what makes him special—or why he's not.

Clyde's Tip

When I was with the Knicks and we played the Baltimore Bullets (now the Washington Wizards), two of the best players at working without the ball went head-to-head: Bill Bradley of New York and Jack Marin of Baltimore. Both were 6'5" forwards who were relentless and indefatigable. They never stopped running, moving in and out of picks until they got open. They were a game within the game.

Watch Your Favorite Position

If you think basketball is a non-contact sport, forget about the ball when a shot goes up and watch the battle for rebounding position instead.

Watch the leaning and elbowing, the pushing and shoving, the hacking and whacking, as two Goliaths battle each other for a better shot at grabbing the ball, should it miss the basket. I marvel when I watch guys like Karl Malone of the Utah Jazz and Charles Oakley of the Toronto Raptors: two huge men with muscular, sculpted bodies, fighting for rebounding position. If you're at a game featuring players like these, keep an eye on them. You'll be glad you did, especially if you sit courtside—they might end up sitting on you, with their hustle and muscle and reckless abandon.

Do you like watching shooters? Then don't wait until your favorite gunslinger gets the ball and is ready to fire away. Watch him away from the ball as he moves around the court, weaving behind picks, trying to get himself free for his shot. This is called watching his play "away from the ball," and it's something coaches are always looking for in their players.

If you like point guards, watch how the players bring the ball up the court. Remember my cardinal rules about staying under control and staying in the middle of the court? See if the players obey them, and see if they get in trouble when they don't.

Try watching a specific matchup. Watch how a center tries to keep Shaquille O'Neal of the Lakers out of his favorite spot in the pivot, or watch how a defender attempts to keep Grant Hill of the Detroit Pistons from slashing and dashing to the basket.

If you appreciate defensive play and are lucky to have a defensive standout such as Eddie Jones of the Los Angeles Lakers in the game you're watching, focus on him when the other team has the ball. Watch how he sticks with his man, while also keeping an eye on the ball so he can anticipate a pass and step in to pick it off. Also, watch a good defensive center such as Dikembe Mutombo of the Atlanta Hawks and see the way he both guards his man and also seals off the lane so opponents can't drive to the hoop.

The opportunity to watch all these antics away from the ball is truly the essence of going to the game.

Watch the Flow

Sit back, take a deep breath, and relax. Forget about watching the ball or any individual player. Just watch the flow of the game, the patterns of the players' movement, the rhythm of the action. This works especially well if you're sitting up pretty high in the arena and can really get a bird's eye view of the action.

Is there a smoothness to a team's movements? Do its players run precise routes, or do they seem to get in each other's way? Does the ball move crisply about the court from one player to another, or does it seem to get stuck in one player's hand for too long while everyone else stands around and watches?

This is akin to seeing the forest rather than the individual trees. By sitting back and watching the big picture, you can get a good idea as to which teams operate smoothly collectively and which are still struggling to form a cohesive unit.

Carly Simon Said It Best: Anticipation

If you really want to have fun, learn to anticipate.

It was often said of Larry Bird, the fabulous forward of the Boston Celtics in the 1980s, that he not only saw everything that was happening on the floor, but he could see what was going to happen one or two passes before they were actually made. Now that's anticipation, ESP, clairvoyance, whatever you want to call it!

It's not easy, but try your hand at being Larry Bird. If a player has the ball, anticipate what he's going to do with it. Will he try to break down the defense by himself? Will he look for a teammate coming off a screen? Will he dump it into the center in the low post?

And don't stop there: Anticipate how the defense will react to the move, and then what the offense will do to counter that reaction. That's prudent thinking, the way coaches and players—especially point guards—try to think. This is what makes basketball a thinking man's (and woman's) game.

Try it for yourself the next time you see a guard bring the ball upcourt. Watch the way his teammates are moving, and try to anticipate where he's going to pass the ball, how the defense will react, and how the offense will counter. When you remember that all these decisions have to be made on the fly while the play is unfolding in front of you, you can really appreciate and admire the point guards of renown who have played this game.

Clyde's Record Book

When I was playing, nearly all the arenas were dilapidated. Except for the Forum in Los Angeles and Madison Square Garden in New York, none had the kind of amenities you see everywhere today. Now the Garden has been refurbished and the Forum is going to be replaced in a couple of years. These new arenas give the league a professionalism it didn't have before. Everything is first-rate. When I stand in some of these places during the National Anthem, I think about what the league was then and what it is now, and it makes me very proud.

About Arenas

It's pretty hard to find a mundane arena around the NBA these days, at least when it comes to creature comforts.

One of the benefits of the league's boom in the past 15 years has been the construction of many new arenas, each of which seems to try to outdo the rest in one way or another.

All arenas are pretty much user-friendly, with good sight lines (the line of vision from each seat to the court), comfortable seats, bright lighting, food courts and other places to eat, nice stores, plenty of bathrooms, and so much else going on in the building. There's even heat and hot running water for the showers in the visitors' locker room, something that wasn't always the case in my playing days.

So what makes a good arena? I think we've all come to expect the amenities: nice seats with a good view of the court, a clean building, convenient parking, appealing places to eat and shop, and plenty of bathrooms. It's unfortunate that we've had to sacrifice intimacy for amenities—and that so many of the new arenas seem relatively sterile compared with their predecessors. Think of Boston Garden and the FleetCenter, or Chicago Stadium and the United Center, and you'll know what I mean.

As a player, I felt an attachment to the crowd, whether it was the friendly crowd at the Garden or the hostile crowd on the road. I don't know whether that exists anymore, whether today's players feel it as strongly as the players who played in my day did.

I relished Boston Garden. I really liked to go into that building. It reminded me of the Roman Gladiators, the Christians and the Lions. You'd be going up against a hostile crowd, the legends, the parquet floor, the banners. It was intimidating but invigorating, and I played some of my best games, my most dramatic games, against the Celtics.

The Least You Need to Know

➤ It's fun to sit courtside, where you really appreciate the size of the players and their skills, but the best place to watch a game is about 10 rows up at midcourt, where you can see the plays evolve.

➤ Watching the ball is a good idea if you're just learning the sport, but if you want to appreciate the complexities and subtleties of basketball, you have to learn to look away from the ball and focus on other things.

➤ To really get into the game, try to envision a play before it happens. Watch the movement of the players, and try to predict where the ball is going to go—and what will happen when it gets there.

Chapter 26

At Home

In This Chapter

➤ Hoops and TV: made for each other, and those replays are great!

➤ See you on the radio

➤ Other ways to follow your team, including hoops in cyberspace

➤ Fantasy leagues: pick your own team

Sure it's fun to watch a game in person, but let's be practical. With the average ticket price in the NBA at $36.32 per seat in 1997–98—and sure to keep climbing—most people can't afford to go to the arena very often, even if they could get tickets. This chapter delves into a few other ways to catch the action.

Most people watch games on television, and that's a good way to follow your team. The cameras zoom in on the players, so you get a closer view than most people sitting in the arena. Best of all, you get all those replays so you are always in the middle of the action and can see details fans watching the game at the arena might miss.

Radio, a medium that has become near and dear to me, is another way to follow the action. There's something almost mystical about listening to the word pictures painted by the announcers and picturing the game in your mind.

Newspapers are perhaps the best way to follow your favorite team during the course of the season, because every major paper in an NBA city has at least one reporter assigned to cover the team on a daily basis. You'll often get two or three stories after games, and Sunday papers usually offer expanded coverage of the team and the league.

With the growth in home computing, a new way to follow your favorite team and sport is developing. Just log on to the Internet, and you can find Web sites from the NBA and each of its teams, every major university, and a host of news organizations, providing you with a smorgasbord of content about basketball.

Clyde's Record Book

The most famous telecast in basketball history took place three decades ago, in 1968, at the Astrodome in Houston. The game paired the local powerhouse, the University of Houston, featuring Elvin Hayes, against the defending national champion, UCLA, featuring Kareem Abdul-Jabbar (then known by the name Lew Alcindor). A basketball court was trucked in from Los Angeles for the event and was set up in the middle of the Astrodome, where second base normally is. There were no seats on the rest of the baseball field, so the nearest of the 52,693 spectators who filled the building were more than 100 feet from the action. Houston upset UCLA 71-69 in the game, which was nationally syndicated by TVS and drew exquisite ratings. That game showed the potential drawing power of a major college basketball matchup to the broadcast industry.

Hoops and TV: Made for Each Other

Basketball is made for TV; everything is right there in front of you, easy to see.

The players are big, there aren't too many of them to keep track of, and they are not hidden by padded uniforms, helmets, and facemasks. You can see the emotion on their faces, the perspiration on their bodies. You can feel what they are feeling, the thrills and the agony.

The ball is also big and easy to see. This may sound simplistic, but it's an important factor. It's annoying to watch a hockey game and lose sight of the puck, as so often happens. The same happens with baseball: When the batter swings, you hear the crack of the bat and then have no idea where the ball went. In basketball, you can always see the ball.

There's also plenty of action and plenty of scoring. Soccer is fun, but you can wait forever for a goal to be scored, and that's a problem.

Everything today is quicker, faster-paced. The profile has been replaced by the sound bite, the hour-long documentary by the 12-minute magazine show segment, the essay by the factoid. We have drive-thru banks and restaurants and express checkout lanes. The same applies to sports. Today's fans want action, and that means scoring; basketball has it.

Basketball is a game of finite length as well. NBA games end after four quarters, except for a rare overtime, and fit into a two-and-a-half-hour time slot. College games are even handier, fitting into a two-hour period. Look at the way ESPN lines up games on Big Monday—bam, bam, bam, one after another every two hours. For the fan, it's heaven.

Finally, basketball is played indoors, which makes life easier for TV types. Program directors don't have to worry about rainouts. Directors can set up camera positions all around the arena, capturing the action from every angle. And announcers can count on calling the game in air-conditioned comfort, with all their information and technical gear set up around them, while sitting in the best seats in the house. What's not to like?

Love Those Replays!

Basketball, especially at the NBA level, is a fast-paced game—almost too fast for its own good. Great plays happen so quickly that they can be gone in the blink of an eyelash. Often I've seen something happen on the court and been left bewildered, wondering whether it was an illusion. Did I really see what I think I did, or is my mind playing tricks?

That's why replays are invaluable. You can really appreciate the amazing abilities of NBA athletes when you watch them in slow motion as they shake and bake on their way to the basket. You can watch them gyrate in mid-air with gymnastic acrobatics and uncanny dexterity, moving the ball from one hand to the other to avoid defenders, then finishing off plays with remarkable shots.

Clyde's Record Book

NBA games have been nationally televised since the 1950s and the old Dumont Network. I grew up with ABC's *Game of the Week* with Chris Schenkel and Jack Twyman, which seemed to feature the Boston Celtics every Sunday afternoon. As recently as 1981, however, NBA Finals games were not televised live but were taped and shown after the late-night news on CBS. Now NBC shows every game of the NBA Finals—and most of the Conference Finals—live in prime time or on weekends. And between NBC and the Turner networks, TBS and TNT, every single game of the NBA Playoffs is televised live nationally. Turner boasts of showing as many as 40 games in 30 nights, enough to delight the insatiable appetites of the most ardent hoop aficionados.

Replays also help you understand just how difficult an NBA referee's job is. He (or she, because women were added to the staff in 1997–98) must make hundreds of instantaneous decisions in every game, all while keeping the game moving and the players and coaches under control. Every ref will blow a call once in awhile—they're only human, after all—but replays constantly prove just how many of those calls they get right. I think they are the best in all of sports.

Clyde's Rules

Often fans talk about using instant replays to help referees review calls, but so far it has never gotten off the ground in the NBA because the game is so fast-paced and because so many calls are judgment calls. One instance where you might someday see instant replays used is in game-ending or period-ending shots, when the question is whether there was still time left when the shot was taken. A wide shot can show the clock and the player shooting the ball in the same frame, and officials could review it during the break between quarters or immediately after the game.

Replays also make great visual aids, especially with today's telestrators that enable analysts to draw on the screen while a replay is being shown. Instead of trying to verbalize a complex thought, a good analyst will find a play that embellishes his point and then use his telestrator for authenticity and emphasis so the viewer can see what he's getting at.

A good television director will use replays judiciously. More is not necessarily better; showing the same play from different angles is pointless unless each new angle reveals something new about the play. And because the game moves so fast, a director must know when to call up a replay so as not to miss live action. But there's no question that, when used properly, replays galvanize a game and make it more invigorating to watch.

In fact, for a time it seemed like the TV viewer had a better deal than the fan in the NBA arena. He could watch the game in the comfort of his own home, shown by cameras strategically placed throughout the building, while enjoying the benefits of instant replays and the announcers' commentary. That's why today's NBA arenas all include gargantuan video screens, so fans in the building can enjoy the benefits of various camera angles and replays as well.

Clyde's Tip

Before I became an announcer, I watched games on TV like any other fan. I'd sit and look, but not think. Now I have to articulate what I'm seeing, so I'm more in tune to the strategies. I try to stay ahead of the coach and think of what he might do, why he calls a timeout or puts a certain player in. I realize the average fan just watches a game and doesn't critique it, but I think you get more out of it if you put a little more into it.

See You on the Radio

Generations of fans in New York grew up with Marv Albert describing Knicks games on the radio, while in New England everybody listened to the gravely tones of Johnny Most broadcasting the Boston Celtics. Similarly, when the Lakers moved out to Los Angeles, Chick Hearn taught Californians the nuances of the pro game. Bill Schonely in Portland and Bob Blackburn in Seattle won legions of fans for those expansion franchises in their early years, helping those teams prosper in the Pacific Northwest.

Basketball is made for radio as well as television. For a radio play-by-play man, there's so much action to describe. Just calling the play ensures there will be virtually no dead air, those dreaded moments of silence when the announcers run out of things to say and listeners wonder if their radios have gone haywire.

Because it is so action-packed, basketball is a challenging game for a color commentator (either on the radio or on television), whose job is to provide the analysis. While the play-by-play man tells you "who," "what," "where," and "when," the color commentator explains the "why" and "how."

One of the difficult things I found, as I began working Knicks broadcasts, was learning how to make my points concisely and profoundly enough so that I would add to the broadcast without getting in the way of my partner describing the action. You really have to know what you want to say and be prepared to say it quickly—in and out, with no extraneous verbosity.

Good radio announcers paint word pictures so listeners can use their imaginations instead of their eyes to reconstruct the scene in their minds. They must always remember that while they can see the action in front of them, their audience can't, so their descriptions must be rich and detailed, enchanting and enthralling.

Clyde's Tip

Many times I'll be watching a game and I'll turn the sound off. When you're not listening to the announcers, and when it's just you, you become more attentive. Nobody's telling you what to look at—it's up to you. And when you turn the sound off, you can hear yourself think.

Clyde's Record Book

Radio is very powerful because it calls on your mind to provide the picture. To this day, the image people have of the Knicks teams I played on is what Marv Albert was saying on the radio. Whether it's Willis Reed limping onto the court, or DeBusschere bounding, or Bradley swishing, or Earl the Pearl shaking and baking, or me wheeling and dealing, those images are indelibly etched in their heads because they had to create the picture themselves from Marv's words. That picture in the mind is how fans remember our team, and they recall it like it was yesterday.

Clyde's Tip

One of the truly extraordinary broadcasters in NBA history is Chick Hearn of the Los Angeles Lakers, who is known for his rapid-fire delivery and unique phraseology. Hearn's unwritten rule is that the commentator he's working with must make his point quickly; once the ball reaches the half-court line and goes into the offensive zone, the microphone is his. The long-standing joke is that Hearn's partners (a list that includes current Miami coach Pat Riley) only need to know four words: "Right you are, Chick."

Marty Glickman, a broadcast pioneer who now works as an announcing coach, helped me get started in the business. He taught me to assume that the audience is blind and to be descriptive. A player is not along the baseline, he's along the right baseline 15 feet away. Most of all, he said, just be yourself and trust that your knowledge of the game, and love for the game, will come through.

For many years, teams had just one radio announcer, who would serve as both play-by-play man and color commentator. That wasn't for any technical reason, but just because it was cheaper to operate that way. Sometimes the announcer was even called upon to do a simulcast, where his call of the game would be used on television as well as radio.

Thankfully, for those of us in the industry, those days are largely gone. As the NBA has prospered, broadcasts have become more lucrative, and teams and stations are more willing to spend money on announcers and game production.

Nearly all NBA teams now have separate radio and TV announcers, and often have additional announcers for cable TV or Spanish broadcasts.

Clyde's Rules

A good announcer will give directions to help his audience see its way around the court and picture a play. Instead of saying, "Miller shoots from 20," he should say, "Miller, to the left of the key, shoots from 20." Similarly, instead of "Bryant drives into the lane," he should say, "Bryant, from the right side, drives diagonally into the lane." The shorter calls are fine for television, but the longer, more descriptive calls help a radio listener envision what's happening.

Following Your Team

One of the best ways to follow your favorite team—especially if you live in or around that NBA city—is also the oldest: your daily newspaper. (While my focus here is on following NBA teams, the same tips apply to your favorite college team.)

Most papers assign a beat reporter to their local team, and he or she will write news stories and features about the team on nearly a daily basis from the start of training camp in October through the end of the season, which for some teams means mid-June. As you might expect, reporters on the NBA beat tend to take nice, long summer vacations!

Between these daily updates and other stories written by columnists or feature writers, newspapers provide extensive coverage of a team over the course of a season. Writers from different cities also tend to network with each other, so you often will get to read what's going on elsewhere around the NBA as well.

Women have found their way into the media coverage of teams as well. It's not uncommon these days for a paper to have beat writers or columnists who are women, something that didn't exist in my playing days when all the writers were men. In addition to stories about the local team, major papers carry wire service reports on games involving other teams, plus occasional features or news stories. Some big-city papers even have a beat writer assigned to cover the NBA as a whole, in addition to the team beat writer. This NBA beat writer focuses on league-wide issues and trends and adds significant depth to a paper's coverage, but not every newspaper feels it has the resources for such a luxury. *USA Today*, as a national newspaper, provides coverage without a local orientation and thus gives a good overview of the league-wide news and trends.

Clyde's Tip

Because you don't have to watch anything when you're following a game on radio, try keeping your own stats. Keep a scoring tally for your favorite players (or all players, if you like), or keep track of something more esoteric, such as fast-break points or scoring within a certain matchup. It will add to your enjoyment of the game.

Periodicals are another way to keep up with the league as a whole. National weeklies such as *Sports Illustrated, the Sporting News*, and the new *ESPN: The Magazine* all provide extensive NBA coverage, focusing on newsworthy trends, analysis, and features. *Basketball Times* and *Basketball Weekly* are two more specialized tabloids that also cover the sport, including the NBA.

If you're a devotee of a certain team, write and see if the team publishes its own newsletter or magazine (see Appendix B for NBA team addresses). Most NBA teams have some sort of in-house publication that is used as a premium for season-ticket subscribers and that's also sold by subscription. The same is true for major colleges. Write away for a sample copy, and then see if it's worth subscribing. While you won't find any negative news or controversial issues in these team-produced publications, you will find features and off-court news about your favorite team and its players.

Finally, a host of magazines come out in late summer, before the start of each season, offering team-by-team previews and feature stories. These are a fine way to get back into shape for the coming season. *Street and Smith's* is the oldest and still one of the best, but *Sports Illustrated* and *ESPN* have been publishing annuals for a few years now, and there are about a half-dozen others on the market. Check out any good newsstand or magazine store starting in mid-August and take your pick, but don't necessarily grab the first magazine you see; by mid-September you'll have a potpourri to choose from, if you don't mind waiting a bit, and the later ones will have the most current trade and player-signing information.

Hoops in Cyberspace

Print resources are fine, but in this computer age the World Wide Web is absolutely the best place for keeping tabs on news about your favorite NBA team or the league as a whole. (Once again, my focus here is the NBA, but the same information applies to major college basketball as well.)

Just about every major newspaper runs a Web site as well, with most of them carrying versions of their print product. So from your home, school, or office computer, you can dial up whatever paper you want (assuming you have Internet access, that is) and read local stories about last night's games for any team in the league. And on Sundays you can read the NBA news and notes columns that the big-city dailies all have.

There are far too many sites to list here, but if you play around with some version of the newspaper's name (such as www.chicagotribune.com or www.nypostonline.com), you should find it. You can also call up the paper and get their site address, which is known in the Web business as their URL. You can also try using one of the online search engines.

For the national picture, you can choose from a host of sites, the best of which include those run by *USA Today* (www.usatoday.com), ESPN (www.espnet.sportszone.com), CNN/SI (www.cnnsi.com), *The Sporting News* (www.sportingnews.com), and CBS/ Sportsline (www.cbs.sportsline.com). All offer constantly updated news, features, analysis, chats, and much more.

The NBA also runs a terrific Web site (www.nba.com), as well as collaborating with its teams on 29 team-specific sites (linked from www.nba.com, or go directly to www.nba.com/hawks and so forth). These provide player information, game-by-game stats, and extensive linked archives and also feature live chats with NBA players, coaches, and broadcasters on a regular basis. You can listen in to the radio broadcast of any NBA game as it is being played, or you can watch a scoreboard that is updated almost constantly to see how your favorite team is doing.

Major event coverage by NBA.com, such as All-Star Weekend, the NBA Finals, or the NBA Draft, is particularly extensive and includes pre-game and in-game analysis by guest experts and live audio and text from post-game and off-day news conferences.

There are many more sites worth knowing about, including those run by the Basketball Hall of Fame (www.hoophall.com), the International Basketball Federation (www.fiba.com), and the two women's leagues (www.wnba.com and www.abl.com). For historical material, one of the best sites is the pioneering Web site founded by the Raleigh (N.C.) *News and Observer* (www.nando.net).

Happy surfing!

Living in a Fantasy World

So you think you're an expert? Well, prove it! Try being a general manager, and see how you do.

Because you probably can't get the job for real, enter a fantasy league. They're not hard to find—many of the Web sites I've listed also run fantasy leagues, and you probably can find others listed in the sports section of your local newspaper.

All run along similar lines. Each entrant picks a team and competes against all other teams picked by league members. Usually each player is assigned a dollar value; you're given a "salary cap" on how much you can spend on your entire team, so you have to choose some stars and some role players. Your players' stat lines from their actual games determine how your team does, based on whatever statistical formula the league uses.

Some formulas are simple, just adding together points, rebounds, assists, steals, and blocks for a point total, for example. Others are more complex, taking away things such as turnovers, missed field goals, or free throws before determining a player's point total for a given game.

After you know your league's formula, just grab the previous night's box scores and tabulate the point total for each player on the team. Your total score over a given period—it may be a week, a month, or the entire season—determines how you rank in the league.

Some leagues allow roster changes, so you may add or drop a player at a given time based on injuries or performance. Some even allow, and arrange, for trades between team owners.

One thing running a "virtual" team does is get you to follow the game closely—sometimes a little too closely. One warning sign that you are a little too involved is when you know more about the health of the players on your team than you do about your own family's health.

The Least You Need to Know

➤ Basketball is a perfect game for television because the action is non-stop and easy to follow, and because replays enhance viewers' understanding and enjoyment of the game.

➤ Radio broadcasts leave more to the imagination, but good announcers paint word pictures that bring the game across vividly to fans listening at home.

➤ Newspapers and periodicals provide a wealth of information about the NBA and your favorite team, but for the most current news plus extensive features, commentary, and even live audio and chat sessions, turn to cyberspace and the World Wide Web.

Chapter 27

Don't Just Watch, Play!

In This Chapter

➤ Basketball is a game for life

➤ Where to find a game

➤ H–O–R–S–E and other games to enjoy

In Chapter 25, I told you that basketball was a game for all ages and that you can truly be a fan for life. Well, you can also be a player for life. Playing ball is a marvelous way to stay in shape, to socialize, and to compete—at any age, as long as it's done sensibly.

In this chapter I'll discuss how to get enjoyment from playing the game, at any age. Much of it involves common sense, but I've found that common sense just isn't as common as it should be.

I'll also give you some tips on where to find a game that suits you, both physically and emotionally. And I'll introduce you to some games you can play either on your own or with a limited number of opponents. Not only will these give you a chance to work on your skills, but you'll also enjoy them.

A Game for Life

The love of basketball can begin early, as early as a toddler tossing a Nerf ball through a plastic hoop. There's no reason why that love can't be infinite—and not just as a spectator, but as a player.

I know men in their 50s and 60s who play regularly, once or twice a week. And when you think about it, if men play tennis and racquetball at that age, why not basketball?

The play has to be done sensibly, of course. As with any form of exercise, basketball should not be undertaken without clearance from a doctor who is familiar with your physical condition and medical history. If you had a trick knee that gave out and required surgery 25 years ago, it's important to make your doctor aware of that when he evaluates your readiness to take the court.

And while basketball is a game, it should be treated like any other form of exercise. That means gradually building up the amount of playing time and level of competition, not trying to do too much too soon. You wouldn't expect to just lace up sneakers and go out and run a marathon, and you shouldn't expect to put on a basketball jersey and play a full-court game with former varsity players half your age.

But don't let that stop you. No matter what your age, basketball is an invigorating way to get exercise, to satisfy those competitive instincts, and also to meet and hang out with people who share your passion for the game. Just do it sensibly.

Start out slowly. Find a half-court game, preferably in an air-conditioned gym, with players roughly your own age. Check out the intensity of the game—are the players having fun, or is it a win-at-all-costs struggle? Watch the style of play—do they share the ball, or is it one-on-one? When you're comfortable with the style, the intensity, and the skill level and age of the players, then get going. Call out "I got next!", pick your teammates, and start playing.

Of course, if you know you want to play with certain friends and there are enough of you for a three-on-three game (with a few extras for those who can't make it on a certain night), try to reserve a court as a group and play among yourselves. But it's not often you'll find that many people starting from scratch at the same time, so it's more likely you'll have to try to fit yourself (maybe with one or two others) into an existing game. Look for a game that suits your ability and conditioning.

If you feel like it, you can gradually get involved in a more competitive game against more skillful players. And when you're ready, you can start playing full-court ball. That's up to you and how you feel. There's no shame in finding a level you're comfortable with and sticking with it; it *is* a shame, however, if you don't get out and try to play.

Clyde's Tip

There's nothing like actually playing the game, dribbling a ball, and shooting it through a basket. When watching an NBA game, everything looks so easy. If you go out on the court and try it yourself, though, you'll quickly learn how deceiving looks can be—don't be surprised if your first try from three-point range is a UFO that falls embarrassingly short of the rim! But be persistent. There's nothing like that feeling when your home-run bomb finally goes in.

Where to Find the Right Game

I know, you can't find a game—you either have one or you don't.

Hey, you know what I mean. Not "game" as in the Spike Lee movie title, *He Got Game*. I'm talking about "game" in the more conventional usage, as in, "Let's find a game to play."

The first place to start is your neighborhood school gym or recreation center. (I suggest starting indoors because the conditions invariably are better.) Many gyms are open in the evening, and while sometimes the courts are reserved for organized league games, there's often a period of free time or open time when anyone can play. Call or drop by to find out if this is the case at a gym near you, or whether someone there knows where you can find such a game. And while you're asking, see if you find out anything about the level of the game—the age and condition of the players and their competitiveness. Then go check it out for yourself to see whether it's right for you.

If you belong to a health club, take a look at the games on the courts there. Find out the ages of the players and watch the level of play; if you find a match you're comfortable with, hook up with someone after the game and let him or her know you'd like to get involved. Chances are these players are always looking for more people, so they'll welcome your interest—especially if you make it a point to pass the ball to your teammates a little more than usual the first time you play.

If you'd you prefer to play outdoors, check out the action at your neighborhood playground or any others nearby. Stand along the fence and watch the games on the different courts—many playgrounds have an etiquette that a certain court is reserved for the best players and the most intense game, and that's not where you're going to want to start out. If you can't find a game that's right for you, try a different playground. If after awhile you still can't find a game that suits you, then spend some time practicing on your own, improving your game and conditioning until you're ready for the level of competition.

But I think you'll be able to find a game at one of the places I've described, or else your local YMCA, religious center, or a facility run by the parks or recreation department in your community. Also, don't forget about the colleges and universities in your area—many make their courts available, generally for a nominal fee, when they are not being used by students.

Here's the view from behind the backboard of a playground court in the Roxbury section of Boston, Massachusetts. Associated Press

H–O–R–S–E and Other Games to Enjoy

Say you show up at a playground and only one or two others are there. That's not enough for even a good half-court run, but you can still work on your game.

One of the most enjoyable ways to do so is a shooting game called H-O-R-S-E, which may be as old as basketball itself. A player shoots the ball from any location; if he makes the shot, each succeeding player must duplicate that shot or else earn a letter ("H" if it's the first miss, "O" for the second, and so on). If the first shooter misses, the next player in line attempts a shot, and so forth. After you get five letters—H-O-R-S-E— you're out of the game; the last player remaining is the winner.

What makes this fun is that you can develop your own repertoire of special shots to make it difficult for others to match you. Because everybody today shoots layups and jumpers, try a hook shot or a bank shot.

You also can put a special twist on an otherwise ordinary shot to make it more difficult for your opponents. Try shooting with your left hand (or your right hand, if you are a lefty) or while facing away from the basket; those who follow you will have to shoot the same way. You also can call "bank" or "swish," and everyone will have to make their shots that way.

Another popular shooting game, Around the World, involves shooting from designated spots on the floor. The shots range from layups to long jumpers, and the game gets its name because you start at one side of the floor and work your way around to the other, as the following illustration shows.

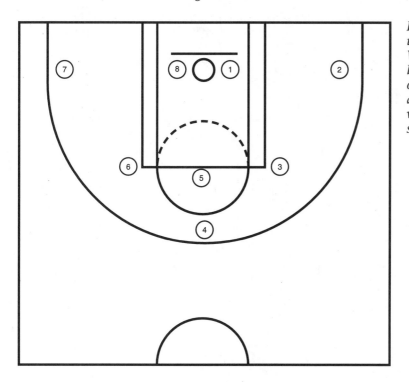

Here are eight shots often used to play Around the World, starting with a layup from the right side of the basket and going around until you finish with a layup from the left side.

The rules of Around the World are simple. If you make a shot, you advance to the next spot. If you miss, you can either wait on that spot until your turn comes again or you take a second shot; you advance if you make this shot, but you start over in the very first spot if you miss.

In addition to playing H-O-R-S-E or Around the World, you always can work on other aspects of your game. You can practice rebounding by throwing the ball against a rim or backboard and then going up and grabbing it. For variety, you can practice offensive rebounding by trying to tip the ball into the basket or catch it in midair, and then shoot it either before you come down or after you go back up.

Practice passing with a friend, working on various kinds of passes such as bounce passes or touch passes off a dribble. And always work on your dribbling until you're comfortable using both hands and not looking at the ball.

The Least You Need to Know

➤ Basketball is a game for life that can be played at any age, as long as you use some sagacity and don't try to do more than your body can handle.

➤ Try your local school or rec center gymnasium, health club, or neighborhood playground to find a pickup game to suit your level of talent and conditioning.

➤ H-O-R-S-E and Around the World are fun ways to work on your shooting, but you should also practice other aspects of the game, such as rebounding, passing, and dribbling with both hands.

Chapter 28

Basketball's Shrine and Other Fan Fun

In This Chapter

➤ The Hall of Fame

➤ Nicknames: who put the "Doctor" in Dr. J?

➤ Basketball on the screen

➤ A hoops reading list

You now know enough to be able to hold your own when it comes to hoops. You know the difference between a pick and roll and a dinner roll, and you know how to tell a point guard from a shooting guard from a lifeguard.

Don't stop now. In this final chapter, I'll show you some ways to increase your enjoyment of the game and build upon your newfound knowledge.

The Shrine

Situated in Springfield, Massachusetts—the birthplace of basketball—is the Naismith Memorial Basketball Hall of Fame. It's the game's only shrine honoring and celebrating all levels of basketball—professional, college, high school, amateur, international, and the women's game.

Strolling through the Honors Court, you will find yourself surrounded by the men and women who made basketball universal. A total of 222 players, coaches, referees, and contributors have been inducted into the Hall of Fame (not counting the members of the class of '98, who were scheduled for induction in September), along with four teams: the first team, the Original Celtics, the Buffalo Germans, and the New York Renaissance Five, commonly known as the Rens.

The 1997 inductees to the Hall of Fame were (front, from left) coaches Pete Carril, Antonio Diaz-Miguel, and Don Haskins and (back, from left) former players Joan Crawford, Denise Curry, Alex English, and Bailey Howell. Associated Press

But the Basketball Hall of Fame is far more than a museum. In fact, one of the first things you see as you enter the three-story building along the Connecticut River in downtown Springfield is an array of hoops, nets, and backboards set at various distances and heights for visitors to shoot at from a moving walkway. Pick up an official Spalding ball off the rack, take aim, and let it fly—don't worry about form, nobody's giving out style points here. But if you're on target, a scoreboard will record your basket and give it a number for posterity.

Clyde's Tip

Pete Maravich's floppy socks, the original 24-second shot clock, Bob Lanier's size-22 sneakers, and the jersey Wilt Chamberlain wore on March 2, 1962—the night he scored 100 points—are just some of the basketball memorabilia on display at the Hall of Fame.

Shooting hoops is just the beginning. Want to know what it's like to have a Hall of Famer take you one-on-one? Step onto a pressure sensitive floor, and suddenly you're being schooled by some of the game's all-time greats. Thanks to the wonders of virtual reality, you can put your best move on Bill Walton—at Boston Garden, no less, which may be gone but thankfully is remembered here.

I was elected to the Hall of Fame in 1987, and that has to rank as the compelling honor of my career—along with being named one of the NBA's 50 Greatest Players of All Time by a panel of experts in conjunction with the NBA's 50th anniversary celebration.

I remember when I got the call telling me I'd been elected to the Hall of Fame—I was mesmerized. My whole athletic career flashed before me. I thought of

Mom and Dad, who provided the impetus. I thought of all my teammates, my coaches, my opponents, people I hadn't thought about for years—it became a very poignant moment. Yes, I cried.

Red Holzman, my coach with the Knicks, inducted me, which was all the more special because he had such an impact on my career. In my acceptance speech, I talked about my teammates—guys who didn't begrudge my celebrity, who didn't mind my being "Clyde." We never had a problem with egos. I thanked all my coaches who stressed discipline and teamwork and strove to make me a complete player. Some of my family was there, but I knew I couldn't mention my parents or I would have broken down. I would not have made it through the occasion. I would have been overcome with emotion. It was a night I'll always cherish.

Clyde's Tip

The Basketball Hall of Fame is open year-round and is a great place to visit. It's located within a couple of hours drive of New York or Boston and you can see it all in one day. For more information, call 413/781-6500 or check out its Web site, www.hoophall.com.

Some Great Hoops Nicknames

You probably know that I got the nickname "Clyde" from the bank robber character, Clyde Barrow, played by Warren Beatty in the movie *Bonnie and Clyde*. Danny Whelan, long-time trainer for the Knicks, hung the tag on me when I showed up at the arena one day wearing one of the wide-brimmed hats Beatty wore in the movie, and the nickname stuck.

Nicknames are one of the lovable things about sports. In what other field of endeavor would some of the all-time greats be known as Dr. J, Wilt the Stilt, the Big O, or Zeke from Cabin Creek? Nicknames are fun, and if you drop a few into the conversation, you're sure to impress.

Basketball is a sport rich in nicknames. Some come from stature, such as Elvin "The Big E" Hayes, Wayne "Tree" Rollins, or Charles "Stretch" Murphy. Others come from hair color, such as Arnold "Red" Auerbach and William "Red" Holzman—although in both cases their hair turned white long before they finished coaching. Some are plays on their real names, such as "Bells" for Walt Bellamy or "'Zo" for Alonzo Mourning. Some are appropriate rhymes, such as my former teammate Earl "the Pearl" Monroe, who truly was a gem of a player.

Often nicknames describe the way players play the game. Two of the clever guards from the NBA's early years, Bob Cousy and Dick McGuire, were nicknamed "the Houdini of the Hardwood" and "Tricky Dick" for their ballhandling wizardry. Chet "the Jet" Walker had some speed, David "the Skywalker" Thompson could get up in the air, Harry "the Horse" Gallatin was a rugged rebounder, and "Easy" Ed Macauley made the game look simple with his smooth style. But you wouldn't want to run into Len "Truck" Robinson or mess with "Jungle" Jim Loscutoff or Larry "Mr. Mean" Smith or my former teammate Mel "Killer" Davis!

The coolest hoops nickname belonged to George Gervin, who won four NBA scoring titles with the San Antonio Spurs in the 1970s and 1980s. He was known as "the Iceman," or simply "Ice," because he always looked so calm and unflappable on the court, showing no emotion no matter how tense the situation. (When he had a son, by the way, the youngster was quickly dubbed "Ice Cube.")

Good nicknames often get recycled, as in the case of my teammate, Dean "the Dream" Meminger and the current version, Hakeem "the Dream" Olajuwon. The NBA also had a pair of "Kangaroo Kids," nicknamed for their leaping ability: Jim Pollard in the 1940s and '50s and Billy Cunningham in the 1960s and '70s.

On the other hand, some nicknames are best forgotten. Who would want to recycle Billy Paultz's nickname, "the Whopper," or Jim Barnes' moniker, "Bad News?" And it took Charles Barkley years to live down his college nickname, "the Round Mound of Rebound."

Here are some stories behind some of the game's other unique nicknames:

➤ **The Big O:** While Oscar Robertson was big for a guard at 6'5", that's not why he got the nickname. It came from a James Thurber story, "The Disappearing O," that was popular in the 1960s early in his playing career.

➤ **Hondo:** Celtics legend John Havlicek got this nickname from Ohio State teammate Mel Nowell. Havlicek liked reading Western novels and bore a facial resemblance to a young John Wayne, who starred at that time in a film called *Hondo*.

➤ **Dollar Bill:** Sure Bill Bradley signed a $400,000 contract when he joined the Knicks—quite a sum for the mid-'60s. But some of us liked to joke that he got the nickname because he was so cheap that he still had the first dollar he ever made. When he was at Princeton, by the way, Bradley was sometimes called "Mr. President" or "the Secretary of State" by his teammates.

➤ **Dr. J.:** When Julius Erving was growing up in Roosevelt, New York, he had a friend with whom he played playground ball, and the two of them went on to the University of Massachusetts. The friend called himself "the Professor" because he thought he could take opponents to school, and he dubbed Erving "the Doctor" because he could really operate. "The Doctor" quickly became "Dr. J," or simply "Doc."

➤ **Spud:** Anthony Webb, who won an NBA dunking contest despite standing only 5'7", got his nickname from a cousin. When Webb was born, his cousin thought his head looked like Sputnik, the first Russian space satellite. Because "Sputnik" was no nickname for a youngster, other family members quickly changed it to "Spud."

➤ **Ack Ack:** Tommy Heinsohn of the Celtics never met a shot he didn't like or wouldn't take, so he got the nickname from the sound made by a machine gun.

➤ **The Big Dipper:** Wilt Chamberlain, 7'1", never liked to be called "Wilt the Stilt" (one of his other nicknames), but he didn't mind "the Big Dipper." When he was 10 years old, Chamberlain bumped his head on the top of a door frame and was told he had to dip to get through. Friends began calling him "Dip," or "Dippy," which became "the Dipper" and finally "the Big Dipper." The late Dave Zinkoff, legendary Philadelphia public address announcer, called Chamberlain's stuff shots "Dipper Dunks."

➤ **Penny:** When Anfernee Hardaway was a youngster, his grandmother called him "Pretty," but with her Southern accent it sounded like "Penny"—which is probably just as well.

➤ **The Human Highlight Film:** At the University of Georgia, Dominique Wilkins made so many spectacular dunks that he began showing up regularly on the sports clips on the nightly news. He was dubbed "the Human Highlight Film," even before the days of *SportsCenter* and *Play of the Day*.

➤ **Muggsy:** Tyrone Bogues, the shortest player in NBA history at 5'3", got his nickname when growing up in Baltimore. He was so quick and adept at stealing the ball that a friend said it was like he was mugging you. From that came "Muggsy."

➤ **Zeke from Cabin Creek:** Lakers teammate Elgin Baylor thought Jerry West needed a nickname. West came from Cheylan, West Virginia, a town so small it had no post office, so his mail was delivered to Cabin Creek. Because Baylor liked to call country folk "Zeke," he dubbed West "Zeke from Cabin Creek." One of the game's all-time great guards, West's other nickname is more appropriate: "Mr. Clutch."

➤ **Blue:** When current NBA player Theodore Edwards was a baby, an older sister found him choking; his blue face earned him his nickname.

➤ **Band-Aid:** Derrick Chievous, who didn't last long in the NBA, always wore a Band-Aid for good luck.

➤ **The Black Hole:** Celtics teammates hung this one on Kevin McHale because of his propensity to shoot the ball. Once they threw it in to him, it never came out.

➤ **The Admiral:** David Robinson of the San Antonio Spurs got this name for his two-year stint in the Navy, even though he never achieved such high rank. I guess it sounds better than "the Ensign."

➤ **Magic:** A sports writer who covered Earvin Johnson's high school games in East Lansing, Michigan, first dubbed him "Magic" because "Dr. J" and "the Big E" were taken. To his teammates on the Lakers, Johnson was known as "Buck" or "E.J.," but rarely "Magic."

➤ **Captain Late:** James Silas, who starred for the San Antonio Spurs during their ABA days, was at his best in the closing minutes when the game was on the line—hence his nickname.

➤ **The Rifleman:** Veteran NBA scorer Chuck Person's full name is Chuck Connors Person because his mom was a fan of the old TV Western *The Rifleman*, which starred Chuck Connors. But that's not all—the 6'7" Connors actually played three seasons of professional basketball and is credited with breaking the first backboard in NBA history, during warm-ups prior to the Boston Celtics' first-ever game in 1946.

Want some more great nicknames? Here, in alphabetical order, I give you Greg "Cadillac" Anderson, Ken "the Animal" Bannister, Jerry "Hound" Baskerville, Darryl "Chocolate Thunder" Dawkins, Clarence "Bevo" Francis, Artis "A Train" Gilmore, Travis "Machine Gun" Grant, Darrell "Dr. Dunkenstein" Griffith, Darnell "Dr. Dunk" Hillman, Gus "Honeycomb" Johnson, Bob "Butterbean" Love, "Pistol" Pete Maravich, Cedric "Cornbread" Maxwell, Bryant "Big Country" Reeves, Glenn "Big Dog" Robinson, Dennis "Worm" Rodman, Tom "Satch" Sanders, Bobby "Bingo" Smith, Donald "Slick" Watts, Jamaal "Silk" Wilkes, and Bill "Poodles" Willoughby.

They're all true, believe me. I couldn't make all this up.

Basketball on the Big Screen

For many years, basketball movies were synonymous with box-office bombs—and deservedly so. There have been some terrible movies made over the years using basketball as the setting, usually because nobody bothered to write a good script for them. I hope, for your sake, you don't remember *The Fish That Saved Pittsburgh*.

This trend seems to be changing somewhat in recent years, perhaps because some filmmakers and stars are true basketball fans.

Spike Lee's recent film *He Got Game* received solid reviews, while Billy Crystal starred as a basketball referee in a romantic comedy, *Forget Paris,* which also was well-received. Two other recent films with a basketball setting were *Eddie* with Whoopie Goldberg and *Celtic Pride* with Dan Ackroyd and Damon Wayans, though neither was exactly a box office smash.

One basketball movie worth looking for at the rental counter is *Hoop Dreams,* a well-praised documentary that captures the spirit of the game and the hold it has on youngsters. Check it out.

And while *White Men Can't Jump,* starring Woody Harrelson, wasn't a huge box office hit, it has developed a certain following.

Because of Leonardo DiCaprio's starring role in the mega-hit *Titanic,* his earlier film, *The Basketball Diaries*—which was more about personal problems and substance abuse than basketball—has received renewed attention as well.

On the small screen, basketball hasn't really shown up that much. One TV series that lasted awhile was *The White Shadow,* about a white ex-pro player who coaches a team at a racially mixed high school. While the plots and characterization were relatively simple, the show did display a sense of humor and often delivered a positive message. There are worse things to watch should you happen upon it.

Recommended Reading

Many excellent books have been written about basketball over the years, from biographies and autobiographies, to reference works, to social treatises, and each season brings new volumes. These are some of the best, including one by an ex-teammate of mine:

➤ *24 Seconds to Shoot* (Leonard Koppett): An informal history of the early NBA that's hard to find but worth the effort if you want to learn about early NBA history.

➤ *Basketball, its Origin and Development* (James Naismith): Who better to write about basketball's early years than its founder? Naismith's book first appeared in 1941 and was reissued in 1996.

➤ *The City Game* (Pete Axthelm): Written in 1971 and reissued in 1992, Axthelm looked at our 1970 NBA Champion Knicks in the context of playground ball and the stars of the street, such as Herman "Helicopter" Knowings and Earl "Goat" Manigault.

➤ *Hang Time: Days and Dreams with Michael Jordan* (Bob Greene): With remarkable access to Jordan in 1991 and 1992, the *Chicago Tribune* columnist offers an insightful look at the game's greatest star and what it meant to be Michael Jordan—on and especially off the court—before his early retirement and comeback.

➤ *Heaven Is A Playground* (Rick Telander) and *The Last Shot* (Darcy Frey): These two portraits of youngsters growing up in Brooklyn, N.Y., and the role basketball plays in their lives were written by writers who spent extended periods with them. Published nearly two decades apart—*Heaven* in 1976, *Last Shot* in 1994—they show how little things change.

➤ *Life on the Run* (Bill Bradley): My ex-teammate was unique among NBA players. Here he talks about his life in the NBA in a thinking man's guide to the sport, written in 1976 and reissued in 1995. *A Sense of Where You Are*, a profile of Bradley at Princeton by John McPhee, is another interesting look at the beginnings of his career.

➤ *Loose Balls* (Terry Pluto): This book is a hilarious history of the wild and wacky ways of the ABA, the league that battled the NBA for nine years before folding in 1976. It's written in the words of those who were part of it.

➤ *The Official NBA Basketball Encyclopedia* (Alex Sachare): This most complete reference work about the NBA was edited by my co-author.

➤ *The NBA Finals* (Roland Lazenby): This year-by-year look at the NBA's championship series focuses on its title-winning teams.

➤ *Take It To The Hoop* (Daniel Rudman) and *We Came to Play* (John Ross and Q. R. Hand, Jr.): These two outstanding anthologies of basketball writings are worth whatever it takes to find them. They are musts for any hoop fan's bookshelf.

➤ *Tall Tales* (Terry Pluto): Similar in style to his earlier *Loose Balls,* this book about the history of the NBA complements Koppett's work nicely. Others of this genre include *From Set Shot to Slam Dunk* by Charles Salzberg, *Vintage NBA* by Neil D. Isaacs, *From Peachbaskets to Slamdunks* by Robert D. Bole and Alfred C. Lawrence, and *Cages to Jump Shots* by Robert W. Peterson. All are recommended.

➤ *A Season on the Brink* (John Feinstein): Indiana's controversial coach, Bob Knight, gave total access to Feinstein for this portrayal of a season—and probably wishes he hadn't.

The Least You Need to Know

➤ The Naismith Memorial Basketball Hall of Fame in Springfield, Massachusetts, is a great place to visit to learn more about basketball—or just to have fun.

➤ Nicknames are fun, and basketball has more than its share of colorful monikers. Learn to toss a few into the conversation, and you will sound like an expert.

➤ While basketball hasn't fared too well on the silver screen, many outstanding books have been written about the sport and will enhance your understanding and enjoyment.

Appendix A

Hoops Glossary

ABA   The American Basketball Association, a professional league that existed for nine seasons from 1967–68 through 1975–76 and featured Julius Erving; David Thompson; and a red, white, and blue ball.

ABL   The American Basketball League. Several pro leagues have used this name, including one of the strongest of the early men's leagues that was founded in 1926 and operated through the 1930s. Another ABL existed for one-and-a-half seasons in the early 1960s; today it's the name of one of the two women's pro leagues, the one that plays a winter schedule.

Above the rim   If a player can really jump, he is said to play the game "above the rim."

Airball   A shot that misses the basket and the backboard completely, hitting nothing but air. It's very embarrassing.

Alley-oop   A pass that is lobbed toward the basket, in which a teammate catches the ball in midair and puts it through the hoop before coming back down to the ground.

Assist   When a player throws a pass that leads directly to a teammate scoring a basket, he is credited with an assist.

BAA   The Basketball Association of America, the forerunner of the NBA.

Backboard   The flat surface to which the basket ring is attached. In the pros and colleges, it's made of plexiglass, but it can also be made of wood or metal.

Backcourt   Another term for the guard position, as in "He plays the backcourt." Also, the defensive half of the court (see also *frontcourt*).

Back door play   One of the basic plays in basketball, in which the ball is passed into a pivotman and a player (either the passer or another teammate) fakes to the outside, away from the basket, then makes a sharp cut to the basket and takes a quick pass for a layup or dunk.

Ball fake   Using the ball to fake an opponent off balance. A player with the ball fakes either a shot or a pass to get his defender out of position, leaning in the wrong direction or jumping into the air.

Bank shot   A shot that is directed off the backboard and into the basket.

Baseline   The border line at each end of the court, under the basket, that connects the two sidelines (see also *end line*).

Basket   The metal ring that is the target for the shooters. A shot that goes through for a score is also called a basket.

Basketball   OK, what part of this don't you understand? If it's *basket*, see above. If it's *ball*, well, figure it out.

Block   To deflect a shot away from the basket.

Blocking   A foul in which a defensive player moves into the path of an offensive player, creating contact and blocking his path.

Boards   Short for *backboards*, as in "hitting the boards." Also, slang for *rebounds*.

Bounce pass   A pass in which a player advances the ball past a defender by bouncing it to a teammate.

Box out   The act of positioning your body between an opponent and the basket to get into better rebounding position. It's something of a lost art today.

Brick   A wild shot that slams off the backboard or rim. The shooter is known as a *bricklayer*. This is just about as embarrassing as an airball.

CBA   The Continental Basketball Association, the sport's primary minor professional league.

Center   One of the three basic positions, usually manned by the tallest player on the team who plays closest to the basket. Another word for center is *pivot*; another term for the person who plays the position is *pivotman*.

Charging   A foul in which an offensive player runs into a defender who already has established his position on the floor and creates contact. It's the opposite of *blocking*, and deciding between the two may be the hardest call for a referee to make—it's tough to tell whether a player was stationary or who initiated the contact.

Chucker   A player who shoots a lot, whether he's hot or not (also, *gunner*). It can be frustrating to have a chucker for a teammate.

Coast to coast   From one end of the court to the other, as in "He grabbed the rebound and went coast to coast to score." It's always a lot of fun!

Collective bargaining agreement The labor agreement between the NBA and its Players Association that spells out things such as free agency rules and working conditions.

Commissioner The head honcho of the NBA, currently David Stern.

Court The 50-by-94-foot rectangle on which the game is played.

Cut A quick run to the basket by an offensive player without the ball. If you've got the ball in your hands, you should look for teammates who are cutting to the basket—when one is free, pass him the ball.

Deny the ball Prevent an opponent from catching the ball by guarding him closely and trying to play in the passing lane between him and the ball. This can be a very effective defensive tactic and can frustrate an opponent.

Dish Pass. As a good point guard, you should dish before you swish.

Double-double Scoring 10 or more in two of these statistical categories: points, rebounds, assists, steals, and blocks.

Double dribble Once you start to dribble the ball, you may not stop and then start again. It you do, it's a violation and the ball goes to the other team.

Double figures Scoring 10 or more in a statistical category. After a player grabs his tenth rebound, he is said to have reached double figures.

Double-team When a second defender comes over to help the primary defender guard a man, they are said to double-team him or trap him.

Downtown Slang for beyond the three-point arc, as in "he hit one from downtown."

Dribble To bounce the ball in order to advance into better position.

Drive A fast move, with the ball, toward the basket.

Dunk A basket scored by throwing the ball down through the hoop. Also called a *slam-dunk*, a *jam*, and many other things. It's sure to bring fans out of their seats.

End line The border line at each end of the court, under the baskets, that connects the two sidelines (see also *baseline*).

English Spin on a ball when it is released by a shooter. If a player tries a bank shot from an awkward angle and gets it to go in, one might say, "He really put some English on that ball."

Fast break When one team attempts to score quickly by moving the ball downcourt before the other team can set up in defensive position.

FIBA The International Basketball Federation, the sport's global governing body.

Field goal A basket, worth two points (or three if taken from behind the three-point arc).

Final Four   The Semifinals and Finals of the NCAA Basketball Championships are commonly referred to as the Final Four, although the term could be used for the last four teams in any tournament. The Final Four is one of the most enjoyable weekends in sports.

Flagrant foul   In the NBA, unnecessary or excessive contact committed against an opponent. Too many of these will lead to a fine or suspension from Rod Thorn, the NBA's Senior Vice President, Operations (a.k.a. the "Dean of Discipline").

Floor burns   The bruises and scrapes a player gets by diving and sliding along the floor chasing loose balls. Coaches love players who pick up lots of floor burns—it means they're hustling.

Forward   One of the three positions in basketball, generally a midsized player who combines some of the size and rebounding skills of a center with some of the ballhandling and outside shooting of a guard. In today's age of specialization, we have small forwards who are primarily shooters and power forwards who are primarily rebounders.

Foul   An infraction of the rules, such as hitting a player while he is attempting a shot or charging into an opponent who is standing still on the court.

Foul circle   The circle around each foul line.

Foul line   The line that is 15 feet from each backboard, from which free throws are attempted (see also *free throw line)*.

Foul shot   Another term for a *free throw*.

Free throw   A shot made after a foul, from the foul line or the free throw line, while play is stopped. See also *foul shot*.

Free throw line   The line 15 feet from the backboard from which free throws (a.k.a. foul shots) are attempted (same as *foul line)*.

Frontcourt   A team's center and two forwards are known as its frontcourt. Also, a team's offensive half of the court.

Full-court press   A defensive tactic in which a team's players guard their opponents closely over the entire length of the court, hoping to harass them into making mistakes and turning the ball over.

Game clock   The clock that shows how much time remains in the current quarter (or half, in college) of the game.

Give-and-go   Another of the basic plays of basketball in which a player passes the ball to a teammate and immediately breaks toward the basket, taking a quick return pass for a layup or dunk. The play works so often because a defender's natural instinct is to turn away from the passer and follow the ball after it leaves his hands. That's enough give the passer all the time he needs to break free to the basket.

Glass Slang for *backboard* because, in the pros and colleges, the boards are made of plexiglass. A good rebounder is said to "really clean the glass."

Goaltending A violation in which a defensive player interferes with a shot on its downward arc toward the basket, or when a player from either team interferes with a shot while it's in the imaginary cylinder directly above the basket. Depending on who committed the violation, it's either defensive goaltending or offensive goaltending.

Guard One of three positions in basketball, generally played by the smallest players on the court (yes, I know Magic was 6'9"!) who usually play farthest from the basket. The position is often subdivided into point guards, whose primary job is to handle the ball and run the offense, and shooting guards, whose primary job you can guess. As a verb, to guard means to defend. If you want to see it in action, check out Gary Payton, Scottie Pippen, or Dikembe Mutombo.

Half-court press (or trap) A defensive tactic in which a team's players guard their opponents closely after they cross the midcourt line, double-teaming the player with the ball and trying to create turnovers.

Hand-checking Impeding an offensive player's progress by keeping a hand on him. This was a common and permissible defensive tactic when I was playing, and after a game I'd often have the bruises to prove it. Today it has been disallowed by the NBA in an attempt to increase scoring by making the offensive player's life a little easier.

Hardwood Slang for the floor or court on which the game is played, as in "Let's hit the hardwood!"

Head fake When a player with the ball moves his head quickly in one direction, in an effort to get his defender to react and either step or lean in that direction. The player with the ball will then go the other way to get off his shot.

Held ball When two players grab onto the ball at the same time and neither has clear possession, the referee blows his whistle and calls a held ball. In the NBA, the result is a jump ball from the nearest foul circle or the midcourt circle.

High post A pivot position above or alongside the foul line.

Hit the open man Find an unguarded player and pass him the ball. It's always a good idea—and a great way to make a teammate happy.

Hook shot An effective, if underused, weapon in which a player shoots the ball with a sweeping motion, with his arm extended over his head, while standing either sideways or with his back to the basket. This shot can also be taken while running or jumping. However you shoot it, it's almost impossible to block because it is released from high above a player's head.

Hoop Slang for *basket*.

Hoops Slang for *basketball*, as in "Let's go shoot some hoops."

Illegal defense   In the NBA, when a player violates the guidelines for playing defense, which state that he may not guard an area of the court or double-team a player without the ball. Actually it's more complicated than that, but most NBA players don't fully understand the rule, so don't worry about it.

In the paint   In the free-throw lane, the rectangle beneath the foul line that is painted a different color than the rest of the court (to make the referees' job easier).

Isolation   When a team sets up its offense so one player is left alone to work one-on-one against a defender, it's called an isolation play.

J   Jump shot, as in "He can really shoot the J."

Jump ball   When a referee starts or resumes play by tossing the ball up between a player from each team, who try to tap it to a teammate. A *held ball* is also called a jump ball.

Jump shot   A shot taken while jumping in the air, ideally while at the top of your jump so it's hard to block. Also known as a *jumper*, it's the most common shot you'll see today.

Key   Early slang for *lane* (see below).

Kill the clock   Run out the remaining time on the clock, or as much as possible, by dribbling and passing and maintaining possession rather than attempting a shot. This is done to protect a lead; until the shot clock was introduced, teams would do this for several minutes, much to the chagrin of fans craving action.

Lane   The rectangle on the court, below the foul line, that is painted a different color than the rest of the court. You'll find one at each end of the court. Also called the *free throw lane*, the *foul lane*, or (slang) the *paint*. Originally the lane was called the key because in the early years it was only 6 feet wide and the combined lane and foul circle was shaped like a keyhole.

Layup   A short shot in which a player lays the ball into the basket either directly or by banking it in off the backboard. Every player should practice his layups, with both hands.

Loose ball foul   A foul that is committed while neither team has possession of the ball.

Low post   A pivot position close to the basket. Also called the *low box* because of the boxes that are often drawn on the court along the lower part of the foul line to help the players line up correctly.

Man-to-man   The type of defense in which each defender is assigned a specific player to guard (as opposed to *zone* defense).

Midcourt line   The line that divides the court in half, between the frontcourt and the backcourt (also, *half-court line*).

Mismatch   When one player has a clear advantage over another, it is said to be a mismatch. This usually refers to height—as when a 6'2" player is asked to guard a 6'8" opponent— but it could also be applied to quickness, strength, experience, or overall talent (as in "Michael Jordan against just about anybody is a mismatch").

NBA   The National Basketball Association, the major professional league in the United States and Canada, consisting of 29 teams as of 1998.

NBA Finals   The NBA's championship series between the winners of the Eastern Conference and Western Conference playoffs.

NBL   The National Basketball League, a prominent Midwest-based pro league in the late 1930s and 1940s whose survivors were eventually absorbed into the NBA.

NCAA   The National Collegiate Athletic Association, the major governing body for intercollegiate athletics. Also, the name of the collegiate championship tournament.

Net   The cord that hangs from the basket ring, or rim. Also, a shot that goes through without coming in contact with the rim is said to have hit "nothing but net."

NIT   The National Invitational Tournament, the oldest post-season college tournament (founded in 1938) but now of secondary importance to the NCAA tournament. There's also a Preseason NIT.

Non-shooting foul   A foul committed against a player who is not in the act of shooting. The player who is fouled is not awarded any free throws unless the opposing team is over its limit of team fouls for that quarter.

One-on-one   When one offensive player maneuvers against one defender without help from a teammate, he is said to go "one-on-one." It's good for a player to be able to beat his man one-on-one, but trying to do it too often can break down a team's offensive patterns.

Open man   A player who is unguarded.

Outlet pass   A long pass thrown by a player after grabbing a rebound to a teammate who is near or beyond midcourt, to start a fast break. Wes Unseld was the master of the outlet pass.

Over the limit   When a team is above the permitted number of team fouls for a quarter (four), it is said to be "over the limit."

Overtime   An extra period played when a game is tied after four quarters (or two halves, in college ball). In the NBA, an overtime period lasts five minutes; if the teams are still tied when it's over, additional overtime periods are played until a winner is determined.

Palming   A violation in which a player dribbling the ball moves his hand under the ball and scoops it to gain better control and change directions. Also called carrying the ball, this violation is about as extinct as the dinosaur.

Penalty situation   When a team has exceeded its allotted number of four team fouls per quarter, it is said to be "in the penalty situation." The penalty is that any subsequent foul in that quarter is automatically a shooting foul (see also *over the limit*).

Penetrate   Drive through the defense toward the basket. A guard who can penetrate will always have a job in the NBA—or at any other level of basketball.

Personal foul   A foul committed by an individual player, such as blocking an opponent or charging into him. In the NBA, you're disqualified after six of them; in college, it's five and you're out.

Pick   When a player positions himself between a teammate and the man trying to guard that teammate, he is said to be "setting a pick" so his teammate can get free from the defender to get off a shot. Also called a *screen*.

Pick-and-roll   Another of the fundamental plays of basketball in which one player sets a pick for a teammate and then rolls toward the basket, taking a pass for what he hopes will be an open layup or dunk. Anybody who has watched John Stockton, Karl Malone, and the Utah Jazz for the past decade knows what I mean!

Pill   Slang for *ball*.

Pivot   A position taken by a player with his back to the basket, or another term for center. As a verb, it's the act of turning, usually toward the basket.

Playmaker   A team's point guard, its principal ballhandler who sets up and runs the team's offense.

Point guard   One of a team's two guards, the better ballhandler whose job is to run the offense. This was my job with the Knicks in the good old days.

Post up   A player positions himself against a defender with his back to the basket and maneuvers his way in close before attempting a shot.

Power forward   One of a team's two forwards, usually the better rebounder. Maurice Lucas created the mold for the modern power forward, and Karl Malone shattered it by adding the dimension of scoring.

PPG   Points per game, a player's scoring average. You'll see the averages for other categories also listed this way, as in rpg (rebounds), apg (assists), bpg (blocks), spg (steals), and mpg (minutes).

Press   As a verb, to guard closely.

Pump fake   To fake a shot so as to get a defender to jump in the air or lean in the wrong direction. The faker often can then get an unobstructed shot.

Quadruple-double   Scoring 10 or more in four statistical categories, from among points, rebounds, assists, steals, and blocks. To do this in one game is extremely rare—so rare that it has only happened four times in NBA history.

Rebound   A missed shot. When it is recovered by the team that shot the ball, it is an offensive rebound; when it is recovered by the opposing team, it is a defensive rebound. Also a verb: To rebound is to recover a missed shot.

Referee   The official who conducts the game, calling fouls and violations. Three of them work an NBA game.

Rim   The basket ring.

Rock   Playground slang for *ball*, as in "Gimme the rock!"

Run-and-gun   A fast-paced offense based on the fast break, where shots are taken quickly.

Screen   See *pick*.

See the ball   My coach Red Holzman's favorite phrase, it meant "Don't just watch your man while playing defense, but also see where the ball is." That way, you not only can overplay the passing lane and keep your man from getting to the ball, but you are ready in case a teammate needs help because you know what's going on around the ball.

Set shot   A shot taken from a set position on the floor. This was common in the early years of the game but is now virtually never attempted because it is easily blocked.

Shaking and baking   Putting on fancy moves and fakes while trying to get to the basket on a drive.

Shooting foul   A foul committed when a player is in the act of attempting a shot. The shooter is awarded two free-throw attempts.

Shooting guard   One of a team's two guards, and the title says it all regarding his primary responsibility. Reggie Miller is a shooting guard.

Shot clock   The clock that shows how much time is left for a team to attempt a shot before it loses possession. It's known as the 24-second clock in the NBA because that's the time limit.

Sixth man   A team's key reserve, the first player who comes in off the bench.

Sky   As a verb, to jump high.

Sky-hook   Kareem Abdul-Jabbar's favorite shot, a hook taken from so high up it seems to come down from the sky.

Small forward   One of a team's two forwards, usually the better shooter and ballhandler. Some of the great ones included Julius Erving and Larry Bird. They're not necessarily small, though—some in the NBA stand 6'9" or 6'10".

Steal   To take the ball away from your opponent. It's a big plus for your team because it can be disheartening to an opposing team. Also a noun for doing so successfully.

Strong side   The side of the court where the ball is (as opposed to *weak side*).

Switch   To change defensive assignments, so as to keep an offensive player from getting free for a shot. Often when an offensive team tries a pick-and-roll play, it's easier for a defensive team to keep both players covered if the defenders switch assignments.

Team fouls   The total of individual fouls committed by a team. After an NBA team has four team fouls in one quarter, all subsequent fouls in that quarter become shooting fouls.

Technical foul   A violation, generally for unsportsmanlike conduct, verbal or otherwise. In other words, it's a no-no. A technical foul may be called against any player or coach, whether on the court or on the bench. A technical foul carries with it an automatic $500 fine in the NBA; a player is ejected from the game after two technicals. In addition, a team is assessed a technical upon its second illegal defense violation and receives an additional technical for each succeeding violation.

Three-point arc (or line)   The marking on the court beyond which a player who attempts and makes a shot is awarded three points. In the NBA, it is 22 feet from the basket along the sidelines to an arc that measures 23 feet 9 inches.

Three-sixty   When a player spins completely around, he is said to "do a 360," as in 360-degree spin. Usually it's used in slam-dunk contests, when a participant does a mid-air spin.

Tip-in   A field goal that is scored when a shot is tipped into the basket by an offensive player.

Tip-off   The jump ball that starts a game, period, or half. Also called the *opening tip* or *opening tap*.

Trailer   A player who follows up a play, usually a fast break. After the first wave of offensive players gets downcourt and the defenders scramble to cover them, another offensive player who follows the play downcourt often finds himself left open for a shot.

Transition   The act of getting back into the offense after regaining possession of the ball on defense, or vice versa. Teams try to score baskets "in transition" before the opposing defense has a chance to set up.

Trap   When a second defender comes over to help the primary defender guard a man, they are said to trap or double-team him.

Traveling   A violation in which a player with the ball takes two full steps without dribbling. Also called *walking*, and not called enough in today's NBA.

Triple-double   Scoring 10 or more in three statistical categories, from among points, rebounds, assists, steals, and blocks. It's a measure of versatility that came into vogue when Magic Johnson was playing, but almost two decades earlier (in 1961–62) Oscar Robertson became the only player in NBA history to average a triple-double for an entire season. Now that's versatility—and consistency!

Turnover   Losing the ball without getting off a shot attempt. Too many of these will kill a team.

USBL   The United States Basketball League, a summer professional minor league.

Weak side   The side of the court away from where the ball is (as opposed to *strong side*).

WNBA   The Women's National Basketball League, one of the two major women's professional leagues in the United States. Its teams are owned and run by NBA franchises, and it plays a summer schedule.

Zebras   Slang for *referees*, because they often wear vertically striped shirts (but not in the NBA).

Zone   The type of defense in which a player is assigned a specific area of the floor to guard and picks up any offensive player who comes into that area (as opposed to *man-to-man* defense). It's often favored by high school and college coaches but is illegal in the NBA.

NBA Team Addresses

National Basketball Association
645 Fifth Avenue
New York, NY 10022
212-407-8000

Team Addresses and Phone Numbers

Atlanta Hawks
One CNN Center
Suite 405, South Tower
Atlanta, GA 30303
404-827-3800

Boston Celtics
151 Merrimac Street
Boston, MA 02114
617-523-6050

Charlotte Hornets
100 Hive Drive
Charlotte, NC 28217
704-357-0252

Chicago Bulls
1901 W. Madison Street
Chicago, IL 60612
312-455-4000

Cleveland Cavaliers
One Center Court
Cleveland, OH 44115
216-420-2000

Dallas Mavericks
777 Sports Street
Dallas, TX 75207
214-748-1808

Denver Nuggets
1635 Clay Street
Denver, CO 80204
303-893-6700

Detroit Pistons
Two Championship Drive
Auburn Hills, MI 48326
248-377-0100

Golden State Warriors
1011 Broadway
Oakland, CA 94607
510-986-2200

Houston Rockets
Two Greenway Plaza, Suite 400
Houston, TX 77046
713-627-3865

Indiana Pacers
300 E. Market Street
Indianapolis, IN 46204
317-263-2100

Los Angeles Clippers
3939 S. Figueroa Street
Los Angeles, CA 90037
213-745-0400

Los Angeles Lakers
3900 W. Manchester Blvd.
P.O. Box 10
Inglewood, CA 90306
310-419-3100

Miami Heat
SunTrust International Center
One Southeast 3rd Avenue, Suite 2300
Miami, FL 33131
305-577-4328

Milwaukee Bucks
1001 N. Fourth St.
Milwaukee, WI 53203
414-227-0500

Minnesota Timberwolves
600 First Ave. North
Minneapolis, MN 55403
612-673-1600

New Jersey Nets
405 Murray Hill Parkway
East Rutherford, NJ 07073
201-935-8888

New York Knicks
Two Pennsylvania Plaza
New York, NY 10121
212-465-6000

Orlando Magic
One Magic Place
Orlando, FL 32801
407-649-3200

Philadelphia 76ers
1 CoreStates Complex
Philadelphia, PA 19148
215-339-7600

Phoenix Suns
201 E. Jefferson
Phoenix, AZ 85004
602-379-7900

Portland Trail Blazers
One Center Court, Suite 200
Portland, OR 97227
503-234-9291

Sacramento Kings
One Sports Parkway
Sacramento, CA 95834
916-928-0000

San Antonio Spurs
100 Montana Street
San Antonio, TX 78203
210-554-7700

Seattle SuperSonics
190 Queen Anne Avenue North, Suite 200
Seattle, WA 98109
206-281-5800

Toronto Raptors
20 Bay Street, Suite 1702
Toronto, Ont. M5J 2N8
416-214-2255

Utah Jazz
301 W. South Temple
Salt Lake City, UT 84101
801-325-2500

Vancouver Grizzlies
800 Griffiths Way
Vancouver, B.C. V6B 6G1
604-899-7400

Washington Wizards
MCI Center
601 F Street NW
Washington, DC 20071
301-622-3865

Index

O

U

X-Z

About the Authors

Walt "Clyde" Frazier embodied 1970s cool, leaping off the pages of *Sports Illustrated* and onto the cover of *Esquire*—and taking the NBA with him. The stylish point guard for the New York Knicks—the thinking man's team that won NBA Championships in 1970 and 1973—he is not just a former basketball player but also a mainstream celebrity, a man about town who helped make cheering for the Knicks the "in" thing among the city's status-conscious. Frazier's style was matched by substance. A native of Atlanta, Georgia, Frazier led Southern Illinois to the 1967 NIT championship and was a first-round draft choice by the Knicks. He joined a team on the rise that included Willis Reed, Bill Bradley, Cazzie Russell, Dick Barnett, and Phil Jackson. When the team obtained Dave DeBusschere a year later, all the championship pieces were in place. The Knicks put it all together in 1969–70, winning a league-high 60 games during the regular season and then beating the Los Angeles Lakers in a classic seven-game NBA Finals for their first NBA Championships. While Game 7 of that series is best remembered for the inspirational lift provided by the injured Reed—who hobbled onto the court just before the opening tip and scored the Knicks' first two baskets—it was Frazier who would not be denied that night, scoring 36 points, handing out 19 assists, and playing his customary superlative defense in one of the greatest performances in NBA Playoff history.

Frazier excelled at both ends of the court, running the offense with his playmaking and savvy as well as wreaking havoc on defense with his quickness and instincts. He played 10 seasons with the Knicks, helping them to another championship in 1972–73, before finishing his career with Cleveland. A seven-time NBA All-Star and a four-time All-NBA First Team selection, the 6'4" Frazier remains the Knicks' all-time leader in assists (4,791) and ranks second behind Patrick Ewing in seven other categories, including points and games played. He averaged 18.9 points, 6.1 assists, and 5.9 rebounds per game in a total of 825 NBA games. He also ranked as high as second in the league in steals in 1974–75.

In 1986, Frazier was elected to the Naismith Memorial Basketball Hall of Fame. In 1996, he was chosen as one of the 50 Greatest Players in NBA History, in conjunction with the league's golden anniversary celebration.

Frazier, who also has been a sports agent, has been the color commentator for Knicks radio broadcasts for the past nine seasons, delighting fans with his insights into the game as well as his wordsmanship as he liberally sprinkles phrases such as "dishing and swishing" and "driving and jiving" into his commentary. He lives in New York, where he is active in promoting literacy among youngsters.

Alex Sachare is the author or co-author of eight books on basketball, including *The Official NBA Basketball Encyclopedia* (Villard, 1994) and *The Chicago Bulls Encyclopedia* (Contemporary, 1998). He was a sports writer for the Associated Press for 10 years and worked for the NBA league office for 15 years, heading its publications department as Vice President, Editorial. A frequent contributor to *Hoop* magazine and several online sports services, Sachare has a B.A. degree from Columbia and a M.A. degree from the New School for Social Research. He currently is the Director of Communications for the Columbia College Office of Alumni Affairs and Development, and the editor of *Columbia College Today*, the school's alumni magazine.